Readers love *An Alzheimer's Primer*

by Joanne Niswander

"The book is both inspiring and heart-tugging, especially powerful in conveying the reality of Alzheimer's and yet maintaining a positive outlook."

"This is a book that will help many, many people."

"The book is full of wisdom, encouragement for others, and happy memories."

"What a lovely, beautifully written book!"

Copyright © 2015 Joanne Niswander
All rights reserved.

Published by Workplay Publishing
Newton, KS 67114
workplaypublishing.com

ISBN 0-9905545-2-X

Cover design and photograph by Alison King
Interior layout by André Swartley

PRINTED IN THE UNITED STATES OF AMERICA

from Maple Crest Pond

Joanne Niswander

WORKPLAY PUBLISHING

To all the flora, fauna and folks
who have prompted these reflections

Introduction

Ordinarily, books are expected to be read beginning at page one and continuing on until the end. Yearly journals are expected to begin on the first day of January and go through the year until the last day of December.

This book of daily reflections is an exception to normal beginnings. The first entry is dated April 29 and the entries continue for a year, until the following April 28. The reason? April 29, 2014 was the first day of my personal challenge to write one purposely-concise thought piece daily, for an entire year. Writing through the ensuing 365 days proved to be an unforgettable, enriching experience.

Most of these reflections originated from my apartment in a small retirement community in Bluffton, Ohio. However a good number of them were written from other locations— from wherever I happened to be on that particular day. My children are scattered across the United States so, when I travel to see them, my notebook and pen travel along.

In addition to musings about life in the Ohio landscape, I will share special thoughts and adventures from Colorado, Illinois, Kentucky, Maine, New Mexico, North Carolina, airports, lakeside cottages and several other places in between. You will be with our family as we mourn the sudden death of a son-in-law, spend Christmas in Santa Fe, celebrate at a family reunion. You will be invited to marvel with me at the beauty, and the wonders, of the world just outside whatever window happens to be at hand.

So I suggest that you, my reader, turn to the present day's date to begin your readings. The reflections written here have much to do with daily discoveries, often tied to the everyday world of nature and the seasons, so it is appropriate to read about Thanksgiving Day in late November and spring's awakening in April. However, since this book is now in your hands, not mine, you may read in whatever order you wish.

Many of these 365 reflections stem from seemingly insignificant happenings that, in one way or another, have opened my eyes and mind to new insights as well as to nearly-forgotten memories. Perhaps they will inspire you, also, to look more closely at the many little things that help to make a day special and confirm, each and every day, that life is well worth living.

April 29

I wasn't looking for him but there he was, on the branch outside my window. What a welcome sight! A belted kingfisher just like the one who appeared one day last spring and who, a few days later, disappeared. Was he the same one, back from his winter quarters? I didn't ask, and he didn't say.

For two days I watched that distinctive big-headed body rocket itself down across the pond, skim the water, then land on the top of the birdhouse on the other side of the water. Back and forth he would fly, snatching the early insects who were just starting their spring appearance. Alas, too soon he was gone—probably heading farther north for the rest of his summer stay.

Just like my kingfisher, there are people who periodically fly in and out of my life. They don't stay but, in their passing by, they add to my perception of the world. I remember Phyllis, whose discerning comments over coffee challenged me to really think. And Rich whose wide and always genuine smile lightens up any room. And Karen with the soaring soprano voice. Is she still singing? I hope. Altogether, they bring color and life and a special kind of beauty into my days.

Thank you, kingfishers and people alike, who fly in and out of my world while adding those special spots of color that keep life interesting. My days continue to be blessed by your presence.

APRIL 30

The Canada geese are back. Yes, back with their babies. They are innocently teaching their offspring to navigate in the pond outside my window. They are happy. We are not. They have insinuated themselves into our "perfect" world and have, once again, messed up our sidewalks and disturbed our peace.

How is it that some of God's creatures, through their own instincts and fecundity, have made themselves less than loveable to us humans? What have they done to deserve our wrath? Or, to look at the problem another way, what have we done to make this happen?

Well, for one, we've provided a perfect spot for them to land and settle. The grass is green and tender, the water is calm and non-threatening, they are relatively safe from dogs and other animals. In addition, we don't charge rent.

Along with watching the geese and numerous other sedentary activities, I've been doing a bit of research on our ancestors. Those hardy souls who left their homes in Europe to settle in the new country of America. They found a perfect spot, northwest Ohio, to settle. The soil was fertile, the trees were plentiful and the land was relatively cheap. Ohio looked like a good place to start a family.

I take for granted my right to be living here, in this country, in this place. Can I not grant the same privilege to even the least of these?

May 1

Are you old enough to remember May Baskets? Do you recall carefully folding and cutting the colored paper, pasting at the corners, adding a handle, then filling it with flowers (real or paper—whatever was at hand)? Remember giving it to Mom on the first day of May? Remember her surprise (even if she knew what we were up to and wasn't really surprised)?

Is there anyone in the world still delivering May Baskets? I have the feeling that we tend to let our florists do our work for us these days. After all, they're the experts. And it all looks so much more beautiful—so much more professional.

But wait! May baskets were never meant to be professional. They were meant simply to be a gift from the heart. So maybe it's time to resurrect the old tradition. Time to bring back the home-made and homely. And, if it should be done, then who will do it? Guess it has to be me.

Flowers? Oh, I have some tiny but oh-so-bright-blue grape hyacinths outdoing themselves in a corner of my garden. And this morning I saw some dandelions out by the street. Blue and yellow—a good combination. Nice and bright. Now, all I need is a recipient. How about my friend Anne? She's old enough to remember the tradition and young enough to be delighted. I'll set the basket beside her door, ring the bell and hide around the corner. Later we'll laugh about it—together.

MAY 2

Mother's Day is coming up and, once again, I must pay tribute to that special person who birthed me, raised me, then let me soar. For she truly did allow me to find my own path in life.

Widowed before the age of 40, my mother guided my brother and me through our teen-age years and then encouraged us both to follow our own paths. Although her life changed directions several times during her 95 years, she accepted those changes with grace and whole-heartedly embraced new challenges as they came.

Moving from the home farm, she found fulfillment—and many new friends—in a college campus setting. And, after 20 years of widowhood, she married again and learned to enjoy pastimes she had previously only read about—like playing golf, fishing, and painting. She was not afraid to learn new ways of doing things and was very adept at adjusting to life as it presented itself around her.

One special thing my brother and I knew, from the very beginning, was that she was there for us if and when we needed her. She was always available but she would never dictate our lives. We also knew that she "prayed us home" whenever we were away. In my heart of hearts, I know that she's still praying us home.

Thank you, Mom!

MAY 3

It's nice to live in the town where, at one time, you went to college—especially when commencement weekend comes around and one has a chance to reminisce with old college friends. Such was the case today, when I enjoyed catching up on the lives of several friends who live a long distance away.

Now, back at home after a day filled with good conversation, I'm starting to marvel about how fortunate I was to have had the chance to go to college. Even today, when higher education seems to be almost a necessity, not everyone has that chance.

In my family, my brother and I were the first of our generation to go to college. My paternal grandfather, an immigrant at age 24, was an Illinois farmer and Mennonite minister—one generation away from Amish. My father went to school only as far as eighth grade. My maternal grandparents were one generation ahead in coming to America but, even then, my mother's education extended only through high school.

My father did not live long enough to see my brother and me go off to college, but I know he would have been as pleased as my mother was. Our small high school was not noted for sending many off to college—of the 37 who graduated high school with me, only 11 of us managed to go on into higher education.

Yes, I was fortunate. Thank you again, Mom!

MAY 4

Today I had the privilege of viewing a world of beauty I would have completely missed, had someone not brought it to my attention. That previously-unnoticed world was contained in a photograph album filled with pictures of fungus or, to use a more common term, mushrooms.

Mushrooms, some of the earthiest, underappreciated and elusive forms of forest life. Just mushrooms and the forest floor surrounding them. All were photographed growing in their natural habitat, not plucked and posed on a table. Straight from nature, surrounded by nature, with nothing artificial to break the spell.

The photographer, herself as unassuming as a woodland mushroom, has gone to great lengths (most times on hands and knees, or *as low as* belly and elbows) to find just the right angle, the best backlighting, to make that reclusive woodland denizen show off its own particular and distinctive beauty. I am still in awe at her ability to help us become more aware of such astounding beauty in the ordinary.

But, come to think of it, isn't that what every one of us should be doing? What if each of us would, in one way or another, get down on our own hands and knees to help someone else bring out his or her own particular, distinctive beauty? Our world, and our own individual lives, would certainly be better for it.

MAY 5

A melody has been singing in my head all day today. The tune goes away for a little while, then returns. Sometimes this "I can't get it out of my mind" syndrome can be most exasperating. Sometimes, but not today. Instead, this song keeps on giving me a lift and a smile.

It all started yesterday afternoon when I attended a musical program put on by members of a music fraternity from a nearby university. Among the individual pieces presented, one of the performers sang for us "A Simple Song" from Leonard Bernstein's *Mass*. That number has always haunted me, and it has particularly done so today.

"Lauda, lauda, laude. Lauda, lauda, di-da-di-day."

Why is it that a person can sometimes be especially open to certain external stimuli and, at other times, be completely untouched? What is it that causes some things to remain with us longer and more intensely than at other times? What made one small segment of yesterday's music program extend all the way into today for me, and probably well into tomorrow?

Perhaps I needed it right then. Even though I didn't realize that I needed it. My heart and mind must have been ready. The music was there. I took it in. It has stayed with me.

"Lauda, lauda, laude. Lauda, lauda, di-da-di-day. All of my days."

MAY 6

Did you ever wonder what you would have been like if you had been born 200 years earlier? If you had been born of the same parents, with the same personality and abilities that you have now, but had been plunked down in a completely different century. What would be different?

Well, of course, your clothing would have been different. Your schooling would have been different. But if, inside, you were the person then that you are now, what would you be doing? Would you be driving a covered wagon across the prairies, or would you have opted to stay in Boston? Perhaps you might still be across the oceans, unwilling or unable to test out the new world of America. Would you have been content to stay with your ancestors? Maybe you would never have had the choice.

Whenever I have driven across the wide expanses of Nebraska and Kansas, I marvel at the perseverance of the pioneers as they traveled mile after mile after mile of the prairies, then bumped up against the mountains of Colorado to top it all off. How did any of them ever survive with body and mind reasonably intact?

Were our immigrant ancestors adventurous or desperate, leaders or followers? Were the personalities of those who came to America that much different from those who stayed behind? What immigrant ancestor are you most like?

It's a question impossible to answer, but a good question to ponder. I wonder . . .

MAY 7

Sometimes it takes just a little curiosity to find a gem. Such was the case recently as I discovered an awesome spot—just outside the Dayton airport. My curiosity had been sparked a couple of years ago, when the airport shuttle took me to my overnight motel west of the airport (which, before, I had always approached from the east). To my surprise, we crossed a dam, the sides of which dropped precipitously on either side. What was this??

The next year, I had a chance to discover a bit more as a granddaughter's plane flight was delayed for two hours. Jessie and I drove to the dam and discovered a road leading down to the river—into part of the area's metroparks system. We spent the next hour enjoying the river instead of watching cars go in and out of the car park at the airport.

Then, last Palm Sunday, two of my daughters were flying home through the same airport—with four hours between the two flights. What better place to go than the park so near the airport grounds? Lee and I dropped Jeanne off for her flight, then drove to the park to walk, this time, through the Aullwood Wildflower Gardens. There, on a sunny and mild mid-April day, we reveled in wildflowers—hills chock-full of daffodils and paths lined with bloodroot, trout lilies, anemones, spring beauties, Dutchman's breeches.

What a way to spend an afternoon in spring!

MAY 8

The thermometer topped 80 degrees again today, the second day in a row. A perfect day for a long walk, except for a bit too much wind.

There I go again, tacking on a bit of a complaint when I should be just enjoying the day with no exceptions. So let's begin again.

It was a perfect day for a long walk. No sooner had I gone out, I spied neighbors across the pond sitting on their patio and enjoying the afternoon. So, of course, I stopped to say "hello" when I got to their house. Which led to a good 15 minutes of pleasant conversation before I continued my walk.

Not much farther along my way, a car pulled into a driveway. Naturally, the driver and I had to exchange greetings before we went on our separate ways. A little farther on down the street, two strangers were walking their dog. We waved and the dog barked his greetings. And later on, I shared a porch swing and good conversation with another friend.

And so the afternoon went. What started out as a long, solitary walk became a not-quite-so-long and definitely-not-so-solitary walk. Then, to top it all off, I sat down, put up my feet, and immediately took a delicious afternoon nap.

As I said, it was a perfect day for a long walk. No exceptions.

MAY 9

I made a phone call this morning to one of my special girls in Maine—my great-granddaughter Virginia. Today is her 11th birthday and she's spending the first part of it doing her regular morning chores. She reported that these duties included helping with breakfast and tidying up the house for expected weekend visitors.

Unlike Naomi, her live-every-moment-like-it's-your-last younger sister, Virginia is my quiet but assertive when necessary, bright but soft-spoken *Little House on the Prairie* girl. Virginia became acquainted with Laura Ingalls Wilder's tales early in life, first being read to and, soon, learning to read those stories herself. Virginia seems to have absorbed some of that pioneer character that was so vital in early days and is still appreciated today.

In the kitchen, Virginia can cook and clean nearly as efficiently as her mother. To her younger sister and brothers, she is her busy mother's willing right hand. She's a quiet bookworm and a quick learner, but you'll also find that she plays "for keeps" when she's at the euchre table. She is not averse to competition!

In this beautiful and amazing world, we have so much to be thankful for. Today, I'm thankful most of all for the special person that is Virginia. May she continue to grow in grace.

MAY 10

Now I truly know that spring is here and summer on its way. I've been to the Farmer's Market. It's good to be back.

Every Saturday morning that I'm not out of town, from now until the end of October, you should be able to find me at Bluffton's traditional Farmer's Market. With my red lobster-trap mesh bag over my shoulder and wallet in hand, I'm there for one purpose: to find the special home-grown and home-baked foods that have been absent all winter. As an added bonus, I always meet friends that I seldom see except at that Saturday morning ritual.

What a wealth of early spring offerings were there for my choosing today! Bright red rhubarb, fresh asparagus, radishes, early lettuce and spinach. Farm-fresh brown eggs. There was even a nature-loving entrepreneur selling just-unearthed-from-the-woods morel mushrooms, pretty as a picture in their distinctive wrinkled beauty and about as special an offering as one can find at a public market.

One stop I always make is at my favorite home-baker to purchase my Sunday morning sweet roll. And then there are the varieties of breads in all shapes and textures, from soft and fine-textured to dark brown and hearty. Home produced jams and jellies to go with whichever bread you prefer.

Here's a salute to Farmer's Markets everywhere. Think Fresh!

MAY 11

I have a little plaque propped up next to my computer that, I keep telling myself, I should hang permanently somewhere. But no, I really need to keep it where it is. I want it here, next to the computer, because I can't help but see it every day. Reading the words always gives me a lift.

It's just a little 5-inch square framed piece that, I'm sure, was quite inexpensive. But the message is one that somehow speaks the right words to me. In calligraphy are written these words:

Wishing you always
Music in your life,
a Song in your soul
and Harmony in your heart.

I don't think I've ever told my niece how much I appreciate that little impromptu gift she gave me. I must do that, especially now that I've committed myself to paper. I'm sure she'll say, "oh, it was nothing—just something I saw in the store and it made me think of you."

But it *is* something. Something special that just happened to hit the mark for me. And so I give thanks for thoughtful nieces and loving family and all that makes my world a special place.

MAY 12

The big lilac bush on the corner is in full bloom. The fragrance of lilacs is all around me. I gaze at the dark green of the leaves, the profusion of tiny flowerets that create a handful of lavender loveliness. Opulence without arrogance.

We had a similar lilac bush next to the garden at my childhood home. I think my mother had rather a love-hate relationship with the lilacs, primarily because the bush shaded her carefully planted vegetable beds—which held another type of beauty.

Yes, our garden was more than just a place to grow vegetables. My mother went about her gardening with a definite plan. Each carefully laid out rectangular bed was planned with a purpose. Utility and beauty combined to place just the right size and shape of vegetable plant into that particular bed, outlined by a row of lettuce or spinach of another particular size and shape.

Of course, when I was a kid, I didn't realize that a vegetable garden could also be a work of art. I didn't appreciate that fact at all when I was assigned the task of scraping the weeds from the paths that surrounded the beds. It was only later, when I went about the task of planting my own garden, that I realized the artistic genius in my mother's plantings. And now, it's too late to tell her.

Why do we always wait so long to get it all figured out?

MAY 13

The world outside my window has suddenly changed personalities. Over the past hour it has become a different place, switching from windy and restless to calm and serene. I not only see the difference, I feel it.

All day the wind had been blowing like a gale at sea, the trees outside my window bowing to its fury, waves had been constantly pushing at the rip-rap lining the pond. Although the sun was bright and the temperature conducive for a long walk, the wind dampened my enthusiasm to venture outside. Now, as evening makes its appearance, nearly all movement has stopped. It is a transformed world outside my window. I marvel at how things can change in such a short time and give us a different outlook on the day.

I am reminded of the days when my children were young and, finally, bedtime arrived. After a day of "Mommy" this and "Mommy" that, noses to wipe and tears to dry, too much to do in too little time, at last the house quieted. All the noise, movement and activity of the previous hours turned off. It was a time to breathe deeply and to catch up with my frazzled self.

The world outside my window is catching up with itself now, too. After a day of furious activity, it has calmed for what portends to be a quiet night. I'm not sure what tomorrow will bring but, for right now, all's well. That is enough.

MAY 14

The sun is warm, the outdoors beckoning and, as usual, I answer the invitation. First I take a short walk, but soon find myself bending over my raised garden. In it is a smattering of spur-of-the-moment plantings from an accumulation of years, plants that weather the seasons of Ohio. My beautiful little grape hyacinths have finally bloomed themselves to obscurity and the verbena is just starting the blooming process. Chives are sending out their purple blossoms. This week I must pick some of those blossoms to put in a jar of vinegar—for color and aroma, a trick learned from a former resident.

And then there is the milkweed, already sprouting out between the blossoms and working to hover over the garden soon. Even though the milkweed will soon be too tall and ungainly to be called beautiful, it is there to provide a haven for our monarch butterflies. It's a small patch, but the butterflies found it last year and we'll hope for the best again this year.

So I pull the weeds that threaten to take over the few flowers that bloom, then run my fingers through my clump of sage to take home that distinctive aroma. My fingers may be dirty but my hands will retain the fragrance of sage long after the dirt goes down the drain. And my body will remember the walk, my eyes will remember the verbena, and I will still have a smile come bedtime.

MAY 15

This morning when I opened my eyes I thought I must have overslept. The light seeping in through the blinds was twice as bright as usual. But, no, I hadn't overslept. It was a mirage, of sorts. I was seeing the early morning sun as through a mirror.

You see, the living room of my corner apartment has a three-bay window. The view is north, north-west and west. Because of this, I have been blessed with many beautiful evening sunsets but I don't experience anything like sunrise from my apartment. Until this morning, that is. The reason? Reflection. Or is it refraction? I'll let you scientists decide on the terminology. I just know that I experienced a sunrise that wasn't really there.

My west window looks out across the lawn toward two villas with white siding. The sun was just at the proper angle to bring an intensely bright image of morning sunlight directly into my windows. In addition, the pond to the north was calm and extra-reflective as well. Result? Sunrise flooding my apartment—from the wrong direction. A beautiful surprise.

I need to tuck that visual surprise somewhere in my memory bank, to be taken out some day when the skies are gray and I need a pick-me-up. It's always good to have a lovely memory to look back on when you need it.

MAY 16

After a long, long winter it has been good to see the grass greening again, to feel the air begin to soften from its bitter chill. And, with the rise in temperature, we once more shake our heads at our intrepid teenagers who bare their legs and arms to welcome in spring long before the thermometer settles into its above-freezing indicators. Watching students walk home from school with bare legs and arms when it's two degrees above the freezing mark makes me shiver.

Has it always been so? Did my brother and I defy the odds and shed our coats as early in the year as the kids do today? I don't think so. I question whether we even thought about it very much, being "farm kids" and rather bereft of fashion sense. We did have, I suppose, a certain sense of teenage conformity by the time we got to high school. But without television to dictate what was "in" and what was "out" across the country (and in the malls which, of course, we didn't have either), we were blissfully unaware.

However I do remember, when I was in elementary school, sometimes rolling down my thick brown stockings after I got to school—then rolling them back up before I walked home. My friends did the same. I guess, in a way, that was our statement. So maybe I'd better just keep my thoughts to myself. I survived childhood and I suppose today's children will, too.

MAY 17

Graduation time! It comes every year—that time when, in every community across the United States, we celebrate the achievements of our youth with high school and college graduations. Then we launch them out into whatever corner of the world is calling to them.

Ah, but then there are all the rest—the forgotten remainder. Those who have already dropped out of school or are in the process. Add to them the children around the world who have never even had a chance to be in school. Children who are learning how to survive in a world we can't even imagine. What about all of those children? We read about them, but can't relate. We hear, but have a hard time understanding. Those children are a part of our world, yet they are not a part of *our* world. We don't see them, or at least they are not in our back yard.

Again, maybe some of them are.

I have a granddaughter who, while in junior high, was taken out of a dangerous home situation and placed in foster care—into the home of my daughter and son-in-law. Not long after, she and her older brother were adopted as part of my daughter's family. Yesterday, that girl graduated from university—magna cum laude. And what is she planning to do with her life? Help other people (which she has been doing ever since she's had the chance). One saved, now saving others.

MAY 18

I got my lift-of-the-day this evening as I attended a piano recital given by a highly talented high school senior. He comes equipped with a smile that can charm any old grouch and a shock of red hair that won't quit curling. To top it all off, he's a good kid—a boy who would make any parent or grandparent proud. No, he's not mine, but I'd claim him if he didn't already have enough family to go around.

That recital has gotten me thinking about his future. Where will he go with this talent? He's going off to college to pursue a double major, in music and mathematics. Which will win out (because one of them eventually will)? Will he become a college professor, like his father, and play the piano purely for his own enjoyment? Will he make piano his profession and, in the meantime, be able to manage his checkbook better than some? Perhaps, once he's in college, he will find another interest and take an entirely different career route.

That's what is exciting about seeing our young people go off to college—the many possibilities that are out there for them. And that's what keeps the gleam in their eyes as well— the many possibilities that are out there.

How does it all turn out in the end? We'll just have to wait and see. And breathe a prayer once in a while that they don't get lost on the way.

MAY 19

This morning I moved the chrysalis of a swallowtail butterfly from my unheated garage (where it has been sitting all winter) to a sunny spot on the front porch. I hope my incipient butterfly is still alive and viable within that dull brown overcoat, although the only way I'll be able to know is to wait and watch.

I had "mothered" several of the big, striped green-black-and-yellow caterpillars to maturity last summer. I watched them spin their temporary raiment before emerging, a good many days later, transformed into beautiful butterflies. Then I watched them fly off to wherever swallowtails go. But this caterpillar-turned-chrysalis was a late-in-life guy (or gal) that chose to make an over-the-winter stay.

The year before had been a disaster. Not familiar enough with how swallowtails developed, I brought a late-fall chrysalis into my apartment and waited to see what would happen. It was warm and safe there and, eventually, the butterfly emerged. A real beauty! But it was already winter outside. How could I feed it? Unfortunately, I couldn't. I still have guilt about that.

This time, if my butterfly emerges and flies away, I'll know I did the right thing to let it winter-over in my garage. If nothing happens, I will have learned to let the next late fall caterpillar make its own decision on where to go for the winter. I'll be disappointed but I will have learned another lesson about life. Don't mess with Mother Nature.

MAY 20

This morning I woke up to gray skies and rain. Oh, no! What a dismal day to run all the errands that have been crowding my must-do list! But now, two hours later, the sun is peeking out and the clouds are lifting—a welcome sight. Now I can finally get on with my day!

But why should I let the weather dictate my mood, as well as my actions? Am I so dependent on what goes on outside my window that my insides are affected by it? That happens sometimes, I guess. But as a rule I try not to let the weather make my plans for me. I try to stay positive on rainy days.

My mother was a very positive person—at least, that is how I best remember her. It reflected in her face and in her conversations. She was not one to join in the latest gossip—far from it. In turn, I don't think she ever gave people much food for gossip.

In that same positive way, my mother guided my brother and me through childhood and teenage. Yes, she had certain expectations of good behavior and demeanor but the guidance was gentle and fair. We grew up with positive reinforcement. How good it is to remember back to smiles and not frowns, gentle words instead of shouts.

How will my children and grandchildren remember me when I'm gone?

MAY 21

The forsythia bushes at one end of our pond endured a hard winter, which turned into a spring bereft of the familiar bright yellow blossoms. Those flowers were sorely missed. But now, in leafing time, the bushes are more than making up for the loss of blossoms. It is as if all the plant's strengths are, now, going into producing extra-healthy leaves. The bushes are alive and well—just different this year.

Maybe that's what happens to us humans as well. Through events, many times beyond our control, we find one of our strengths diminishing and we have to find something else to keep us balanced. I find that particularly true as I get to the age where my body does not always keep up with what it used to do.

My left knee now complains when I head down the stairs, but that does not stop me from taking walks. My singing voice does not perform as well it used to do, but I sing anyway. Reading and writing keep my mind at work even when my body is relaxed. I still feel like I'm a viable human being, even thought I may not be able to do all I did 20 years ago.

So I'm relatively content with the life stage I'm in right now. If the forsythia bushes could talk, I think they'd echo that comment as well. With the right weather, they'll bloom again next spring. Who knows what blooms, or leaves, will emerge from me?

MAY 22

My favorite inspirational calendar was lying on the floor this morning. I'm not surprised that it fell. In fact, I'm surprised that it stayed up as long as it did. I was reluctant to put a nail on the side of a cabinet where I wanted the calendar to hang, so I just tacked it up with Scotch tape. After a couple of months the tape finally succumbed to gravity. I put the calendar up again, with more tape, but it promptly fell again.

So I did what I should have done in the first place. I found a small nail in my tool box, grabbed the hammer and secured the calendar to the side of the cabinet where it had hung so precariously before. Now it will stay. It finally has permanence—at least as much as a yearly calendar can have.

I think back to one of my sisters-in-law who had a beautiful picture of a landscape that, for years, was propped against the wall above her spinet piano. For one reason or another, about which I hesitated to ask, the picture remained in that temporary state. It was in its designated place but gave the impression of impermanence.

I know that I will not be in this world forever, but while I'm here I need to feel that wherever I am is where I am supposed to be. I'll find my niche, then try to add a bit of beauty where I can. That's permanence enough.

MAY 23

When I was a child, going to Aunt Ruth and Uncle Clarence's house was a treat to look forward to. Since they lived two states away, we didn't visit them often. But when we did, it was a time for special memories.

Memory #1: There were seven children in their family. One of the boys was exactly my age and one girl was just a bit younger but close enough that we looked forward to playing together. What a treat!

Memory #2: They had a huge (to me) kitchen table that held all nine of them, plus our family of four. Unheard of!! And what a rollicking time we had around the table at meal-times! Quite a change from our small, and relatively sedate, household.

Memory #3: Uncle Clarence could draw. Today, after being shown some of his impromptu caricatures, I realize that he was a talented but unsung cartoonist. He was really very good at capturing the essence of an individual. But back then, all this little girl knew was that he was the person I wanted to sit beside in church. Being a visiting niece, I evidently pulled rank and usually got my wish. He entertained me during the entire church service with his drawings of people in the congregation.

In my estimation, Uncle Clarence was pretty close to being God. When you're a kid, God can come in many forms. It's too bad we tend to lose that as we get older.

MAY 24

If you walked into my apartment, one of the first things you might notice is a jigsaw puzzle under construction on the table. Not a little one—definitely not! It's always a thousand-piecer. That's because my children, for the last four years, have sent me a puzzle-a-month. It's one of their ways of saying "I love you" at the same time as they make sure I keep busy and don't spend my days with what has become America's favorite pastime—television.

Puzzles weren't always so ever-present at our house because Dean, my late husband, shared little of my interest in them. Anyway, we had plenty of other things to do and places to go in our younger years. After their father's death, the children came upon this puzzle-a-month plan, to keep Mom's mind and spirit occupied. It has.

I've had fun anticipating what's going to be coming in the mail. It's like Christmas 12 times a year! Now I have a game closet lined with puzzles, ready to loan out to my puzzle-loving friends. Sometimes, if I get my monthly puzzle finished early, I'll pull out one from the "stash" for a second or third time around.

So if time gets heavy on your hands, pull out a puzzle. Or read a book (which is also on the top of my "to-do" list). Or pay a visit to your neighbor. Or knit, or sew, or play solitaire. Get involved. There are so many things to do without turning on TV.

MAY 25

At last, the porch is fully occupied again. It has been a long time.

Here at Maple Crest, the retirement complex where I live, we have a long porch at the front of our main building (not rivaling Mackinac Island's Grand Hotel, but big enough). In spring, summer and fall, you will find many of us there on balmy afternoons and evenings, enjoying the breezes and the conversation. It is a gathering place. A good place to be with friends.

After an especially grueling winter, followed by an off-and-on spring with more wind than is tolerable to most, Memorial Day weekend turned out to be ideal. Everyone was ready for this reprieve and the "porch people" took every advantage of the change of scenery. It's like old times again. Smiles and laughter, bantering back and forth, telling stories, remembering old times and relating new experiences. It feels good to be back on the porch again.

Yes, I know, we have been together all winter. We have seen each other day after day—inside. Today was the grand beginning of a special season—the porch season. Not all of us will be part of it. Some residents think it's too hot, or too cold, or too windy, or too . . . whatever the excuse is. Porches and conversation are not for everyone.

But for us "porch people," today was the beginning of a new life once more. "God's in His heaven, all's right with the world."

MAY 26

Today, Memorial Day, I have such mixed feelings that I don't know what to write. So I'll just pour out some of my thoughts and together we can sift through them.

You see, I grew up in a Mennonite family. Mennonites don't believe in participating in war. I was in elementary school on Pearl Harbor day, so was only marginally affected by what was going on. My awareness of the war was that of an immature 12-year-old. I'm still sorting it all out.

I saw some young men from our church enter the regular armed forces, some into non-combatant overseas services like ambulance drivers, while others served their country in Civilian Public Service in mental hospitals and the like. Being too young, and a girl, I did not have to make those decisions. But I was aware that there were divergent opinions in the community as to what was the "right" way to serve our country. Those opinions resonated through the church, and the community, for some time.

Today, I wonder what I would have done had I been forced to make a decision about serving. Could I carry a gun, and use it? No, I could not take a life—neither then nor now. Could I go into a war zone as a non-combatant? I think so. Could I have enough resolve to be jailed if the draft board rejected my plea to be a true conscientious objector? I doubt it.

I guess I'm still in the middle.

MAY 27

Do you ever get the feeling that you have lost something and won't ever find it again? That's how I felt this afternoon when I was walking at the edge of the Nature Preserve close to my home. I heard a bird call, high up in the trees, that was both familiar and unfamiliar. A musical series of notes I had not heard in a long time. An oriole, I thought. A Baltimore oriole. Was I really hearing an oriole, or was it just wishful thinking on my part?

You see, it has been a long time.

Forty years ago my husband and I were knee deep into birding. We had purchased a home in the woods and a wonderful variety of birds came with the mortgage. We delighted in identifying warblers as they passed through each spring. We faithfully monitored bluebird trails. We came to recognize a great number of bird calls. Each year we looked forward to adding new birds to our life list as we traveled across the country. But a lot of life—and illness and death—has happened since those heady birding days. Yes, it's been a long time.

I never spotted the oriole, if that's what it really was. But that's all right. That song from the treetops brought back a treasure trove of good memories. And, at my age, memories are enough.

MAY 28

It's a perfect picture. A young child, about six years old. A mother who is probably 35 (but we won't ask). A grandfather not yet to retirement age. All three have big smiles and are intent on throwing stale bread cubes into the pond to entice fish to the surface. They are having a quiet "together" time there in the morning sunshine. I am only a spectator, watching from my window.

However the picture is marred because I know a tiny bit of their story. The mother and her son are there because granddad needs a break. He needs to get out of his room, into the outdoors and lift his face to the sun. He needs to be outside and dissipate some of his pent-up energy. But he cannot go alone. His mind, all too prematurely, has turned from productive to disabled. Too soon, much too soon.

What is there to say? It rends the heart, this family story that does not have a happy ending. The young grandson, enjoying the outing without feeling the heartache, will never know his grandfather in his prime. The grandfather, also oblivious to the heartache around him, will not remember feeding the fish. The mother will remember it all and, every day, try to cope with the challenges that come.

Care-giving is a special art. How well I know, as I watched Alzheimer's disease slowly take over my husband's mind and persona. Care-giving is not for the faint-hearted but still it comes, even to those whose hearts are unprepared. Life is not always fair.

MAY 29

The heavy machinery moved in today, and it is a welcome sight. Welcome because a construction project is finally getting underway again, after being halted last fall when winter came early and stayed around much too long. Maple Crest's dream of a fishing pier, deck and screen house by the pond is getting one step closer to reality. I welcome the noise because it means progress, and I'll try not to complain about the mess in the meantime. I am anticipating good summer evenings visiting with friends in the screen house by the pond—when it's finished.

Any project, whether it is building a house or moving or cleaning closets or organizing files, involves a mess. Our familiar surroundings become unfamiliar. We experience an upset in our daily schedule that can be very disconcerting, even while it promises to enhance our lives—once it is done. It is that upset of routine that throws us. It's more comfortable to stay within the status quo.

But status quo can be stifling, too. The same old, same old, can lead to boredom and depression. Our minds and bodies—at least, my mind and body—need stimulation to keep going.

Help me, God, never to complain when something, or someone, interrupts my routine. Help me to keep looking forward to change and welcome new ideas, new friends, new experiences. Help me to keep living until I die.

MAY 30

Today I watched a ballet, of sorts. No music, no stage, no costume, no final bows. But an artist was definitely at work on the sidewalk below my window. He was a cement finisher, just doing his job. But there was definite artistry in what he was doing.

His sun-browned, muscular arms strained when scrubbing at a rough spot, but turned gentle when that particular flaw was set right. His knees dug into the kneeling pad as he stretched to reach a place in front of him, then flexed as he rose to move backwards to the next spot. I watched as my cement artist finished his work in that particular area and rose, circled his shoulders to relieve the strain, then got back onto his knees again until the job was finished to his satisfaction.

Every job has its artistry, some much more obvious than others. I remember my mother as she made noodles—her rolling pin forcing the dough into an ever-so-thin sheet, rolling that sheet into a tight scroll, finally slicing that scroll into the slimmest noodles possible. She was an artist with noodles. I remember watching my great-grandson, not yet in his teens, precisely folding paper cranes from tiny one-inch squares of origami paper. He was an artist in miniatures.

Sometimes, on our way to artistry, we give up. Maybe it's too hard, too time-consuming, too…any excuse will do. What will they say about me when I'm gone? Was I an artist in anything?

MAY 31

"Always leave a place looking a little better than you found it."

That's a saying my late husband used to repeat every so often, to our children and grandchildren. But he did much more than just say it—he *did* it. Perhaps it was the Boy Scout training in him, perhaps the influence of his parents. It was definitely something he had learned from little on up, and he demonstrated it throughout his life.

If we went on a picnic, he always made sure than our site was cleaner when we left it than when we had arrived. He wasn't averse to stooping to pick up litter on the sidewalk. And, of course, he bent down to pick up every penny, nickel or dime that was left lying in his path. "Pennies spend, too," he'd say.

I recall one Saturday morning in particular—a morning our children have never forgotten. We were living in Okemos, Michigan, a suburb of Lansing. Dean got all of us out of bed (including our high schoolers) and into the car along with rakes, shears and digging tools. We headed to a small highway island with a "Welcome to Okemos" sign. The vegetation on that traffic island had been severely neglected and the once-attractive area was growing up in weeds. But not for long! When we left for home, there was a cleaner, friendlier site announcing the town where we lived.

No one thanked us. No one gave us a good citizen plaque. Maybe no one even noticed. But our town, and all our family, were better for it.

June 1

Whenever I flip the wall calendar to June, I can't help but sing (in my head or, sometimes, out loud) "June Is Bustin' Out All Over." That song from the musical *Carousel,* popular more than half a century ago, brings back wonderful memories.

When my husband and I were busy and ambitious young marrieds, we were part of an eight-voice singing group. We called ourselves the Goldenaires and, for about ten years, presented musical programs to groups in town, around the county, and beyond. We enjoyed learning the music, we had fun at our practices, we looked forward to traveling to give our programs and meeting new people. It was a very special time with a very special group of amateur musicians.

One of the Goldenaires' favorite numbers was a medley of songs from *Carousel,* which ended with, yes, "June Is Bustin' Out All Over." That particular song provided an exuberant and splashy ending to the medley. The last chord included a high A for the high soprano—yours truly.

No longer can my voice produce a reasonable high A. No longer do I have the voice control and range I once had. And, of the eight singers, only three of us are still living. But the good memories are still there, the words still resonate, the feelings of exuberance continue, and I can't help but sing when June comes around once more.

JUNE 2

The month of June is, in more ways than one, a month of promise. And the promise I'm thinking of right now is fresh strawberries. I can hardly wait. Shipped-in California berries are better than none at all, but strawberries picked fresh at an Ohio farm can't be beat.

We are blessed, in our community, to have a strawberry farm just a few miles out in the country. Everyone in the area knows the name "Suter's" as the place to go to pick your own strawberries. Or, if you prefer, let them pick for you. In addition to the strawberries in June, Suter's fresh sweet corn and melons are staples during the months of July and August, all the way to Labor Day. What riches—right in our community!

In addition to summer produce offered daily from their farm, we have the Suter family to thank for another type of service. Suter's Farms provide good summer jobs for a multitude of local school students. And, when I say "good," I mean good in more than one way. To Jerry Suter, each of those kids is like one of his own family. He not only pays them, but he cares about them. They reciprocate by coming back to work the following years as well. That's the way it has been at Suter's farms for many, many years.

Knowing about that kind of caring makes the strawberries, corn and melons even sweeter.

JUNE 3

Books have always played a big part in my life and, if you have this book (or any book) in your hand, you probably feel the same way. When did a love affair with the printed word begin to take shape for you?

For me, it started in a tiny, dark building in rural Illinois—my first introduction to a public library. Today, we would probably classify that building as unfit for public use. Too small, too forbiddingly dark, inadequate ventilation, plus a non-credentialed librarian. But that little old library building looked, felt, and smelled just right to me at that age of innocence. In addition, tiny Miss Neuhauser always had a ready smile when I walked in—waiting just for me, I thought, to help find the perfect book for this budding bookworm. I still get a warm feeling thinking about that place, even though it must have been rather more like a hole in the wall. That tiny library was all I needed at the time.

Public libraries have come a long way since those days. So many books, so many services, so many conveniences for every kind of library patron. Stories and crafts for the young children, computers for everyone else. Prizes for the most prolific readers, contests and fun nights. And, we hope, a kindly librarian who is willing to guide the uninitiated.

Thank you, Miss Neuhauser, for being a guiding light in my library. You started me on the right path.

JUNE 4

Have you ever seen a flamingo close-up? Really close-up? I haven't, but my computer screen-saver has a photograph that reminds me every day. It's an intriguing photo taken by my son Mark, with a long-lens camera, at the Denver Zoo. Two beautiful pink flamingos, close-up and in profile, have their long necks wound snake-like around their bodies, their bills tucked under their wings. That's all one sees of the birds—their heads, their long sinuous necks and a portion of their wings.

It is if they are twin dancers, posed on a dance floor with bodies synchronized and movement as one. Although I cannot see their long legs, I can imagine their feet placed just so and toeing an imaginary line. But what makes the photo particularly arresting is that one bird has its camera-side eye closed while the other bird's eye is wide open. That one open eye is looking right at me. What does that bird see?

Yes I know, it's just a photograph. Those birds didn't even know they were being caught on camera—the cameraman being far away. But something about the way that one open eye keeps looking at me makes me sit up a little straighter in my chair. It reminds me I that am not alone. There is a whole universe of people, animals, birds—all of creation—outside my door and beyond.

That thought is comforting as well as challenging.

JUNE 5

This is an evening so still, so calm, that I am drawn outside for one more short walk before darkness falls. The pond is almost motionless and the swallows, quite raucous earlier this evening as they swooped over the water catching insects, are settling in for the night. A few low clouds are turning pink as the sun is about to set behind them. I sit on the bench beside the pond, just to drink in the beauty and the stillness.

Just two hours ago, this very place was filled with noise and crowded with families—a host of children of all ages with their parents, grandparents and great-grandparents. Our retirement community was enjoying a family fishing derby with 200-plus people gathered together all around the pond. Plenty of food, activity, laughter, squeals and shouts. Everything was alive with noise and movement.

Now the landscape has been transformed. The families have gone home. Chairs have been stacked, extra food taken back to the kitchen, tables put away. The pond, which had been rippling with plenty of bobbers, lures and fishworms, is still once again. The quiet is noticeable.

And so I sit, marveling at how the natural world can adjust so easily to us humans bursting in with our noise and exuberance, waiting patiently while we roil the waters and trample the grass. When we leave, the pond stills and the birds go to bed.

We all take our rest, readying for tomorrow.

JUNE 6

Every once in a while my friend and I get really hungry for fresh spring rolls as served at our favorite Thai restaurant. Today was one of those days, so off we went. They were delicious, as usual. Little rolls of finely chopped fresh vegetables encased in rice paper, floating in a delectable sauce that melds the flavors. We're never disappointed, either with the spring rolls or with whatever entree we decide to try.

So why don't we go there more often? I guess because letting something get too familiar means losing what was once special about it. What was once something to look forward to as an uncommon treat suddenly would become—well—just ordinary. The food would still be good, but the fun would be gone

And that doesn't just happen with food and restaurants. Losing our sense of anticipation can happen in our work, in our relationships with people, in our homes. It is good to be mindful of the fact that routine can easily become paralyzing, that bad habits can take hold and take over, and that even the best of intentions can sometimes turn sour.

So how to keep the freshness in life? For me, these daily reflections have been an awakening. My mind has been learning to grasp, and appreciate, the moment at hand. I am slowly discovering that there are many little wonders out there just waiting to be noticed. Just outside my window. They are at yours, too.

JUNE 7

With all the construction/deconstruction going on outside my window these days, I keep being fascinated by the artistry involved in working with big, noisy, cumbersome, heavy machinery. Being a woman who is much more versed in taking tiny embroidery stitches than in moving mountains, I have been getting a free tutorial into a different world of work.

This morning I watched as one man operated a big yellow machine. Sitting in the cab, he gently maneuvered the bucket to the ground—to the exact place where he could pick up a heavy block of cement without disturbing the grass beneath or toppling the pile adjacent. This was definitely not the first time he had worked that shovel. He knew what he needed to do and how it needed to be done.

Each of us has, over our lifetime, learned a variety of skills. Some we have mastered well, others remain in the periphery of our knowledge, and still others have never been tried. What you might excel in, I may have no interest in at all. But if we all were good at the same thing, who would do the rest of the work that has to be done? We all need each other.

So today I thank you, construction worker, for lending your skill so the job could be done right. We need you here.

JUNE 8

The day's forecast promised temperatures close to 80 degrees, with rain likely as well. I decided to take a walk before the rain arrived, and before it got too muggy to enjoy being outside. When I returned to my apartment after that walk, I was surprised to find the air decidedly chilly. My desk thermometer indicated that the apartment was colder than the setting on the thermostat. My air conditioner was working overtime to do a job that it didn't need to be doing.

This has happened before. Sometimes, after running for long periods on the same setting, the thermostat gets stuck. I have to fiddle with the controls to get it back to performing its designated task. Once adjusted, we're back in business again. Back to normal.

Don't we humans get stuck sometimes, too? Stuck in a routine that is much too familiar? We go about our tasks automatically and, sometimes, keep on going through the motions without realizing we're no longer on the right track. It takes something, or someone, outside ourselves to bring us back to where we should be. We need a wake-up call, an adjustment to bring us back to our purpose in life.

Maybe that's why Sunday (or whatever day is Sabbath for you) remains a special day of the week. A time to wake up and get back on track.

JUNE 9

Today the sky was a lie-on-your-back-and-find-the-animal-in-the-clouds day. It was a gift. A gift of bright blue sky full of white cotton balls, enough wind to keep the images changing, and the sun warm but not burning. I almost missed it. Busy at the computer this morning, I barely even glanced outside. But a necessary trip to the grocery took me away from my desk. It was only then, when I got in the car and was driving to town, that I realized what I had been missing all morning.

I wonder how many others in my community noticed that gift today. How many children lay in the grass today, letting their imaginations run? How many parents or grandparents were pointing out cloud-animals to their offspring? How many nursery school teachers noticed and then introduced to their children the wonders in the sky? How often was "what a beautiful day" spoken?

I'd venture to say that there weren't a lot of us, although I would be pleased to be told I am wrong. It is so easy to fill our days with "musts" and "shoulds" that we forget to relax and look up once in a while. There is so much that we miss. Days like today don't come when we order them and simple joys don't announce themselves. We just have to be open to their appearance.

May we never be too busy to open our eyes, each and every day.

JUNE 10

This afternoon I was leafing through an old photograph album, searching for a certain picture that I couldn't readily find. However plenty of other photos slowed my search and, suddenly, a search for one picture became a beautiful Sunday afternoon of reminiscing. Old photos will do that!

About ten years ago I finally started a project that had been on the "to do" list for some time. I began going through our boxes of photographs and slides to get them organized into albums, along with identification. It took a lot of work, and made for a long-term messy tabletop, but well worth the trouble. The memories are now there for everyone's enjoyment.

Now that we have cell phones that take our pictures, plus almost unlimited photo storage, will printed photograph albums be a thing of the past? Fifty years from now, when one of my great-grandchildren wants to know what I looked like, where will they find my picture? In someone's cell phone? On a disc? How will they know that picture is of their great-grandmother? What will be the storehouse of memories for the next generations to enjoy?

I guess I'll have to leave that up to someone else to figure out. But I hope that, along the way, my descendants will care to preserve a bit of our family history in pictures, well identified. Memories are important, too.

JUNE 11

Today was a "work with strawberries" day. Not long ago, this term would have meant an all-day job of picking, washing, stemming, freezing the big ones and making jam with the rest. But now I'm a good deal older, less physically agile, perhaps a little wiser. Plus I have only my own mouth to feed.

So today's strawberry day meant driving to Suter's farm, buying a bucket of just-picked-by-someone-else strawberries, stemming and freezing them. All finished before noon, but to be remembered for many mornings to come when I will enjoy homemade granola, yogurt and fresh-from-the-freezer strawberries for breakfast.

I miss the wonderful aroma of strawberry jam cooking on the stove, and the sight of jelly jars stacked away for winter use. But, to me, the reward is not worth the mess and effort anymore. In addition, I don't really crave jam on my toast as I used to.

All through life we pick and choose, and live with the result of those choices. At this point in my life I still want fresh strawberries in June but will forego the jam. Someday I'll be happy just to buy a quart of berries and forget about freezing some for the winter. Then, some later day, perhaps I won't even remember that there are such things as strawberries. But, if you pop one in my mouth, I hope I will remember to smile and say "thank you."

Everything in its season.

JUNE 12

Today was one of those days when people and things you hadn't thought about for some time become the topic of conversation. It all came about when my first cousin and two of her daughters came from Chicago for a short visit. She was returning to this corner of Ohio to reacquaint herself with her home town and, at the same time, introduce the "old haunts" to her daughters. I was there as a quasi tour guide and observer. Such fun!

They say you can't go home again. Sometimes the memories are not particularly sweet. But, in my cousin's case, there were many pleasant surprises and few reasons for regret. The home where she lived most of her growing-up years is still stately and beautifully groomed. There is a brand new school at the edge of town. The cemetery where her parents are buried is very well-maintained. The small church she used to attend has been attractively remodeled into a private home. The physical things that have changed are, for the most part, good changes.

The memories enlivened my cousin as we drove along the streets of town. Memories of playmates, school friends and next-door neighbors peppered her conversation as we made our way through town. Pointing out where her father had his office, talking about the grand house where special parties were held. Good memories kept flowing.

It was a good day. A day of reminiscing. A necessary part of life.

JUNE 13

The sun and clouds made a glorious display this evening as sunset time arrived. Thin clouds drifted slowly in to mute the pinks and blues. As the sun disappeared below the horizon and light began to fade, the pond stilled, the birds stopped their singing, everything quieted. It was as if the entire natural world was settling in for the night. So I found a book and sat in my favorite chair to read—to settle in myself before, eventually, going to bed.

But it wasn't long before a thought came to me—I'm missing something! What is it? It's the sounds of the night creatures. My windows are closed because the air conditioning is on. I have shut away the outdoors, so I can't hear the frogs at the pond, the quiet snuffling of night creatures.

When I was a child growing up on a farm, windows were open wide to let in the evening breeze. We were lulled to sleep with the night sounds. I remember the repetitive sound of the crickets, listening for the owl, hearing the train whistle from the track four miles away, a lone car driving past. Those night sounds were familiar and comforting.

Today we have to work at it to be able to hear nature's night sounds. Even camping is noisy, unless we find a true wilderness, because there's always someone with a portable radio, if not much more.

Ah, civilization!

JUNE 14

I have been eagerly awaiting the arrival of the monarch butterflies to our area. For the last several years I have cultivated—yes, cultivated—milkweed in my raised garden expressly for the benefit of the monarchs who lay their eggs on the underside of the milkweed's large leaves. We watch as the eggs hatch, the caterpillars grow, spin their light green jewel-case of a chrysalis, and finally emerge as a beautiful monarch butterfly.

Last year was a complete bust. I found only two tiny white eggs on the leaves and the fragile caterpillars that emerged lived for only a few days. Something wasn't right and I wasn't sure what to do about it. So we turned to raising black swallowtails instead. There was plenty of dill in the garden, a food the swallowtail caterpillars love, so the summer was not a complete loss. We enjoyed the growing and hatching process, but it wasn't the same.

For the monarchs, I still hold out hope for their arrival even though, worldwide, the fate of the monarch butterfly is tenuous due to the loss of winter habitat in Mexico plus weed killer use on farm fields and roadsides, taking away their food source. How I wish I could put up a big sign in the sky, pointing the way to my garden and stating *FREE OVERNIGHT CAMPING.* But, without the sign, will the monarchs come?

We'll just have to wait and see.

JUNE 15

This weekend, the time to celebrate Father's Day, evokes a wide variety of feelings in me as I think of the special fathers in my life.

First of all, I think of my own father who died of leukemia when I was nine. In memory's pictures I am in the barn with him, chattering as he milks the cows. The only other vivid memory I have is visiting him in the hospital, tickling his toes. My mother loved him very much and always regretted that her children never had the chance to really know him. I regret that, too.

My father-in-law, bless him, was a gem. He was openly welcoming to me from our very first meeting. He played fair, showed kindness to everyone, and provided a perfect example for his son, my husband. He was also a very special "Pop" to our children when they were growing up.

Of course I must list my late husband, the father of our six children. Dean loved them but didn't spoil them, provided for them but also let them try their wings. He also offered a living example for them to emulate, the way his father did for him. Dean wasn't averse to hard work, cleaning out the garage, or cooking special meals. And he loved his wife (I have to add that!).

And today I bless my sons and sons-in-law, those who are fathers and those who are uncles to my grandchildren. Thank you, fathers all, on your special day!

JUNE 16

This morning I heard first, then spied, a song sparrow perched on the top branch of the locust tree outside my window. Head up, throat vibrating, the bird sent its familiar song floating through the air. Three or more short notes, then a distinctive trill. Over and over the song rang out. A good start to the day.

Song sparrows have a way of getting one's attention, often by positioning themselves high on an open branch and then sending out their song loud and clear. It is as if they have a certain pride of presentation about them. "Look at me—here I am!" The elusive catbird, in contrast, will play hide-and-seek with you, staying deep in the foliage and daring you to play the game. Then there are those non-descript, hard-to-identify birds that tease by flitting silently from branch to branch, then flying away before you even have a chance to zero in.

I have human neighbors like that as well. Some hold their heads high and aren't afraid to speak out for a good cause. Some like the neighborhood but want to stay in the background, contributing silently. Others are so busy they never stay still long enough for you to get to know them.

The world is full of all types, some easier to get along with than others. But wouldn't it be pretty dull if they were all like me—or you?

JUNE 17

The suitcase came out of storage yesterday and now it stands open, waiting to be filled with whatever I'm going to need for the next seven days. Tomorrow morning I fly to North Carolina to spend a week with Rick and Debi, my oldest son and his wife. I expect to have a wonderful time as I usually do when I'm travelling, especially when visiting family.

As I pack, I think back to the many places this one favorite piece of luggage has been over its relatively short lifetime. This little copper-and-black case has been lifted into an airplane's overhead compartment several times (before I decided that it was just too much hard work and now check it). It has taken numerous trips up and around the airport's luggage claim belt. Often it has been opened by a security officer, checking to see if I've stashed any contraband. The wheels still move, the handle still retracts, the outside shows no scars. It has been a good and sturdy trip companion.

One of these years I'll probably need to bid my travel companion goodbye. As I get older, I realize that the time will come when I'll not be able to fly all around the country any more. I'll stay home and wait for my children and grandchildren to visit me. That's the way life goes, if we live long enough.

But, until that time, my suitcase and I will remain ready for whatever trip beckons.

JUNE 18

My mother was a great advocate of people-watching. I learned that to my dismay when I was small and had not yet developed the art of sitting still. If we went somewhere in the car and had to wait for someone, she'd say, "Just watch the people. It's always fun to watch people go by." I didn't buy that philosophy—at least until I got much older.

Today I am sitting in an airport having my mother's definition of "fun"—watching people. What a difference a few decades make!

Since my flight is scheduled for 12:15, there are very few men or women dressed in business attire—they would have all been on an earlier flight. Instead there is an energetic and efficient young mother with three boys, ages around 7, 5, and 3. There is one *very* young couple with a two-year-old whose smile could capture the most die-hard of grouches. An elderly woman and (probably) her son are sitting in the handicap section, waiting to be boarded first. There is also a young man taking a look at his passport. I wonder—to what country is he headed?

Then I realize that all the people waiting here are just like me—travelers away from home, destination somewhere else, all with expectations to arrive safely. Because of skilled pilots, attentive air traffic controllers, plus all the service personnel involved, we almost always *do* arrive safely.

Thank you.

JUNE 19

This week I am in Greenville, North Carolina, visiting my son and daughter-in-law. Greenville is not in the mountains to the west nor on the Atlantic coast to the east, but somewhere in between. Greenville is not as large as Charlotte nor is it as small as Okracoke—it's an in-between size city.

Isn't "in between" the sort of place where many of us find ourselves? We dream of the storied places, the glamorous places, places everyone goes for vacation. But most of us find ourselves living most of our lives somewhere in between. In between can be a very good place, an important place, even though we may think of it as unimportant. We cannot expect to live constantly on a high or on a low. The body and the spirit need some of both.

After I take a long walk, my body tells me to sit for a while with my feet up. After attending an exciting basketball game, it's good to settle down with a good book for a while before going to bed. And coffee breaks at work are important as well. Right now, I'm enjoying a season of much-anticipated family time. We'll go places and do things that are different, for me, than the norm. I'll enjoy every minute of it. And, when I get home to the old and familiar, that will be OK too.

Everything in its season.

JUNE 20

Growing up in the Midwest, I was never introduced to the beauty of the crape myrtle, a flowering tree that abounds in more southerly climates. But here in North Carolina they are outdoing themselves in striking white-to-pink-to-purple loveliness. You find them all over town. Most trees are pruned to keep their blooms down to eye level but others are allowed to grow tall as maples, their blooms high in the air. Every part of the tree—trunk, branches, leaves, flowers—is distinctive.

Each area of the world has certain trees endemic to that particular climate. Local trees become "old hat" and we hardly notice their beauty. But we "ooh" and "aah" over blooms in another part of the world. Oleanders in California, palms in Florida, jacarandas in India and cherry blossoms in Japan. Right now I am "ooh-ing" over the crape myrtles in North Carolina.

During the time I'm visiting here in Greenville, I will continue to revel in the beauty of the 100-year-old live oaks, the massively-wide vintage magnolias and the beautiful blooming crape myrtles that grace this city. And I thank the developers who, in many areas, have built around nature, preserving rather than destroying, planting where necessary, and keeping the city of Greenville truly green.

I am reminded of the words of Robert Louis Stevenson: "The world is so full of a number of things, I'm sure we should all be as happy as kings."

JUNE 21

It is always interesting to visit another part of the country to experience both the differences and the similarities—what's familiar and what's unfamiliar. Today, during my visit to North Carolina, I went with Rick and Debi to drive some of the "blue highways" leading to small villages overlooking Pimlico Sound.

I'm used to flatlands, growing up in Illinois and living in Ohio, but this land is truly flat—and very low. Just inches above sea level and subject to hurricanes, the coastal homes are built high, most of them on stilts. Plenty of steps lead to their front doors!

Fields in this area are planted in the familiar (to me) corn and soybeans, plus some wheat. Once in a great while we spot a field of what at one time was "king" here—tobacco. But few fields are as large as those growing timber, the biggest crop in this area. The low-lying areas are populated by trees, some native and natural but many Weyerhaeuser-planted. Fodder for the paper mills.

No matter what our individual feelings are about tobacco or paper mills, we are a society with a variety of wants and needs. In a perfect world, we would all live in comfort in an ideal climate with no one to question our motives or desires. Maybe our creator had it right when we were given freedom of choice. At least, it keeps life interesting!

JUNE 22

Today I'm still on my North Carolina "vacation," sitting alone at the house while my son and his wife are each away tending to Monday morning duties. How did I get here? No, I don't mean that literally. But, thinking back, how many decisions, what kind of influences, were in play to bring me from birth on an Illinois farm to sitting on a tree-shaded patio on a lovely North Carolina morning?

I didn't run away from home in my move away from Illinois. In fact, I intended to attend university at Illinois State, but an invitation to summer camp introduced me to a new set of friends going to school in Ohio. So off I flew to Bluffton College where I met the man who would become my husband.

If our eldest son had not gotten bitten by the ham radio bug in junior high school, he never would have attended Idaho State University, where his radio friend was teaching accounting and where his future wife was a student. And if he had not forsaken a CPA career in Phoenix to go to graduate school, he would never have found himself in administration at East Carolina University today. And I would not be sitting here, on a tree-shaded patio on a lovely North Carolina morning.

Life takes all kinds of twists and turns. Had I made some other decision, way back in time, I would not be here, in this place. But here is where I am and I am content.

JUNE 23

My daughter-in-law and I got out an old Parcheesi board this afternoon. Neither of us had played the game for years so we needed to read the rules again before attempting to play. But soon the memories came back.

"Oh yes, I remember how we used to blockade."

"*Twenty* extra spaces when you land on someone's space and send them home? I forgot it was that many!"

Debi and I had a great time hopping our markers around the board, overtaking the opponent's marker and counting off the rewarded spaces. In the end, we each won one game, then decided it was time to put the game away while both of us were still having fun. Knowing when to quit is sometimes an essential part of a game.

I remember playing Parcheesi as a kid, then playing again with our children, then with the grandchildren. Before the days of television and electronics, board games were the designated special entertainment for the evening, especially when company came to visit. But is there anyone out there who buys those old board games any more? I see such games displayed on the store shelves, but is there still a viable market for the old and unsophisticated? The old games don't beep, they don't blink, they don't move, they don't talk to you. They just sit there and invite you to create your own fun.

Maybe it's time to leave the electronics at home and take an old board game on vacation this year.

JUNE 24

There are times in our lives when we welcome guests into our home and cater to their needs. There are other times when we travel to someone else's home, where we can enjoy being catered to. I have enjoyed the latter this week while visiting my son and his wife in North Carolina. It has been like "Queen for a Day" without the crown.

We have been on a very relaxed schedule. Oh, we went places and did a variety of interesting things, but it was all very laid-back, very casual, no need to impress the friends and neighbors. During the day while Rick was at work, Debi and I put together one fabulous jigsaw puzzle—one of those difficult photo-mosaic ones made up of a thousand color photographs. We needed the full week to get it finished, but what an accomplishment!

Perhaps I've enjoyed this past week a bit too much—this being waited on, fed great food, allowed to relax and be lazy. But I think back to how much I enjoyed just being with my mother as she moved into her later years, taking walks, looking at old pictures, just talking and spending time together. Times like that make for good memories—for both young and old.

So thank you, Rick and Debi. It has been a great week!

JUNE 25

The sun shines just a little too brightly through my west window in late afternoon and evening, so I usually keep one mini-blind pulled down until near sunset. It is then that I take the blind up again to enjoy the colors as the sun goes down. This evening, however, I had a big surprise when I opened that blind. There were mountains looming on the horizon!

Now, I know—we all know—that northwest Ohio has no mountains. Not even hills. But there they were! Mountains were silhouetted against a clear sky, as if the Tetons had moved themselves east just for my benefit. After the initial shock, I soon had the phenomenon figured out. But even then I continued to marvel at the illusion and how it manifested itself in an exceptional kind of beauty.

What really appeared in the sky, hovering over the horizon to create the effect of mountains, were thunderheads. Those massive, but also threatening, clouds that form in summer and sometimes bring strong storms. But this evening, right at sunset, the thunderheads were bringing the mountains to Ohio. What a delightful surprise!

And then I began to wonder. How many other delightful surprises have I missed by not being at the right place at the right time—and in the right frame of mind? I must stay aware, and awake, to the quiet blessings that come when least expected.

JUNE 26

It was a still, still morning. Early fog had given way to sunny skies. The leaves on the locust tree outside my window were not moving at all. It was as if the world were standing still, waiting for orders to start breathing again.

And then I saw it. One lone goose feather floating on the surface of the pond, like an untethered boat. The movement was so imperceptible that I watched for some time before I realized that the feather was making progress, ever so slowly, toward the shore. Yes, it definitely was a still, still morning.

How did the feather get there, in the middle of the pond, this morning? Usually I do not see geese at the pond until late in the afternoon. Had the feather floated there all night? Or did a flock of geese come for a swim earlier this morning, leaving a calling card in their wake?

I don't know what eventually happened to the feather, since I did not have the time to sit and watch until it made shore. I probably would not have had the patience, either, to spend the next hour or two watching one lone feather make its way across the pond. But perhaps, when I'm finished writing this, I might just slip downstairs and check the rocks at my end of the pond. Maybe there will be a lone feather there, finished with its travels and just waiting to be discovered.

JUNE 27

Today a little poem I remember from elementary school has been running through my head. You know how it is—the words are there and just won't go away. Thanks to the Internet, I had no trouble finding that poem and confirming its words as well as the author, Dorothy Aldis.

If I had a spoon as tall as the sky
I'd dish out the clouds that go slip-sliding by.
I'd take them right in and give them to cook
And see if they taste as good as they look.

Along with the words to that poem, I remember an illustration painted by a friend of my mother. Depicted in that small picture is a little girl in old-fashioned clothes reaching high into the sky with a long-handled golden spoon, trying to snatch a fluffy cloud. It was a delightful representation of an equally delightful poem.

But now, I wonder—whatever happened to that painting? When my mother died, was it in her things to be divided up? And, if so, where did it go? I don't have it. Did someone else take that little keepsake? And who was the lucky recipient?

It's easy to lose track of many of those little "somethings" that once had a place in our lives. But the memories sometimes remain vivid. I still see the little girl with the big spoon. The memory will have to suffice.

JUNE 28

I remember it vividly, and yet it seems like a dream from another world. The phone call came yesterday evening. "It's Rick," came my oldest son's voice. But that voice sounded strange—too quiet, too strained. The voice went on. Two words, "Dan died." Stunned, I whispered the first thing that came to mind, "Oh, my goodness." Silence. Then I said it once more, more emphatically this time. "OH, MY GOODNESS!"

Rick's quiet voice continued and my mind picked up snatches of what he was saying. Wheelchair—ramp—backwards—probably instant. My son-in-law Dan, husband of my youngest daughter Kay, was dead. Impossible! But yes. Possible.

After several tries I finally reached Kay by phone in Maine, nearly a thousand miles away. Too, too far away. We cried, of course. I told her I'd be there as soon as I could get plane flights arranged. She told me Lee, her sister, happened to be on the east coast and would be flying up the next day. Kay's daughters and grandchildren were there. Someone would be there with her.

Sleep was elusive that night. So much going on in my head. I already had my ticket to fly to Maine at the end of July, a month from now, for a family reunion. I could change the reservation and fly out over the weekend. But I've never changed a flight before. This is all new—too much, too much.

Help me, God. Help us all.

JUNE 29

Accepting news of a death is never easy. When that news is about someone younger than oneself, it is harder still to accept. When that news is about your daughter's husband, it is doubly hard to get one's mind around the concept. *How can it be?*

My son-in-law, not yet old enough (or ready) to retire, died suddenly, accidentally. The news came as such a shock that it has yet to fully sink in. Dan, the popular teacher, the hard-working volunteer, the proud father, the loyal friend, the advocate for all that's good—suddenly not with us any more. It's just not fair.

No, life is not fair. Neither is death. We scan the obituaries, but usually with dispassionate interest since we seldom expect to see a familiar name there. It's usually someone else's problem, someone else's grief—until one of the listings hits far too close to home.

And what can a mother, talking over the phone with her grieving daughter, do except grieve with her and run to her side as soon as possible? With nearly half a continent between us, I'm not with her right now—except in spirit. I will be at her side as soon as I can get everything arranged. And then, all I can do is weep with her.

I guess that's what mothers are for.

JUNE 30

Everything is finally arranged. Tomorrow morning I'll be getting on a plane again. Less than a week ago I was winging my way through the clouds, heading home after a relaxing vacation in North Carolina. Tomorrow I will be winging my way through the clouds once more, but this time I will be on a different sort of mission.

I know that Kay needs me there right now, but I have just as strong a need, perhaps even stronger, to be there with her. I think that is true with most mothers—when your child is hurting, no matter what age, you need to be there.

All day yesterday I was at loose ends, trying to settle down to accomplish everything I had to prepare in order to be gone from home for nearly five weeks. I wasn't functioning well, my mind wishing me a thousand miles away, with my daughter. Today was better, as I neared the end of my "to do" lists and started packing for the trip. Tomorrow will be better still and, when Kay and her sister Lee meet me at the airport, I'll be able to breathe normally again.

Even though we live miles and miles apart, when disaster strikes there is nothing like family—at least in our family that seems to be the case. We live far apart and don't schedule regular phone calls or visits, but when the chips are down we're there for each other.

We will get through this—together.

July 1

We met at the airport, a sterile, impersonal site that has, I'm sure, been the setting for many an emotional meeting. But the meeting place held much less importance than the meeting itself. There's something about that first hug—the one between mother and daughter following a tragedy—that is longer, more comforting and more needed than any of the many other hugs to follow. That prolonged first embrace says words that cannot be uttered, only felt.

So now I am in Maine, with Kay and her family, plus another of my daughters who arrived a day before me. More family from both sides of the aisle will be arriving during the ensuing days. The house will be full and noisy and bustling with many things to plan and do. For, let's admit it, deaths and funerals are mainly about family and friends and those still living. These elements make for words and stories, laughter and tears, meals and bedtime and all things human.

I remember how important it was to me that my daughter was with me when my husband died several years ago. I hope I can be that sort of anchor for her now—another presence to depend on at a time when physical and spiritual support is so important.

We will hold each other up as we struggle with making sense of an untimely death.

JULY 2

Tonight, after a day of relatives arriving and concluding with emotionally taxing visitation hours at the funeral home, our gathered family experienced one of those "little blessings" that come unexpectedly when most needed. The blessing came in the guise of a dance of fireflies in Kay's back yard.

Darkness had come and, with it, those tiny bearers of fluorescent lights blinking on and off all across the back yard. It was a perfect night for them, and for us, as we stood on the back deck, all interior lights extinguished, so we could enjoy the show.

We all stood in silence for a while but then the explanations began. Some of the science lovers needed to explain the phenomenon of the fluorescent glow. Others of us made comments about the mating dance going on in the back yard. Some of us related our childhood memories of chasing fireflies and putting them in a glass jar to watch them blink in our bedrooms. Others just stood and marveled at another piece of God's handiwork.

Back home in Ohio we keep our world too well lighted and we spray our lawns to keep away the pests. The result? We seldom see fireflies perform. But here they were, in Maine, inviting us to dry our tears, stop our work, lower our voices and just enjoy. Nature was offering us a gift and we responded with gratitude.

JULY 3

Some individuals can move into a new community, live a good portion of their lives there and, when they leave, they are barely missed. Then there are others who, as soon as they move to a new community, get involved to such an extent that their going away leaves a big hole. The large attendance at today's funeral service for Dan, my son-in-law, gives evidence that he will be sorely missed in his adopted community.

Dan's obituary will tell you that he was an EMS dispatcher and firefighter early on, then a dedicated middle school teacher. But that merely tells you where he was employed. The more important information about his life is told in the way he went about his work with enthusiasm and dedication, the way he opened his arms and his life to others, the way he willingly gave of his time and energy to his town, his school, his church, his neighbors. It is those characteristics that drew nearly 600 people to attend a funeral held in a non-airconditioned high school gym on a hot, muggy afternoon the day before Independence Day.

Most of us *do* strive to be good citizens and to make a difference during our years on this earth. Some of us fall short of our goals. Some do better at the task than others. Some of us excel.

Dan was one of the latter. He is already missed.

JULY 4

This morning it was heart-warming to watch Jeanne and Lee, two of my daughters, and Debi, a daughter-in-law, as they worked to give a special gift to their sister. They were creating a new flower bed in her yard.

It started with a small blueberry bush—one of the floral gifts sent at the time of Dan's funeral. To supplement, the girls purchased a bleeding heart, some hostas and Gerbera daisies to be planted with it. Then the girls began digging. Two of them took turns with the spade, turning up the sod while another separated the grass from the topsoil, mixing it with peat moss to make a good planting soil. They laid edging to separate the bed from the rest of the lawn. Then they laid down a weed barrier and topped it all with mulch. Those three women were on a mission and, before long, they had transformed a little corner of the yard into a beauty spot.

How heartening to watch those still-young women, whom I have nurtured and loved for many years, create something special for their bereaved sister! Here they were together, in the state of Maine, after traveling here from New Mexico, Colorado and North Carolina. It was love and family that brought them together, here in this place at this particular time.

One more memory to put in their own books of family memories.

JULY 5

The crowd of extended family that has surrounded us for the past several days has dwindled to the "Mainers" now (except for me—I will stay here with Kay for another month). The family now consists of Kay's four children and six grandchildren, all of whom live here in town or within 90 miles. Our task now, over the next few weeks, is to try to pick up the pieces of our lives again and settle into a "new normal."

The house is quieter—too quiet much of the time. The refrigerator, once bursting with gifts of food, has been emptying little by little. The beautiful floral arrangements gracing most of the tabletops in the house are beginning to fade.

Coming back to a semblance of normal is not an easy task. Our perspective has changed while the world continues on at its normal pace. Things that seemed so important at one time hold very little relevance now. We are all still running in neutral, bodies responding to normal day-to-day tasks while the spirit is still numb.

Next week we must start crossing things off the "must do after the funeral" list, and there will be plenty to do. But right now, on this weekend following the Fourth of July when most folks are vacationing in one way or another, we will cling to each other as we gather strength for the ensuing days.

That's what loving families do best.

JULY 6

There is something special about an outdoor worship service, especially when it is held at a spot overlooking the water. My daughter's church had such a service this morning—a monthly tradition each summer.

We met at the Owl's Head lighthouse park, under the trees overlooking Penobscot Bay. We brought our own lawn chairs, sat on one of some folding chairs provided, or sat on the ground wherever we found space. We had our own natural air conditioning. There was no sound system, only the pastor's strong voice. Hymns were accompanied by a lone guitar. Birds provided the special music. It was a worship service to remember in that special space.

I wonder how many from that congregation attended today especially, since it was an outdoor service. I wonder too how many stayed away especially, since it was an outdoor service. I'm sure the pastor, and the pastors before him, have pondered that question. They know it is hard to please everyone all the time.

But for Kay and her family, and myself, this informal outdoor service was a welcomed respite. After the stressful week of mourning in a formal and more traditional setting, we were able to relax in a way that helped us put aside the sorrow, at least for a little while.

It was a good way to start the healing.

JULY 7

Children have a way of brightening one's day, even when the day is not particularly bright. Their laughter is contagious, their questions can be unexpected, their hugs are heartfelt. The mood of this past week has been lightened with the presence of Kay's young grandchildren (my great-grandchildren). The two-year-old's bright blue eyes grab your heart, the four-year-old is full of questions, the seven-year-old goes a mile a minute and their eleven-year-old sister is her mother's right hand.

As I see my granddaughter caring for her lively children, it takes me back to my early-married days. My, how things have changed! When my children were small there were no Pampers. Cloth diapers, large safety pins and a diaper pail were the accoutrements at the changing table. Car seats and seat belts were non-existent. How did my children ever survive a trip in the car back then? Toys didn't beep or flash or speak, they were just there to play with. Captain Kangaroo was the only TV personality they knew, and he only appeared on the neighbor's TV—we didn't have one early on.

But today, when we as four generations sit around the table, we still hold hands and sing "God is great, God is good." And at night these great-grandchildren of mine will go to sleep with some of the same Bible verses in their heads that I myself learned as a child.

Some traditions stay the same.

JULY 8

I had nearly forgotten the air-fresh aroma of sheets hung outside on the clothesline—until today, that is. Having used a clothes dryer (and the accompanying scented dryer sheets) for so many years, the odor of fresh-air-dried clothes had nearly faded from memory.

Here at my daughter's home in Maine, with a couple of acres of space and plenty of sun and wind, the clothesline is kept busy. "No need to pay to run the dryer on nice summer days," Kay maintains. And I agree. Especially after lying in bed between the freshly-washed and air-dried sheets. The smell and feel reminded me of my childhood home.

But then my thoughts took another turn. Perhaps I wasn't quite so enamored with air-dried sheets back in those days before there were automatic dryers. I remember hanging wet laundry out on the clothesline on cold winter days when everything took all day, or more, to freeze-dry. I remember having to bring the clothes back into the house from the line, all stiff and crinkly and still half wet. Not much fun.

So, even though dryer sheets can't quite duplicate the aroma of the outdoors, I guess I'll stay in this 21st century with all the modern conveniences. But while I'm here in Maine, I'll take advantage of the clothesline and sweet summer breezes.

JULY 9

Today Kay and I were running a variety of errands in town as well as several in the country. I'm glad I was a passenger, as I would never have been able to find my way alone in this countryside criss-crossed with roads winding this way and that and up and over and down. The scenery is beautiful but I think even the best GPS would get confused on some of these Maine roads.

In addition to marveling at the proliferation of winding roads, I have also been surprised at the large number of houses that are hidden away—not at all far off the road but almost completely hidden from view by trees and underbrush. There is very little open and arable land around here. Trees are everywhere, but little lakes (or ponds, as many are called) also dot the landscape. Lovely views of the ocean and its coves may appear just around the next corner.

When my daughter and her husband moved from Ohio to Maine more than 25 years ago, Kay worked as a visiting nurse, traveling to visit her assigned patients over three counties here along the coast. She had not been in her job very long when she exclaimed to me over the phone one fall day, "Mother, it's so beautiful, driving around to see my patients. And I even get paid to do it!"

Kay and Dan's love affair with Maine never diminished. They found their niche.

JULY 10

Life is a series of adjustments. Some are major, such as what my daughter is going through now following the death of her husband. Some adjustments are minor and only a temporary irritation to daily life. I've been working on one of those minor adjustments since I flew to Maine ten days ago.

I still can't get used to morning coming so early. You see, I live in Ohio, a state on the west side of the Eastern time zone. Maine is at the far east edge of the same time zone. Over nine hundred miles separate our two homes, but we occupy the same time zone. That takes some getting used to.

It is most noticeable to me in the morning. I wake up, see that it's light outside and tell myself it must be time to get up. Look at the clock—5:15. Definitely *not* time to get up. It happens every morning, although by now I've gotten used to it enough that I don't check the clock any more, I just roll over and go back to sleep.

The arrival of darkness in the evening has not been so noticeable, perhaps because the sky at my bedtime is dark in both time zones. Since I plan to be here in Maine another month, I'm sure this minor adjustment will soon be forgotten—until I get home and will need a few days to adjust to the time difference once again.

This is a welcome reminder that I am still alive, still aware, and still able to adjust. May it continue.

JULY 11

It has made a grandmother's heart glad to see how her daughter's children have gathered round to let their mother know how much she is loved. Kay's two adopted children, who live in town, are over every day and her two natural daughters who live out of town call every day, come often and, many times, stay the night.

Yesterday and today they were all here, with their children, working on their summer "to do" lists that they want to complete for (and with) their mom. Yesterday's jobs included organizing the workbench in the garage plus clearing out a storage shed—we all know how things can accumulate over time. Today they were cleaning the mini-blinds, trimming the bushes and pulling weeds, followed by a good swim in the above-ground pool.

Two of Kay's children are still here tonight, plus five of her grandchildren, so the house is vibrating with children's voices and activities. Kay loves every minute of it. When the younger children are settled down for the night, the adults will probably have a more serious discussion about future plans. There will undoubtedly be some tears shed before we all turn in.

But that's all right, too, because laughter and tears are both part of the grieving process. We're in this recovery period together. We'll come through all right, with God within us and beside us.

JULY 12

My thumb has never been particularly green, but I do enjoy gardens—both the edible and the floral variety. Today my daughter Jeanne and I spent several hours experiencing a delightful garden tour in the town of Rockland, Maine. With a combination of bright sun and cooling ocean breeze, we couldn't have asked for a more beautiful day.

Eight different settings gave us a variety of garden spots to enjoy—from the more formal gardens tended by professionals to the informal backyard gardens of hobbyists. My favorite surrounded a small Cape Cod built in the late 1800s. The lawn was not smooth or manicured because the limestone bedrock presented a real challenge to cultivation. But every inch of ground that could support growth was filled with color and texture and just plain natural beauty.

A short quote from the tour brochure says this about that garden: "The home had been vacant for several years and was in a poor state, along with the grounds. A builder saw its potential and renovated the inside and left us to do the outside."

What insight that purchaser had—to take a neighborhood eyesore and turn it into a delightful place to live and enjoy! Would that more of us could realize the potential in unappealing places and add a little more beauty to this world.

JULY 13

Twenty-five years ago when I would visit my mother and stepfather at their year-round house in Florida, they would complain about the winter visitors, their cars filling the streets and clogging the intersections. Here in Maine in July, it is the summer travelers that create traffic jams along the coastal roads. And the heavy traffic will continue into fall as the trees begin to turn to gold and crimson.

And yet, these busy tourist seasons are essential to the permanent residents. Tourism is an important industry, not only here in Maine, but across the country. Each area of the U.S. depends on travelers and vacationers to bring extra dollars into their coffers. And each area has its own way of facing the challenge. One accommodation made for residents here in coastal Maine is that the public schools schedule a full week of vacation in late spring because so many families are not able to take summer vacation during the busiest tourist months of July and August.

So, the next time we get stuck in traffic going through Camden, we'll just sigh and know that's how it's going to be until Labor Day. And then, when the leaves begin to turn their gorgeous reds, yellows and browns, the residents here will sigh once again—and go on with their lives.

That's just how it is.

JULY 14

How did you celebrate your second birthday? I suppose almost all of us would answer that we don't remember. In fact, I would doubt anyone who claimed to have a vivid memory of such an event—at two years old.

My great-grandson had his 2nd birthday today. His sisters would say to him, "How old are you, Josiah?" He would break into a grin and hold up one finger (he still hadn't figured out how to raise that second one) and say "two." Then we'd all laugh, including Josiah.

We didn't have a birthday party, as such, for him—with cake and candles and all. We sang to him but he didn't get a heap of fancy presents. But I'm sure Josiah will not grow up to be stunted by that fact. He won't resent it that his parents didn't invite in a half dozen other two-year-olds to celebrate with him. He is not growing up in a family that feels the need to be trendy or to out-do their neighbors. An afternoon swim in grandma's swimming pool and a trip to Dorman's for ice cream was as delightful a day as any two-year-old could dream up.

Next year we'll probably bake a cake and put on three candles. By that time Josiah may be able to blow them out, all by himself. And maybe, some years later, we'll invite in some of his friends. But one small step at a time is good enough right now.

JULY 15

It rained early this morning and now it is very humid, cloudy and cool. The fog rolled in, as it often does on days like this along the Maine coast. So we are inside going through the bookshelves, deciding what to keep and what to give away.

Kay's husband Dan was a teacher, particularly interested in history and social studies. His bookshelves held many books on American history, the Civil War in particular, plus a host of other books as well. But history was Dan's interest, not Kay's. So most of those history books will go to the school or the local library. Others, Kay will keep while some will go home with her daughters. We've also discovered some long-forgotten items. You know how it is with shelves—they have a tendency to accept odds and ends, hiding them from sight until the mind forgets.

When the shelves are put back in order, Kay will have started to make those bookshelves her own. She will continue, over the next weeks and months, to gradually readjust the house to her particular needs and interests. Although the memories of "our" house will always be there, she will gradually make it her own.

I'm glad I am here in Maine right now, as Kay goes through these first weeks of a new kind of life. Actually, right now, I probably need her as much as she needs me. Once a mother, always a mother.

JULY 16

I've been reading a book about immigration to America (one of Dan's books I found on the shelf). It's not a subject I was particularly interested in pursuing, but the book was there, I had some free time, so I picked it up and started reading. Then I was hooked. That's what books will sometimes do.

I am not far into the book, so am certainly no expert on the subject, but I have gleaned some interesting facts. One thing that interested me, from the very first chapter, was that statistics rarely mention the people who come but don't stay— those who return to the country from which they emigrated.

In the 1700s and 1800s, it would have been much more difficult to cross the ocean to America and then decide to return to Europe, or one of the other continents from which they had come. But there are always some who opt to return. Leaving one home for another does not always work out, especially when it involves differing cultures and unmet expectations. Returning to one's former home is an option that immigrants have taken ever since the Americas began to be settled.

My grandfather was 24, and unmarried, when he came from Europe to America with his parents and two younger brothers. Fortunately for me, the family prospered in Illinois and stayed. And that's why I'm here today, reading this book in English and writing these little reflections, also in English. Thank you, Grandfather, for planting deep roots in a new country while passing along your love for the earth and all its creatures.

JULY 17

Today Kay and I drove north to Bangor, where her daughter Jessie lives and works. On the way there, while enjoying the scenic drive, I was also made aware of the contrast between early farmsteads in Maine and in Illinois, where I grew up.

In Illinois, the farmsteads are spread out—the house at one site and the barns and outbuildings some distance away. There was plenty of room to spread out on the prairie. But in Maine there is a saying: "big house, little house, back house, barn." All the buildings are attached—the barn being a part of one continuous building. It makes sense in a state covered in trees and with harsh winters. In the early days of Maine's settlement, fewer trees had to be felled when clearing the land and the animals could be more easily tended in winter.

Today, many of Maine's 200-plus year old buildings are still intact and occupied, although much renovation has taken place. The main house may still contain a fireplace in every room, but most fireplaces do not provide the main source of heat. The attached barn may have been converted to a three-car garage plus plenty of storage above.

The early settlers to America used their "old country" experience, plus their ingenuity, to adapt to whatever land and climate they encountered, whether it was in Maine or Illinois or Georgia. We are living with that legacy now. What will we leave for the generations following us?

JULY 18

All this week Kay and I have been looking at trees. *Really* looking. Not at the tall, tall maples and oaks, pines and spruce that one finds in abundance in this state of Maine. My daughter and I have suddenly become very aware of some of the smaller, decorative trees that grace the lawns in town. Those can also be found in abundance, especially when one is looking for them.

The reason for this special interest is that, in two weeks, our Niswander family will all be here. The last Saturday in July, Kay's five brothers and sisters will be arriving with their families for a week-long special family reunion that has been in the planning stages for a year. We plan to plant two trees in honor of Dan, our recently-deceased son-/brother-in-law. Of course, none of us ever dreamed, in planning this reunion, that planting memorial trees would be part of the schedule.

Kay has selected a white dogwood and a Japanese willow to be the dedicated trees. They will be planted near a tall English columnar oak that my children and I planted here four years ago in honor of Dean, my late husband and their father. I trust that it will be many years before another memorial tree is planted and, when it is, that the tree will be planted in memory of me.

Death should not come to the young.

JULY 19

Today I moved into my daughter Jeanne's house. This is a smaller place, now occupied only occasionally in the summer. Jeanne had lived and taught here in Rockland, Maine, but then she met and married a gem of a man from New Mexico, where they now live. They have kept Jeanne's house in Maine to come back to and enjoy for a few weeks each summer.

So why am I writing about this? In order to make sense of the ebb and flow of life as it presents itself in upsetting previously-laid plans. It's about adapting and moving on.

My original summer plans were to fly to Maine July 23 and return home August 6. All of my family had made plans to come to Maine the last week in July for a much- anticipated family reunion. Then, when Kay's husband died suddenly at the end of June, I quickly changed my flight plans and came to Maine on July 1st instead of the 23rd. I have been staying at Kay's home all this month—until today.

Kay's in-laws had also planned a week in Maine, for the third week in July, so her house is filling up today and tomorrow with Dan's side of the family. Kay needs "my" bedroom so I am making myself scarce and moving to Jeanne's house for the week. After all the emotional stress and busy-ness of the past three weeks, I will relish this time of quiet.

JULY 20

Yesterday I wrote about looking forward to some quiet time during which I hoped to write, read, and relax. And that's certainly what I have experienced here. Jeanne's welcoming house is empty except for me. I slept late this morning, took a long walk, had a quiet morning time of reflection, ate a leisurely lunch, did a crossword puzzle, and now I'm at my daily writing task.

But it's almost too quiet. The phone isn't ringing. No one is talking. I'm having withdrawal symptoms—withdrawal from people and activity. What I looked forward to yesterday is almost too much on this first day of my anticipated hermit experience.

Our lives get complicated like this sometimes. We long for peace and quiet, then chafe at the quiet when it goes on too long. We love people and activity but soon we wish it would slow down. Many times we don't know what we want, but we're sure it's not what's happening at the moment. Some of us make the best of it and go on. Others of us just enjoy complaining.

All right, I've been complaining (and maybe even enjoying it). But now it's time for me to stop the whining and get on with life—to get on with life as it is right now, in this quiet place.

This is the day that the Lord has made. I will rejoice and be glad in it.

JULY 21

So here I am, at Jeanne's summer house until Thursday evening when she arrives. How can I say "thank you" in something other than words?

I look around the house. Everything is in apple-pie order. I notice a bit of dust on the living room tables and take care of that in almost less time than it takes to write this sentence. The windows are clean on the inside and I'm not about to get on a ladder and wash the outsides. Then I see that the window-wells outside the double-hung windows have a coat of winter grime. That cleaning job takes a little more time, but the sills are now ready for next winter.

Friday sometime, after Jeanne arrives, I'm pretty sure she will discover that I cleaned the sills. And I can already hear her say, "Mother! You weren't supposed to do that!" And I'll smile and say something equally as typical. (Or maybe she'll be too busy to notice until I leave, which will be even more satisfying for me.) Over the next few days I may find a few more things to do to "earn my keep," as we used to say. Even though I'm family, I am still a guest here.

In our communities, and even in our separate countries all over this world, all of us are temporary guests. The earth gives to us, we consume. We need to say "thank you" in any way we can.

JULY 22

This morning I was captivated by two books relating the early histories of two adjoining towns, Rockland and Thomaston, Maine. The summer home of my daughter Jeanne is in Rockland while my daughter Kay lives year-round in Thomaston. The two towns' histories, as well as their present-day auras, are dissimilar.

Today, Rockland is a busy harbor town with hundreds of boats of all sizes and shapes moored and waiting for their owners to set out to sea. You'll find a busy downtown with plenty of shops, restaurants, hotels, plus a large ferry terminal to take you to outlying islands. Rockland is the business hub of this area today (although a Wal-Mart opened last fall just across the town line, in Thomaston).

But Thomaston's history goes back much farther—back to early ship-building days. Established along the St. George River, many sailing ships were built, then launched, from the Thomaston shipyards. Driving along Thomaston's Main Street today allows a view of many beautiful, historic homes of early sea captains. You will also see Montpelier, the stately mansion of General Henry Knox, Secretary of War for (and good friend of) George Washington. Thomaston has a small, attractive business block but today's bustle centers on Rockland or Camden, just a few miles to the north.

In another 200 years, what will we find of these towns on the Atlantic coast? Will their characters have changed once again? Will they even exist? Only time will tell.

JULY 23

Today was designated "go to Bar Harbor" day for Kay's in-laws who have been visiting her this week. They invited me to go along and, since I had not been there for 15 years or more, I accepted the invitation. Going to Bar Harbor includes visiting Acadia National Park, and that was the draw for me.

Acadia shows off the singular beauty of Maine's north Atlantic coast. Cadillac Mountain is the tallest spot from which to view the coastline and ocean, but the entire loop road is filled with many beauty spots. The views overlooking Egg Island, Sand Beach and Thunder Hole are spectacular, but a little stony cove that Kay and Dan discovered on their honeymoon more than 30 years ago was a hidden delight.

To appease the shoppers and ice cream lovers, it is always necessary to drive into cars-and-people-crowded downtown Bar Harbor. I'll admit that Bill & Bob's black raspberry ice cream is delicious, but the waiting in line is less satisfying. Walking single-file on the narrow sidewalks, past shop after shop, is far from my idea of a relaxing afternoon. But my spirits were lifted when we found a bench in the shady village square and were well entertained by my great grandson as he delighted in splashing in the water fountain.

Soon the day was over, the clouds moved in and rain dampened some of our drive home. But, all in all, another beautiful day in Maine.

JULY 24

I was taken by surprise this morning. I shouldn't have been, once I digested the surprise. But, when I saw him (or her—for convenience we'll dub him "him") my first thought was, "What are you doing here, in Maine?"

It was a hummingbird nosing around the bushes just outside the kitchen window. The clouds were heavy, rain coming down in a light drizzle, but there he was. No sun to glance off his red gorget, nothing showy to announce his presence, but I just happened to be there at the right time and place to spot him.

He flew up to a low power line leading into the house where I could continue to watch him. Suddenly he was joined by another. Now I had a pair, just sitting there for my delight. And then, too soon, they were off—maybe to find Jeanne's flowers planted right around the corner, or maybe to the next door neighbor's garden. But, for the moment, they had opened my eyes and given me a lovely Maine morning surprise. Enough to give a smile to my rainy morning and a little something to think about for the rest of the day (food for this reflection).

I've thought before and will think again: How many times do we miss those "little somethings" only because they happen out of sight or, more often, out of mind? Oh, for better eyes to see…all around me.

JULY 25

Last night was music night—and what music it was! My daughter Kay and I, both amateur musicians and lovers of good music, had a most enriching evening at the Rockport Opera House. On stage were eleven members of "Curtis On Tour," students and faculty of Philadelphia's Curtis Institute of Music. Playing music ranging from 18th century Vivaldi (Italy) to 20th century Piazzolla (Argentina), the musicians gave us an evening to savor.

The audience at this evening's concert was, predominantly, over 50. But I was pleased to see a representation of young people there as well. Parents with children who are, probably, taking lessons on stringed instruments. We need those parents to keep bringing their children so they learn to appreciate and perform a wide variety of music, including the classical.

These young performers on stage last night, so poised and so talented, delighted the audience. How much practice time, study time, lesson time has already gone into their budding careers? What have they already given up to get to this stage? How much more will be expected of them until they reach whatever goals they have set?

Each of us, at some point in life, has had dreams for the future. Last night I saw students whose goals are much higher than mine ever were. I marvel at their talent, I wish them well, but at the same time I do not envy them. I am content to listen and enjoy.

JULY 26

Today begins the week when my family gets together here in Maine—a reunion that we started planning nearly a year ago. We've rented a large house on the water for the week and, with two daughters and some of my grandchildren already having homes here, we'll have enough room to house everyone. Since my six children and their families are scattered across the U.S. from Maine to Illinois to New Mexico, from North Carolina to Colorado (with me in the middle), the times when all of us get together are preciously few. We've all been looking forward to this time together.

This afternoon the first of our travelers arrived and 12 of us were together for tacos and a trip to Dorman's for ice cream. By Monday nearly everyone that can come will have arrived and, on Tuesday evening, we plan to have one huge birthday party for all 31 of us. My girls added up the number of years old we will all be on our next birthdays. Total? One thousand one hundred fifty-two. No, we won't put that many candles on our two giant birthday cakes. No need to start a 21st century Chicago fire!

In addition to the birthday party, we'll do a few more special things together, including planting two memorial trees honoring my late son-in-law Dan. But much of our time will be spent just enjoying each other's company.

All of it good for a mother's heart.

JULY 27

Our week-long family reunion is off to a good start. The house we have rented promises to be great for us. Right on the water with an expansive lawn complete with playground equipment for the youngest, as well as the young at heart. Trees offer plenty of shade for the large deck, nice spaces inside for rainy days or chilly evenings. All the things one dreams of for that one special week that may not come again for another decade.

Only one day so far, and there has already been enough laughter to dub in a year's worth of sitcoms, plus enough stories told to write the scripts for them. Tonight it was word games that kept more than a dozen adults giggling like the children they used to be.

My husband and I must have done something right, because our children have all found good life-partners and have raised children that truly are assets to this world. It's so good to see them cooperate in planning meals, playing together, showing interest in each other's lives. The cousins, who rarely get together because of distance, are enjoying getting reacquainted. And, because we recently lost one family member in death, everyone is particularly aware of the fact that we must relish and not squander the time we have to be together.

Family life IS precious.

JULY 28

What do you do on a rainy day while you're on vacation? In our family, you don't complain—what good would that do? You adjust. Fortunately for us, it didn't rain *all* day but, when the rain did come, it was in torrents. So we got out the card tables and had most of the family engaged in three separate euchre games. The rest played Scrabble or enjoyed kibitzing.

Euchre is a fast-paced card game. Our children have been, for the most part, hooked on euchre since growing up in Michigan. It has been almost a requirement (but not quite) that the in-laws learn to play euchre before they are officially accepted into the family. My great-grandchildren are learning it also, to keep up the tradition.

Some families play bridge, some play poker, some don't play card games at all. Some aren't happy unless they're in or on the water, some love hunting, some are hikers and bikers, some love to sit and read, some just like to sit and watch TV, some just sit. Every family has its own pattern of living and doing, eating and sleeping, arguing or laughing. The pattern may change a little when on vacation, but the old way of doing things tends to remain constant.

For our family, a rainy afternoon filled with euchre games was one part of the ebb and flow of the tide of life during this reunion week in coastal Maine.

JULY 29

Although the words "planning" and "vacation" do not always coincide, today was more planned than usual. For this is the day our family set aside to honor the life of Dan, my daughter Kay's late husband. Our family focus was to plant two trees in her back yard in his memory. But before that was to happen, we wanted to do a few other labor-intensive projects and, with all the young cousins here, it was a perfect time to put them to work.

After the rains of the previous day, the ground was prime for digging. The boys got started by digging the holes for the two trees. Then they, along with a few females, helped finish an earlier project of a stone path alongside the house. Other little outside projects were tackled by whoever happened along. Meanwhile, some of the women were inside, baking two large cakes for our planned "everybody's birthday party."

By mid-afternoon the family was all assembled to plant the memorial trees. My young great-grandchildren will certainly remember being allowed to put in their shovels-ful in honor of their grandpa. We may have been somber for a few minutes, but our little homely ceremony soon turned into a picture-taking session, to commemorate the afternoon.

Twenty, thirty, fifty years from now my great-grandchildren will be showing those pictures to their own children and grandchildren. And so it goes—generation after generation extending the story.

JULY 30

Last night was lobster night. A time to introduce the un-initiated to a shellfish that was once maligned but now commands respect as well as high prices at the restaurants but low remuneration for the lobstermen.

We got out the tall and fat lobster pot, filled it with water and set it on the outdoor cooker to heat to boiling. Then the greenish-black live lobsters, their strong claws held tightly closed with thick rubber bands, were dropped into the water one at a time. Only a few minutes later the shells turned red. Then the eating began, accompanied by bowls of melted butter (for dipping) and plenty of napkins (for dripping hands and mouths).

There were salads for the few vegetarians in the group, plus bread, but that's about all that was necessary for a feast. At least, until dessert time arrived. It was then that we brought out two huge birthday cakes—one German's sweet chocolate cake plus a carrot cake—each made from "scratch" earlier in the day. Twenty-six of us stood in a wide circle and sang "Happy Birthday to Us" as the wax candles representing our combined age (one-one-five-two) burned brightly.

Smiles all around, voices and hearts in harmony, we were captured on videotape by Greg, one of my grandchildren. Not to be sent around the world on YouTube but to be saved, and savored, by our own Niswander family for years to come.

That's how memories are created. One special day at a time.

JULY 31

If you had been anywhere near the Westkeag River tonight, you might have thought there was an outdoor concert going on, featuring a group somewhere between the Mormon Tabernacle Choir and the Grand Ole Opry. But it was just our family having a sing-along featuring everything from "She'll be Comin' Round the Mountain" to *Amahl and the Night Visitors.*

It never fails to happen when any of us get together. We sing. We've always sung. We sing our table grace. We sing in the car. We sing around the piano, when there is one, and a cappella otherwise. Beautiful sometimes, gratifying always.

My husband and I met through music and lived our lives making music together, not as professionals but as dedicated amateurs. So our children grew up singing and playing instruments at home, at school, at church, and all places in between. Music was an important ingredient in the glue that held our marriage and family together. Listening to the singing and seeing the smiles this week shows that music is still part of that glue.

I have a neighbor whose children and grandchildren live nearby. I can tell by the way he talks about them and the regularity of their visits that there is a lot of love and good feelings of togetherness in that family. Someday I'll ask him what the glue is that keeps them a close family. For them, I don't think it's singing, but something else.

What is your family's glue?

August 1

Late October of last year I visited Boothbay Botanical Gardens, a special beauty spot along the coast of Maine. At that time of year, late fall, I was amazed at how many flowering plants were still vibrant. So I looked forward to this outing when part of our family made a return trip to the gardens, now in full summer splendor.

Each season has its own special beauty and this sunny day in early August gave us much to admire. The Garden of the Five Senses offered a stone maze to walk, herbs to smell, vegetables to savor, unusual flower displays and a sounding stone. We found frogs in the pond and, although there were hundreds of bees in the air, they paid no attention to us humans and concentrated on gathering pollen from every flower available.

Lining the various walkways were head-sized hydrangea blooms, tall armloads of daisies, brightly colored begonias, roses in full bloom. A wide variety of vegetables and herbs, both native and exotic, flourished in the cafe garden. One of several walking paths led down to the water's edge. On the way we could sit in the quiet meditation garden or watch children (and adults) gathering wood, stones and leaves to make one of a hundred miniature dwellings in the woodland fairy garden.

A perfect summer day at a beautiful site—what more could one ask?

AUGUST 2

One of the duties necessary when renting a vacation house for a week is putting it back to the way it was when our family moved in. This large house along the river was an ideal home-away-from-home for our eight adults sleeping there, and worked exceptionally well as others of us came and went during the day. But now was the time to see that everything was in order for the next week's renters.

That's when the teamwork kicked in. Everyone was put to the task, the last dishes washed and put back in the cupboard. Refrigerator cleaned out, the uneaten food plus everything borrowed boxed up to go to home with the family members remaining in Maine. We were finished with the work and out the door fifteen minutes before the 10:00 a.m. deadline, the house looking very much like it did a week ago when we moved in.

But we *did* take something with us from this place that no amount of money could begin to replace: Memories. Memories that will add to the family stories and spark our conversations for the next several decades. And, while saying our goodbyes, we all vowed to not let so many years pass before our next reunion. Though we know that school and jobs and long distances make it difficult for everyone to make it every time, we need to touch each other's lives, in person, as often as we can.

Family truly *is* important.

AUGUST 3

One of the most popular and visible T-shirts we have seen around town this weekend sports the word VOLUNTEER. Worn on one of the biggest weekends for this area, Rockland's annual Lobster Festival, many residents have taken time out to give several hours of their time to a good cause.

And Rockland's fest is only one of hundreds of special weekend celebrations held along the coast and inland, to offer summer vacationers a taste of what is special about Maine. Oh yes, other states have plenty of special weekends. But the lure of the sea, cool summer weather and specialty seafood attracts a giant share of vacationers here. So the volunteers in and around Rockland come out of the woodwork to make things happen. Long-time residents stand shoulder to shoulder with newer summer-only residents to serve up both good food and a good time to visitors.

None of those volunteers would say, "And all I got was this lousy T-shirt," because none of them offered their services for what was in it for them. Some may have volunteered because of a sense of duty, some because "I've always done it," some just because they have time on their hands.

Whatever the reason, let's hope that the "yes" of volunteerism continues to resonate for the next generation. Because every community depends, and thrives, on its volunteers.

AUGUST 4

Kay and I started a new jigsaw puzzle this morning. This one is filled with an array of colors and shapes—all of them seashells. Not being an avid shell collector, my first thought of shells is that they are mostly roundish, whiteish and small-ish. But the picture on the front of the puzzle box shows every color of the rainbow and nearly every shape—except square. There are circles, cones and odd asymmetrical shapes from tiny to large.

Now that my first impression of seashells has been altered, I look more closely. I look at size, at shape, at color with a different eye. I see shells that could pass as Easter eggs, others as pincushions, still others as tree ornaments. One resembles a breakfast roll, another a butterfly. Each kind of shell is distinctively shaped for the crustacean that calls it "home." Now, as I work to put this puzzle together, I marvel at the infinite variety of forms and colors that grace our beaches.

Sometimes it takes a second, and a third, look to make us stop and really appreciate another part of God's creation. Sometimes it takes another person to point out to us what we don't see ourselves. Sometimes we are the ones who have to do the pointing out to someone else.

I learned something today. I'm telling you about it. Pass the word along. It's a wonder-filled world.

AUGUST 5

Tomorrow I fly home to Ohio after a little more than five weeks in Maine. Two weeks were pre-planned, three weeks added because of a family tragedy, unplanned. Looking back, what have I done to warrant my being a guest all that time? Where have I been of help?

During that first week, I could not have been anywhere else than right here. For my daughter, her children and grandchildren—and for myself. I could not dry everyone's tears but I could give hugs. I could help with food preparation and wash the dishes.

Second week: help with business notifications and thank-yous, tend to the many gifts of flowers and planters, help with food preparation, wash the dishes.

Third week: stay out of the way as Kay's in-laws come for the week. Have a bit of quiet time to renew myself.

Fourth week: enjoy all my children and their families as they come for the week. Sit back and revel in their presence, sing, laugh, let them wash the dishes.

Fifth week: move back to Kay's, take her to dinner, play piano duets with her and let her win at cards (??). Just Be There with willing hands and arms, and wash the dishes.

Our last hug at the airport tomorrow morning will be long and with tears, I know. But it's time to go home. Kay will be all right. I've done what a mother needs to do—come when called and leave before she's not wanted.

AUGUST 6

There's nothing quite so frustrating as running into complications on an airline flight. Fortunately for me today, my trip was not only complication-free, but downright pleasant. Thank you, US Airways!

My plane left Portland on time. Occasional light clouds streaked the skies but I had a beautiful view as our flight passed along the Connecticut and Long Island coastlines. Changing planes in Philadelphia, I enjoyed a coffee and biscotti before boarding. And then, the biggest delight of all—no one else claimed the seat beside me. Pure luxury!

To top it all off, after I landed at Dayton airport, again on time, my luggage was already on the carousel by the time I got there to pick it up. Unheard of! It only took a quick call to my friend Mary, waiting for me in the cell phone lot, and we were on our way home. With five weeks of catching up to do, our conversation in the car and over lunch was non-stop.

So here I am, back in my apartment with a pile of mail waiting to be gone through, plus all the little duties that will need to be tended to over the next several days. But there is plenty of time for that. First I must say a quiet "Thank you, God, for being with me one more day."

AUGUST 7

It's good to be back home. After five weeks away, even when surrounded by family, there's nothing quite like getting back to the old familiar haunts and greeting old friends again.

Since I live in an independent living apartment in a retirement village, I found everything just as it was when I left. The office crew was there to greet me with smiles and the latest news of resident friends. Walking down the hall to my apartment, I heard more than one "Welcome back!" from my hall-mates. The only change in my apartment was that my table was piled high with mail that had been delivered while I was gone.

So now it's time to play catch-up. Time to sift through the mail and tend to anything that's urgent, discard any junk mail, and let the periodicals wait for another day. A necessary trip to the grocery, plus a stop to visit my brother and his wife are on today's agenda. Other than that, I will take my time to ease back into life here. At this stage in life, there is plenty of time.

One true advantage of growing older is that few things are imperative any more. The feeling that "I have to do this right now" is from my former, younger life. It's the life my children are still living, but I have graduated to a new stage.

In fact, I think it's time to take a nap. No apology needed.

AUGUST 8

This afternoon I went out to check my raised garden where I raise a few herbs and flowers. But as I've mentioned before, most of the garden is taken up by milkweed—the plant that used to flourish along the fencerows and highways but has been nearly eliminated as an undesirable weed.

I grow milkweed for the monarch butterflies, the sole source of the developing monarch's food. For several years, we have watched the monarch eggs hatch into caterpillars, spin their jewel-green chrysalis, and then emerge as lovely butterflies. It is an intriguing process and one that I hope we can duplicate this summer.

Unfortunately, last year we had no success with the few little eggs we found on our leaves. They did not mature. We're hoping this year yields better success. If the eggs hatch and produce viable caterpillars, I will set up a display in our Family Room. We will watch the caterpillars as they nibble the leaves and grow before their metamorphosis into butterflies. The entire process has made many of us here much more aware of the intricacies of God's creation.

If we have some success again this year, I'll be sure to write about it. Perhaps you too will "get the bug" and try raising a few monarchs yourself. Sometimes Mother Nature needs a helping hand.

AUGUST 9

I'm back to my Saturday morning ritual. It's Farmer's Market day. And what an array of good food was on display this morning! Early August is always a prime growing time for gardeners and the booths set up today showered us with produce.

The sweet corn season is in full harvest right now, and everyone and his brother had sweet corn for sale. Tomatoes right out of the local gardens (such a far cry from those shipped in from afar). Summer squash, zucchini, purple and white eggplant, carrots, beets, green and yellow beans, new just-out-of-the-ground potatoes, cucumbers, everything for a healthy vegetarian meal.

Local peaches are juicy and delicious right now. Melons will be proliferating soon. And then there is the wide variety of home-baked goodies. This morning I brought home a small sour cream coffeecake that smells heavenly and should make my breakfasts special for the next few days.

I marvel at the number of local gardeners and bakers who come, week after week, setting up their stands and smiling as we prod and poke at their produce, looking for quality and a bargain at the same time. They are a hardy lot, working late and then getting up early to bring their produce to those of us who love what's fresh off the farm.

Thank you, good neighbors, for our special Saturday morning treats!

AUGUST 10

Maybe it's just old age creeping up on me, but I have a hard time realizing that it's the first part of August and school has already begun in some areas. I have a grandson in Colorado whose high school classes start this week. My daughter's teaching job in New Mexico begins tomorrow. Does any school district, anywhere, wait to begin classes until after Labor Day, like it was in the dark ages when I went to school?

Ah, those dark ages! School days, especially those in a small rural school such as I attended in the late 1930s, were completely different from those of the city schools that my grandchildren attend. I have, on occasion, mentioned to them an anecdote or two from my school days. But those tales are so far removed from their own experiences that they really can't relate. It will not be until their own grandchildren come along that they realize time makes us all obsolete in one way or another.

And so, even though my memories may seem centuries-old, what I recall needs to be preserved. Otherwise, how can those seeds of remembrance flourish in succeeding generations? How else will my family keep alive the sense of continuance?

So I will keep my family photograph albums up to date, making sure that pictures are identified and dated. I will try to slip in a family story every once in a while, when conversing with my grandkids. And I'll always be ready to talk when someone asks, "Grandma, where were you on Pearl Harbor Day?"

AUGUST 11

It is dark this morning, with rain in the forecast. That is welcome news around here, where the grass has been slowly losing its green-ness to dusty brown. It happens every August here in Ohio, or at least it seems to. Lush summer colors begin to lose their lustre, the soft green carpet of lawn hardens and fades unless it has been constantly watered. Summer starts to turn to autumn.

There are times when we humans also experience Augusts—times when a drought of some sort comes to suck the vitality out of us. Maybe it's an illness, a death, a sudden change of circumstance. Maybe there is nothing that seems to be the cause but we know that something has changed.

We as a family had our own August in late June, when death came calling. We mourned our loss but were well aware of what had happened to sap our strength. We waited for the rain. And the rain came, in the guise of the family reunion we celebrated in late July. We reveled in each other's presence and were rejuvenated. But we also had been made more aware of our own fragility and tenuous hold on life. We vowed to keep in touch more regularly and savor the times when our lives touch.

My hope is to continue to be a good steward of all the blessings that have already come my way and look forward to all that life offers, even if it is another August.

AUGUST 12

My daughter-in-law Nancy is an avid and prolific quilter. Her home contains countless quilts, from large bed-size to medium-sized hangings to tiny miniatures. She has given many away as well. Let me tell you of the latest one Nancy has given me.

It is an abstract flower garden made up of a combination of squares and triangles in green, pink, yellow and white. You can readily spot the flowers, randomly scattered throughout the piece. You soon notice the buttons defining the center of each flower. But it takes more looking before you spot a gray sprinkling can in one corner or notice the varied lines of random machine stitching throughout the piece, both realistic and abstract.

What I like most about this piece is that there is so much to discover. It has been fun to sit and look at every inch of this quilt piece to see what is really there, hidden away. Oh, there's a string of water drops coming from the sprinkling can! My, what an interesting button! She put gold stitching at the corner—nice touch!

There are so many things in this world that we look at only on the surface and never take the time to see what is really there. There are interesting people we encounter but then we pass up the opportunity to really get to know them. We have so many opportunities lost because we don't pay attention.

Looking deeper means finding more.

AUGUST 13

Is it better to go to a meeting and expect to be rebuffed, or to just stay home and save my breath? That is the quandary I am in this evening.

I have been invited to attend a short, half-hour meeting tomorrow with our congressman to ask for his support for additional funding for the Alzheimer's Association (I was the caregiver for my late husband, who had the disease). For the last several years I have traveled to our statehouse in Columbus on Memory Day, to advocate for state funding and, last year, attended one meeting with this same congressman to petition for his support on the national level.

We all went away from last year's meeting feeling that our appeal was to no avail. He politely listened to our stories, as one would expect a congressman to do for his constituents, then told us all the reasons that money was tight (which we already knew). I doubted that our testimonies made much of a dent in his thinking, since he has continued to vote "no" on almost every funding bill.

So, will any good come out of my going to that meeting tomorrow? I doubt it. But yet, if I don't go I will miss the chance to tell the story one more time. And it may be just that "one more time" that will tip the scales for more Alzheimer's research funding.

It looks as if I've talked myself into it.

AUGUST 14

Yes, I went. This afternoon I went to the meeting I was pondering over yesterday—whether it was worth my time to attend or not. It was a meeting with our congressman to ask his support of more funding for Alzheimer's disease. I came home with a smidgen more hope today than I had last year. What made the difference? We got his attention.

We were a motley group of about a dozen, sitting in a circle in a small office. After a short introduction, our group leader was speaking of the National Alzheimer's Project Act, already passed (unanimously) and signed into law. She went on to say that the next step is a proposed Alzheimer's Accountability Act, requiring an annual research budget to be presented directly to Congress. All of a sudden our congressman's eyes lit up and he was full of questions. We had captured his attention.

A busy person trying to keep to a tight schedule is not the best audience to try to persuade. There must be something to make the eyebrows rise. In this case, the word "accountability" must have done the trick. All of a sudden, our congressman was eager to know the details.

Whether he will say "yes" whenever the bill is put to the vote is still questionable. But, for a time at least, we had his attention. He listened. He asked questions. He listened some more. He even said he might be able to help. That's progress!

AUGUST 15

Yesterday was one of those ideal summer days, clear blue skies with enough cotton-y clouds to create a picture, yet cool enough to know that autumn is slowly on its way. But one thing ruined that picture for me.

I had just parked at a small strip mall. Across the street was what used to be a large and very busy shopping mall. Now that mall was a pile of rubble, with the wrecking ball still working on one section. I knew it was happening, but had not been in that part of town to see the walls come down. My heart dropped as I saw that vast space, empty except for the rubble.

Now, I'm not an avid shopper so I had not lost my favorite shopping place. But there has definitely been a loss here. Fifty years ago, this area was a series of green farm fields. The outward push of the city then began gobbling up the land for housing, then services. With the growth came the inevitability of a shopping mall, with more shopping malls going up in other areas of town. Development ran wild and kept running.

It seems that today we build for obsolescence. Build it, use it, tear it down, build something else bigger, use it up because there will always be better stuff coming along. Don't worry about it lasting for your grandchildren. They won't want it anyway.

And so it is with our precious resources. We're users.

AUGUST 16

There is a honey locust tree just outside my window, growing at the edge of the pond. This morning I happened to notice a large seed pod hanging from one of the branches, the sun glinting off its twisted shell. The pod is light brown, such a different color from the green locust leaves that it stands out. The pod is equally different in that it is so much larger than the compound leaves and leaflets around it. It doesn't look like it belongs there. In addition, the seeds inside the locust pod are much larger than those of most trees. Consider the size of a maple seed (part of a tiny airplane), or an apple seed (many inside the core). Why is the locust so different?

I haven't found an answer through Google. I don't know if the average nurseryman would be able to answer that question. It's not one of those questions that demands an immediate answer. It's just something to ponder, and that's what I'm doing right now—pondering.

There are so many questions in life that defy answers, that beg for pondering. Being the age I am, I have time to ponder. To wonder. To zero in on something, mull it around a while and then either find the answer or be content to always wonder. But it is those of us who wonder and are NOT content that discover the next penicillin, the next galaxy.

Will my great-grandchild, or yours, be our next Galileo?

AUGUST 17

What an evening we had! Laughter, singing, hilarious skits. All to say goodbye to a well-loved pastor who is moving on to another church. She's leaving before we want her to, which is the main reason why there was so much laughter and singing tonight. We all wanted to wish her well, to bid her goodbye on a high note, to have a celebration. And that's what it was.

Change happens in every church at some time or another. A pastor retires or moves and another comes. The necessary adjustments are made, some smoother than others. Parishioners also come and go. There are flourishing times and more difficult times. But, for the most part, the church continues on.

This church, my church, has been in this town for more than 100 years. We have a history of strong pastors and a loyal congregation. But it is not the only church in town. There are others with long histories, strong pastors and loyal congregations. Some of those pastors, and a few of their parishioners, were at our church tonight—to join the celebration. They, too, wanted to send best wishes to a fellow pastor who is moving on.

This celebration tonight was a fitting "good-bye" to someone whose laughter has brought a smile to many faces, whose love of singing has enhanced more than one sermon, and whose presence has been a blessing to us all.

Thank you, Louise!

AUGUST 18

Why am I doing this?

Why do I sit at the computer today and tomorrow and the next day, spilling out my wandering thoughts on paper in the hope that, perhaps, someone somewhere will notice and agree that much of life is beautiful? Are these short reflections on life worth anything to anyone other than me? Or are my writings mostly a narcissistic exercise for my ego alone?

What began as a whim of the moment—just a jotting down of some nebulous thoughts at large—has become an eye-opener as to what can emerge if one gives just a bit of time and thought to an otherwise fleeting image or idea. I have been amazed at how I have begun to look at common ordinary things with a wider vision. How normal it has become to want to share a sudden inspiration with you, my reader.

Sometimes it seems so easy. The ideas and writing flow smoothly. At other times the words come with determined effort. However, somewhere along that continuum, thoughts line themselves up and attach themselves to the page day after day.

So I guess I've answered my own question. Why am I doing this? Primarily because it fills a certain need for me. And, in the process, if anything I say brightens your day as it does mine, we're both the better for it.

AUGUST 19

Hurrah! We're back in the butterfly business. After several summers of raising monarch butterflies, and one bust year (last year), we're at it again. Nearly two weeks ago I found a few eggs that had been deposited on the underside of milkweed leaves in my raised garden. I brought them inside.

One of those eggs hatched and that almost-infinitesimal critter has now grown into a recognizable striped caterpillar nearly 3/4 inch long. He (or she—we can't tell at this stage) is happily munching milkweed leaves in a plastic box in our family room. He'll keep eating and growing for a week or more before transforming into a chrysalis.

Yesterday I found another caterpillar, less than 1/8 inch long, on a leaf of one of my milkweed plants. I would never have spotted that tiny creature if it hadn't been for a few pin-prick holes she had made in the leaf while eating her fill. So she, too, has been transferred to the little plastic box in the family room.

To watch the transformational growth from egg to caterpillar to chrysalis to butterfly is so amazing, so awe-inspiring, even to those who don't like "worms," as some of my friends call the caterpillar stage. It boggles the mind to think that each species, including *homo sapiens,* goes through its own distinctive life cycle to create this amazingly diverse world in which we all live. Thank you, God.

AUGUST 20

Today would have been our 64th wedding anniversary. We only made it a little past our 59th before Dean's mind and body succumbed to Alzheimer's disease. So today has been a bitter-sweet day, filled mainly with good memories while giving in occasionally to a tear or two.

But even those few tears were shed because of good memories. When I opened an email from one of my sons this morning, telling me once again how our marriage has stood as an example for him and his wife, those tears were good tears. No regret there. How gratifying it has been today, on an anniversary, to be reminded once again that one's life has been worthwhile.

Did I ever tell—really tell—my mother just how much I appreciated her example? Some years after her death I published a little book about her life and the influence she had on me and others she touched. But did I ever say it directly to her while she was living? Did I ever really put those feelings into the proper words, while she was still able to understand my meaning? Perhaps. But never enough, as I look back.

Time has a tendency to move on and our good intentions sometimes get left on the sidelines. So it's time for me to start making a list.

Whom shall I thank today?

AUGUST 21

It's raining today. Not surprising, since it's County Fair week. I don't think there is any county fair held in Ohio that doesn't get at least one good rain sometime during that special week in summer. However, while rain might dampen the ground, the spirit of celebration continues on, year after year.

Of course, when you think about it, in this part of the country it is unusual to have seven consecutive days of sunshine at any time—or to have a full seven days of rain. We seldom have severe drought, nor do we often experience monumental flooding. That's one of the reasons why Ohio is part of the country often referred to as the "breadbasket." Crops grow and flourish in the Midwest. This results in hundreds of county fairs, all celebrating the bounty of this land.

Some folks go to the fair for the rides and entertainment. Some go for the deep-fried everything. But underneath all the carnival atmosphere lies the initial purpose of these county fairs—to show off the products grown and developed in each area. Young 4-Hers bring their best animals, tended and groomed especially for the fair. Gardeners show off the biggest and best of their produce. Farmers check out the latest in farming equipment and practices.

A county fair is a celebration of the land and its people, living in this particular place at this particular time. A wonderful thing to celebrate!

AUGUST 22

Tomorrow marks the last day that Suter's will open their little red barn for sales of what is deemed by most everyone I know to be the best sweet corn in this part of Ohio. Suter's also have delicious home-grown melons to round out the fresh produce menu. So we're lining up to purchase what will be the last of the really "fresh from the farm" for this year.

Oh, there is still some good corn growing in the fields. But schools are opening and all the high school students who have earned good money working on the farm this summer have other duties to attend to now. Most of them will be back again next year, since work at Suter's is a tradition for many families in this area.

In June I wrote about Suter's strawberries—the produce they're well-known for in the spring. And in late September, when apples start to fall in area orchards, Suter's cider press will be running for the locals to bring in their orchard produce. Another good reason to live in this neck of the woods.

I realize that there are advantages to living in the city, where everything can be found at the fingertips. And I know that there are good farmer's markets there, as well. But for me, I still relish knowing that the sweet corn I ate tonight was still on the stalk this morning.

And it's still the best sweet corn in this part of Ohio. Hands down.

AUGUST 23

Today as I walked past a table in my living room, my eye was drawn to a small stone that has been sitting there, unacknowledged, for some time. It's so small, so insignificant, that I don't often notice it any more. But at one time I carried that stone in my pocket day after day. Several times each day I would rub it. It was my "worry stone."

It is a Petoskey stone, one of many that I have gathered over the years along the eastern shores of Lake Michigan. The stone is made up of once-living organisms—a colony coral. Google can show you a picture and tell you all about how the stones were formed, millions of years ago. But only an experienced eye will help you spot a Petoskey stone on the beach. Why?

When dry, a Petoskey stone looks just like any old gray rock. But when wet, the beautiful honeycomb pattern will reveal itself. If put in a rock tumbler, the stone will not survive—it is too porous and fragile. However, putting it in your pocket and rubbing it with your fingers day after day will eventually bring out a permanent shine and delineate its distinctive colony coral history. The oil on your fingers makes the difference.

That's why this little stone has survived my many years of finding, then eventually giving away, a host of similar Petoskey stones. I tended and "worried" this one into life.

Is there a lesson here?

AUGUST 24

Our monarch caterpillars keep marching along—or should I say crawling and munching their way along—as I keep busy supplying fresh milkweed leaves for their sustenance. The oldest one, now almost fully grown, is getting to the place where he will soon shed his striped skin and go into the strikingly-beautiful chrysalis stage.

Yesterday I gathered some small branches and cobbled together a rather crude jungle gym, created especially for my butterflies-in-utero. I placed the structure inside the large aluminum roasting pan where the growing caterpillars have been eating to their hearts' content. This twiggy structure will provide a place on which the caterpillars can climb to find a spot to fasten themselves and spin a chrysalis.

It is such an amazing process—this creation of a butterfly. From an egg the size of a pinhead, to a squirmy caterpillar, to a jewel-case chrysalis, to a fully-formed monarch butterfly. So many changes in so little time! And each species of butterfly has its own source of food, its own special metamorphosis, its own distinctive markings that make it different from all other species.

This world is so full of so many marvels, from insects to birds to animals to humans. It boggles the mind as one considers the great variety of living things that inhabit this planet, and beyond this planet. We are truly blessed.

AUGUST 25

Although Dean and I traveled many miles and visited many special places during our almost-60 years of marriage, we were not souvenir hunters. We came home from each trip with mostly memories, plus a host of photographs. However, once in a while something special would stand out and call to us. Then we'd decide if we liked it well enough to pay the price.

One such small "find" is a tiny carved hummingbird, life-size, perched for posterity on an interestingly lumpy manzanita burl. Carved from mountain ironwood and signed by the artist, this sleek little hummingbird has graced our living room ever since we brought it home from a trip along the Blue Ridge Parkway more than 40 years ago. Sanded, smoothed and polished to perfection, the tiny bird with its delicately-curved long bill has weathered three or four moves plus being nearly-dropped more than once. Its bill is just as slim and pointed, its pose on the burl still as perky. I love it.

What will happen to this little hummingbird when I die? Probably one of my children will take it, but he or she will never be able to visualize the little shop where we found it or remember our trying to decide whether this tiny sculpture was worth the money we were paying for it. I guess it really doesn't matter. After forty years of enjoyment, I have had more than enough pleasure rediscovering and writing about it today.

AUGUST 26

Hurrah! Our first caterpillar has moved to the chrysalis stage today! Yesterday evening he was crawling around on the branches, exploring (I'll still use the masculine gender until we can determine the sex when the butterfly emerges). This morning he seemed to have settled down to one particular branch on which to spend this stage of life. By noon he had formed himself into a "J" while hanging from that branch and, late this afternoon, he completely shed his caterpillar skin and, in its place, sheathed himself in a beautiful jade-green outer garment.

Now he hangs from that branch, like a diminutive green Christmas ornament with a halo of tiny gold dots, while all sorts of miraculous changes begin inside that chrysalis. He will remain in his miniature dressing room for about two weeks, then emerge clad in full monarch regalia—the striking orange and black markings so different from anything we have seen so far in his short life. We will also be able to see, at this stage, whether this butterfly is male or female. The male has two black dots on its lower wings and the female has none. Otherwise, their markings are nearly the same.

It all seems so impossible—this complete metamorphosis. Changing into something so different from what it was before. But it's possible as I've watched it happen year after year. It never ceases to amaze.

Another of nature's wonders.

AUGUST 27

Today was bonanza day for our small retirement community library. We received, unannounced, several boxes of large print books which were donated by our used bookstore in town. Many of our residents prefer (and need) the large print books, so demand has been higher than our supply—until today.

Since I have volunteered my services for several years at that cozy corner library, it was time for me to get busy and find room on the shelves for the new books. This presented a real problem because my to-do list has had "redo book shelves" written on it for quite some time. So, even though it hadn't been in my plans for today, this was the beginning of housecleaning time in the library.

Good intentions sometimes fall by the wayside when something else better, or more urgent, presents itself. That's why the library shelves had already gotten too crowded. I kept putting off the task of weeding out the unread and keeping the shelves in good order. Now the job became urgent—too many good books and too little room. Get busy!

And busy I was, all afternoon. Pulling books, filling boxes, cleaning shelves, making decisions. Finally, with my back knowing it had done more bending than usual, and the job only half done, it was time to stop and leave the rest for tomorrow. Although the task is not complete, I will rest well. Satisfying work makes for good sleep.

AUGUST 28

Today I finished my library job. By mid-afternoon the library shelves were as tidy as they've been for quite some time and we have doubled our selection of large-print books. That in itself is most satisfying.

This weeding-out process has happened with some trepidation on my part. Did I pull a book that would have been a favorite for someone tomorrow? Have I let my own preferences be too much the judge? I try not to do that, as I realize that not all of us enjoy reading the same sort of literature. There is room in a library for a variety of tastes.

Some of the books pulled will go to our used book store in town, some to the nursing home down the street. Someone will benefit, just as we have benefitted from gifts of books. The joy of reading will still get passed on.

I learned to read at a small country school in Illinois, although I don't remember the learning process. It was all part of that early elementary atmosphere of absorbing everything that was presented to me. The home where I grew up was not filled with books, but I recall fondly the distinctive covers of *Anne of Green Gables* and *Girl of the Limberlost,* along with their fascinating stories. Books of all kinds continue to draw me to them.

I am grateful, every day, for eyes to see and a mind to read and remember.

AUGUST 29

This spring we planted a bed-full of zinnia seeds in one of our raised gardens, hoping to duplicate last summer's crop that graced the tables in our dining hall. Last year's zinnia blossoms were big, colorful and abundant. Each week we had fresh flowers on our tables. They were delightful.

The seeds were the same as last year. We looked forward to producing similar blossoms this summer. But what came up was a surprise. It was as if a magic wand had passed over the garden and—whoosh!—everything was in miniature. Oh, the flowers were colorful, and abundant. But they weren't big. What a disappointment!

So, when life gives you little zinnias, what do you do? You enjoy smaller bouquets. I am enjoying a sample now—a few that were left over after I filled the vases. Up close and personal, these miniatures are a delight. One is like a pink powder puff, rounded and full. Another has a collar of tiny red petals and a round brown face topped with a crown of yellow stamens. One is like a miniature daisy. Each, in its own way, is different. And special.

How often we overlook the little things, the quietly-going-about-their-business things. When I was putting these little flowers in their vases, I had not taken the time to really look. Now I'm looking, and I like what I see.

AUGUST 30

This morning I headed my car north to spend the Labor Day weekend at my son Tom's vacation home on a lake in the southern part of Michigan. Tom and Nancy live and work in the Chicago area, but found this place just a few years ago. Already a family-friendly house when they purchased it, they have spent weekends and vacation time painting walls and adding special touches to the place. They are, little by little, making it their own.

Sitting on lawn chairs at water's edge, we talk of further plans for enhancing their little corner of the world. Replacing carpet with tile in the sunroom that overlooks the lake. Removing the rotting railroad ties that, at one time, framed a stairway leading from the deck. Creating a new flower bed near the garage. The list will probably never have an end, as home ownership always seems to demand to-do lists.

I remember those days of dreams and doing. Redecorating, creating, turning ideas into reality. I enjoyed those busy years. But now I am content to keep my surroundings pretty much the same. I no longer feel a need for change. I must wonder again whether I am getting "set in my ways," as we used to say. Perhaps I am. But I hope not so much that I discourage my children and grandchildren from following their own dreams. I may not have the energy to move mountains any more, but they do.

I wish them well.

AUGUST 31

This morning's quiet is welcoming after the winds and rain of yesterday evening. The lake is calm, if not completely still, and the surrounding world is early-Sunday-morning quiet. The neighbor boys, busy with back yard baseball yesterday, are nowhere in evidence. It's time to sit here for a few minutes and savor the morning's peace.

Were I at home in my apartment, I would be having breakfast alone at my glass-topped table overlooking a small pond. Here, my breakfast was with my son and daughter-in-law at their own glass-topped table overlooking a largish lake. There is something similar, and soothing, about both scenarios—both settings involving water and glass. Transparent and conducive to reflection, the two similar settings beckon to me to sit and think about something more than what is happening the rest of today.

Maybe that's why I'm enjoying this time of life—this period of taking time and slowing down. Time to breathe, time to think, time to enjoy the little things that don't always fit into a busy world. Some individuals choose the slower, more contemplative life early on. But most of us wait until our bodies demand that we slow down. And, even then, we give in reluctantly.

In a few minutes, I'll be getting dressed and ready for church. But right now, in this quiet setting, I am reminded that moments of peace can be found in many different places and at many different times. I must not forget.

September 1

Fog and mist hang over the lake this morning. No bright sunshine to wake the body and mind. It's a morning to sleep. But Mitch and Domino, the two basset hounds who are an important part of my son's family, are patiently waiting for their morning walk. So Tom and Nancy, while walking the dogs, will enjoy their own private time to talk over their plans for the day. Were it a regular working day at home in Illinois, rather than a lazy weekend of vacation in Michigan, Tom would be off to work early. No time for leisurely discussion. Nancy would walk the dogs alone. So today they relish this vacation time of walking and talking together.

It is good to see them enjoying each other in a vacation setting. They work together well as they replant, replace, weed, paint—all interspersed with boating and relaxing by the water. This weekend, with two sons and a girlfriend also spending time here, there has been less work and more water skiing and fishing. Everyone has been enjoying it together.

In another ten years, things undoubtedly will have changed. Some, if not all, the children will have married. Young grandchildren's voices will probably be heard, such as I hear coming from the neighbor's house today. There may be less painting and more playing. But, from what I see today, I predict more love, not less, and plenty of happy years ahead. May it be so.

SEPTEMBER 2

An email just arrived, bringing good news from my grand-daughter and her family. They have arrived safely at their destination after two full days on the road. Mark and Sara, with four children (plus one on the way) are relocating. So they drove a car, plus a van pulling a large trailer loaded with their worldly goods, the 1,000-plus miles from Maine to their new home in Kentucky. I was relieved to hear the good news of their safe arrival. I had waited only two days, but I kept thinking of them throughout the time they were on the road and praying for safe travels.

How did the extended families of the early pioneers, the ones left behind, ever manage to survive the suspense—wondering if their loved ones ever arrived at their destination? I can't imagine the emotions of seeing your children embark on a journey across the ocean, or across the country, knowing that it would be months before you might hear from them. Plus the possibility that you might never hear from them again. How could they live through that wait? How?

We are so spoiled, as we have grown accustomed to this phenomenon of instant communication. We have so easily lost the ability to wait, to pray, to have faith that good news will come. We want it RIGHT NOW.

Today I got my good news. I must give thanks.

SEPTEMBER 3

This afternoon I went to the nursing home to see my brother, Norman. He has Parkinson's disease. Some days when I visit he is sleepy and lethargic. On other days he is more alert and responsive. Today was a good day, so I began reminiscing about the farm where we grew up.

"Remember how we used to sleep on the screened porch when it was really hot upstairs in the summer?" Norm's face broke out into a big smile as he nodded in remembrance. He asked if I remembered mowing our big lawn with the little reel-type lawn mower. "Oh, yes," I replied. We agreed that neither of us liked that mowing job. Then we moved to the subject of the barn and the cows we used to milk by hand. And on to the tiny baby chicks we raised every year.

On we talked, for at least half an hour, reminding each other of little things we remembered about our childhood home. Norm was as animated as I have seen him for some time. It was a very special afternoon for both of us.

This probably won't be the scenario the next time I visit. Norm may not be as responsive, or I might not be in the frame of mind to set the stage for a meaningful conversation. But I hope to remember today and the warm feeling I had as I left—that this was a very good day.

I must try to make it happen again.

SEPTEMBER 4

Today was "clean up the garden" time. The raised garden I have tended for nearly a dozen years had taken on a very unkempt and ungainly look over the last month. This is primarily because at least half of the garden is overgrown with milkweed. Milkweed for our monarch caterpillars to eat—a primary necessity for their existence and growth.

Since we now have successfully raised two caterpillars that have gone into the chrysalis stage, with only one more caterpillar munching away at the leaves, there is no more need for the tall milkweed plants to tower over the garden. So, after a great deal of cutting and chopping this afternoon, my garden now has only two small milkweed plants, one sweet-smelling sage, two very productive bunches of chives, and a tiny verbena that is trying to hang on until frost.

A few years ago, before we started our project of raising monarchs, that little garden produced some lovely lettuce and onions in the spring plus a variety of summer flowers. Now the summer vegetables have been nearly bypassed as the garden produces what farmers tend to call "weeds." Has it been worth it—this turning the garden plot from beautiful and delicious to ungainly, productive and necessary for the butterflies?

Just ask the next monarch you see.

SEPTEMBER 5

Lightning has been dancing around in the sky tonight. It is not the usual kind that accompanies a rainstorm, with sudden bright lightning bolts heading down to earth with a loud boom of thunder to follow. The lightning tonight makes no sound but just appears suddenly and disappears just as suddenly, as though afraid of staying too long. It is most beautiful.

There is a quiet kind of dance going on in the sky right now. Somewhat like white and orange spotlights flickering on and off, appearing here and there across the night sky, sometimes illuminating a fluff of clouds hovering near the horizon. I stand at the window, fascinated by the light show going on outside.

The kind of lightning we see tonight is what my mother used to call "heat lightning. " My brother and I would stand next to her on our screened porch and watch displays like this quite often when we were growing up on our Illinois farm. But I haven't seen this kind of lightning nearly so much here in Ohio. I almost forgot how beautiful heat lightning can be.

The forecast calls for rainstorms tonight, but so far there has been no rain, no noise and no storm. Instead, we have received a special kind of beauty. We need the rain, but we also need nights like this to remind us, once again, that this universe is beautiful in all its forms. Thank you, God.

SEPTEMBER 6

A whisper of fall was in the air this morning and it livened up my trip to the Saturday Farmer's Market. The feeling that summer will not be around for long prompted me to search for the veggies that will soon disappear from the booths. No more sweet corn, but melons still in good supply. A beautiful purple eggplant, perhaps the last until next year. Farm-fresh tomatoes and summer squash still plentiful, at least until the first really cold spell. Will the first frost come next week or not until next month? One never knows in Ohio.

But even in late September and throughout October there will be plenty of good fresh produce available at our Farmer's Market. Winter squash, cabbages, potatoes, apples and pears and pumpkins. And don't forget sweet apple cider, fresh from the cider press just down the road. Then, week by week, the air will turn cooler and the number of vendors will lessen as the winds grow sharp. But booths will still be offering farm produce as well as freshly-baked cinnamon rolls and pies to tempt our taste buds.

Then, when November comes and the outdoor market is closed, the local grocery will have to suffice. And even though there will be plenty of produce available on those shelves, as well as plenty of freshly-baked goodies at the bakery, it's just not the same.

You can take a girl off the farm, but she's still a farm girl at heart.

SEPTEMBER 7

It was an unforgettable Sunday afternoon. For three hours we sat, entranced, as our first monarch butterfly of the season emerged from its chrysalis and, after a long period of drying, was finally ready to test its wings. As I am writing this, our female butterfly is checking out little blue flowers in the planter on the porch. Perhaps, before I am finished writing, she will have taken wing to check out other flowers nearby.

We gathered on the front porch after lunch, marveling at her emerging. One tiny leg appeared, then the edge of a wing, and suddenly our butterfly was out. But it was so small! Not the full-sized monarch we expected. The distinctive orange and black markings were there, but in miniature. It took nearly half an hour for the wings to fill to full size, but even then our monarch was not ready to fly.

The "blood spot" dropped from her body—not the last of the liquid to be expelled, but the most obvious. The wings still had more moisture than they could hold. It was more than two hours before our butterfly was able to hold her wings steady and crawl around on my hand. Finally we decided to put her on one of the planters. She will probably stay there for quite a while yet, allowing her wings to dry more fully before taking off to meet friends and get ready for the long flight to Mexico.

Bon voyage, little one!

SEPTEMBER 8

Our local writer's group met today, the first since our summer break. It was refreshing to meet again with old friends as well as greet a newcomer. We are a motley crew—more women than men and more of us well matured than wet behind the ears. Some of us have written "forever" while others of us have come lately to that discipline. Our only criterion is a love for the written word.

So why do I tell you all this? To celebrate the fact that we, as writers, still feel the need for each other. We are not solitary authors and poets, hunched low over our lengthy manuscripts and scribbling away on faded parchment. Writing instruments have evolved, styles of writing come and go, the publishing business has completely changed, but the art of writing is still an art. And the need to write and share our thoughts is still as human as it was in the time of Chaucer.

So we writers relish this time of coming together to read our works aloud and to learn from each others' strengths. Although we all have dreams of seeing our own writings in print, we rejoice when someone else is published or has won a prize in a contest. We feed on each other's successes and encourage one another. Each monthly meeting gives us impetus to keep on writing.

We do not expect to get rich, but we are enriched.

SEPTEMBER 9

This afternoon the rafters would have been ringing, if we had such things here, as about forty of us "old timers" had the time of our lives singing the old songs we used to sing when we were kids—and the ditties we sang along in the car with our own children. No pesky song sheets, no accompaniment, no one to give us a pitch. All we needed was someone to start the next song. What a great time we had!

Maybe the ones who think they can't sing any more stayed home. Maybe all the old grouches did the same. But every person that came was singing, smiling, laughing. If everyone went home this afternoon feeling as I did (and I think they did), our sing-a-long was a huge success.

Too many times we depend on others, from outside, to provide entertainment for us. We think we don't have any talent, we don't have the time, there's something better on TV. We can think up all sorts of excuses to keep from getting involved. But staying involved is what helps retain the youth that we all wish we still had. We let it slip through our fingers through neglect.

This afternoon proved that just a simple sing-a-long can keep the heart pumping, help the lungs expand and stretch those smile muscles. Better than any doctor's prescription, any day.

SEPTEMBER 10

What makes a friendship last? What is the glue that holds some unlikely-to-mesh individuals to each other for a lifetime while other friendships, seemingly strong at one time, dissipate slowly before dying altogether? What is the chemistry that binds?

I'm thinking about this right now, after a brief conversation in the hall with a friend I first met at summer camp, then roomed with in college for a year. Our backgrounds were dissimilar but we found an appreciation for each other then that has lasted. We both married, lived thousands of miles apart for almost all of our "working" lives, and eventually ended up in the same town in retirement.

Throughout those years, our paths crossed primarily through Christmas cards and occasional letters. But those Christmas cards and letters must have been enough to cement a relationship that had its start nearly 70 years ago. Now, even though we live in the same town, we don't see each other that much. When we do stop to talk, it's always when one or the other of us is on another mission so we chat briefly and go on with our lives. We don't go out to dinner together (except on our birthdays—three days apart), but my spirit always lights up when I see her. I think she feels the same way.

What makes a friendship last? I guess I don't really need to know. I just know it has happened here, and give thanks.

SEPTEMBER 11

Today I put my amaryllis bulb "to sleep" in a dark spot in the garage, hoping that it will rest peacefully for the next couple of months until I bring it out to bloom again. I should say that I *hope* it will bloom again. My history of successes hasn't been too good, but I hope this will be the year.

Isn't that a big part of all of our lives—the hope that lies there within us? The hope that things will be better next time around. The hope that this or that will happen and make things come out right. But we really have to do more than just hope. With my earlier failures at keeping an amaryllis bulb productive, I didn't do much except read what was on the tag—and that tag contained very little information. Basically, I just hoped. Now, with all the assistance one can get on the internet, there is plenty of information on just what to do to make that bulb flower over several seasons.

So I've done my homework more thoroughly this time around. I have a plan. Oh, there is still a lot of hope involved, but there is a method in what I'm doing to make the blooming happen. If I fail, it won't be the end of the world. I'll just get another blooming bulb at Christmas and try again.

And learn a little more each time around.

SEPTEMBER 12

Is it the person I am today, or the day itself, that is getting in the way of a "have a good day" day? Yes, it's cloudy and chilly outside—not conducive to taking a long walk. But it's cloudy inside myself today, as well. I don't like how I feel.

Part of this unsettledness has to do with waiting for phone calls and emails from volunteers I'm trying to line up for a special celebration two weeks from now. I'm impatient, wanting to hear "yes" from a number of people and dreading the "no" that might come instead. "I'm getting too old for this," I tell myself. "Next year I'll let someone younger do this job."

And maybe I will. Maybe that would be the best thing. Sometimes we hold on too long to a job that we think no one else can do as well as we. We pride ourselves in all our "doing" and sometimes forget that "being" is also important. Letting someone else take a turn at a job that, until now, we have hoarded to ourselves is a vital step as we get older.

But, for today, I still have the challenge of being patient. Perhaps right now is a good time to call a friend and suggest we get together for tea and conversation. My email messages and phone calls can wait for me to return. Perhaps then I will have returned to normal. It's certainly worth a try.

SEPTEMBER 13

Last spring, when the Canada geese were multiplying and bringing their babies for swimming lessons in our pond, you found me waxing less-than-poetic about them. Today, as I look across the pond, I see those families sitting in the sun and enjoying an early fall day. They haven't ventured over to our side for some time now.

What has brought on this change of habitat for the geese? Did we shoo them away so often that they finally got the message? Possibly, but I rather doubt it. Has the grass suddenly become tastier on the other side? Whatever the reason, all of us who use those sidewalks for our daily walks are most appreciative that the geese no longer use them for their private dumping ground.

Soon it will be time for the geese to fly south. We already see signs of their restlessness as they practice their take-offs and landings. Will we miss them when they're gone? For most of us, probably not as we remember what pests they seemed to be at one time. And yet, if the geese would not come back in the spring, wouldn't we all have to pause and wonder what happened? Wouldn't we get the uneasy feeling that something just wasn't right?

It's hard to have everything exactly to our own particular liking. So it might be best just to appreciate our natural world as it is. Even the Canada geese.

SEPTEMBER 14

How can an attitude change so fast? Yesterday I was commenting that we'll be happy to see the Canada geese go south for the winter. Then, this morning, my sympathies suddenly turned. What precipitated that change of heart?

It was one solitary goose, standing at the edge of the pond. No compatriots to be seen anywhere. One solitary goose, possibly one of those who have mated for life and the mate is no longer living. I've seen him/her standing alone before, but this morning I felt a certain kinship. It must have been my mood. My mate is no longer living, either.

Now, as I write this afternoon, there are a few other geese in that same area in which the solitary goose was standing this morning. I count seven. An uneven number. Is my solitary goose of this morning among them? Will they fly south together? What will the lone one do this winter? Will he/she find another mate for another season, or remain alone?

I myself, a widow for too long, feel alone sometimes, even with people next door and plenty of activities going on around me. I have no intention of looking for another mate. This is a personal choice. Still, I feel a kinship with that solitary goose. The one who doesn't quite fit in any more.

Each in our own way, we go on with life.

SEPTEMBER 15

The sunset draws me to the window this evening. And here I stand, watching as the sun goes down and tints the sky a familiar *fireandsmoke*. Hmm. That's a word I haven't thought about for a long time. It's a color I coined back in my much earlier, waxing poetic days. I had rather forgotten about that made-up word but, looking out the window this evening, *fireandsmoke* popped into my mind right away.

Can I describe that color to you? No. It's one I can't explain except to say that I recognize it when I see it. And now I am reminded of another color I coined, again back in my poetry days, describing the early morning sky. One word: *pinkwhiteblue*. Can you see it?

There are some things that are never describable in normal words so we have to make up words to bring them alive. Children are better at it than adults. Most young children are still imaginative enough to coin a word now and then. But, much too soon, some adult laughs at their attempt to describe the indescribable so they learn to shy away from anything too creative. What a loss!

I don't make up words any more. Not often, anyway. But I am getting older by the day and they say that our inhibitions sometimes melt away in old age. That we aren't nearly as afraid of what other people think. So maybe there's hope for me yet.

Maybe there's hope for all of us.

SEPTEMBER 16

Another monarch butterfly, also female, emerged today from her chrysalis. We had checked the darkening sheath when going to lunch but nothing was happening at that time. Yet, by the time we had finished eating she was already out and clinging to a branch. The wings were nearly fully expanded. So we took the branch outside into the sunshine, giving her time to dry her wings before flying away. By mid-afternoon she was gone.

How many more experiences will she have before she arrives at her southern destination? Will she survive? None of us knows. We only know that we have tried to provide her with a good start. Now it is up to her. It's rather like parenting, without the conversations and confrontations. We protect, we provide, we hover, we do the best we can with what we know and feel at that particular time and place.

With our butterfly, we tried to give tender loving care as best we knew how. But then we knew it was time to let go. It's the letting go of our children that is the real test. To trust that what we have done is the best that we knew how. And then to loose the strings. To let that child fly when we know how many challenges and obstacles there are between where he is and where he is drawn to be.

Trust, and a few prayers, is about all we can do.

SEPTEMBER 17

Yesterday afternoon I made granola—one of the very few things I still make "from scratch." Living in a retirement village, with each day's main meal provided, there is little need to be busy in my kitchen. But granola is one of the foods I will not buy at the store—it needs to be made from scratch, from my recipe. Actually, the recipe came from my daughter but I have adopted it as my own. Simple to make, delightful to smell as it is baking, granola is my favorite breakfast food when combined with yogurt and fresh fruit.

One of the benefits of creating something in the kitchen is the aroma that is part of the cooking/baking process. Yesterday my apartment was blessed with wonderful aromas when oatmeal, nuts, brown sugar, honey and butter combined with oven heat. This morning's breakfast featured the newly-baked granola and strawberries. Mmmm.

I'm taken back to earlier days, when I was busy cooking every day for our family of eight. I can't forget the smell of fresh bread, right out of the oven. Of tomatoes cooking down for catsup. Of soft sugar cookies from Mom's recipe. Of vegetable soup simmering on a cold winter day. It's enough to—almost—make me want to gather up all my veggies and concoct a hearty soup right now.

But the sun is shining, the air is warm, the outdoors is beckoning. Maybe tomorrow…

SEPTEMBER 18

A great blue heron has joined the Canada geese across the pond this afternoon. The geese go on nibbling grass, paying no attention. I reach for my binoculars and watch the heron as he/she preens in the sunshine. It has been some time since I have seen a heron here at our pond, since there is much more seclusion, and possibly better fishing, in Riley Creek just a few wing-beats to the north.

Usually, when a heron visits our pond, I see the bird standing in or alongside the water while stalking fish. Occasionally I have seen one catch a fish, then craftily transfer the catch from bill to gullet—a sometimes time-consuming maneuver. Today our heron must not be hungry but more interested in oiling its feathers and smoothing them down. The long and supple neck curls around to reach a certain spot, then another. The movements resemble ballet.

Suddenly, around the corner comes one of our maintenance men on the riding lawn mower. Oh, don't frighten my heron away! The mower is on my side of the pond, a safe distance away from the birds, but I fear the noise will chase my heron away. The geese start to waddle away, but the heron remains stationary.

For several minutes my heron continues to preen, as if unconcerned about the noise and movement under my window. But then, with an opening of wings and a graceful take-off, my heron moves on to quieter ground. Come again soon!

SEPTEMBER 19

My lone goose, the one I reflected on recently, is still here by the pond. But there is more to the story than I first noticed. The goose's left wing hangs to the ground—it is injured. My instinct is to help and yet I know that the goose would not welcome my intrusion. I watch as it feeds, then walks to the edge of the water. Soon it will enter and swim to the other side—I've watched it before.

Feeling the need to do something, I call the park district. "What do you do if someone calls about an injured Canada goose?" I ask. I am informed that there are few wildlife rehabilitators in the area so the district confines any rehab efforts to the rarer species. "For geese, we just let nature take its course."

Naturally, that is what I must do as well. I must let what is to happen, happen. But it does not make it any easier—this watching as the goose makes its way into the water. Swimming, it looks fine. But I know that on land it will struggle. When the rest of the flock flies south, will there be a place of refuge?

I must let go, but it will take time. My earlier complaint about the proliferation of Canada geese has turned into sympathy for one in particular. In Sunday School we used to sing "God sees the little sparrow fall." Does that include geese?

SEPTEMBER 20

Today I was part of a round-table discussion on genealogy books and family trees, held at our local used book store. There were just three of us there, but we had no trouble keeping the conversation going over a three-hour period. What did we learn? That there are myriad ways of tracking and recording family history with none of them superior to the other, just different.

One of us is, at present, recording her family history through photographs, although she intends to flesh it out with words later. Another will use mainly the written word to make her history come alive. What work I have done is a combination of both in a variety of styles. The three of us bounced ideas back and forth, each of us gaining a little better idea of what might be our own best way of recording our histories.

Whatever results arise from this afternoon's discussion will come as individual stories, not a composite. We three are distinct individuals with entirely different life stories. What we produce will vary. Sharing ideas only helped solidify what each of us already knows—that "my story is my story." It is that unique, individual story that needs to be preserved whether in black and white or color, written word or voice.

Every family should have one storyteller willing to record the past, whether it be in pictures or words. I'm the one in my family. Are you the one in yours?

SEPTEMBER 21

The third of our three monarch butterflies emerged from chrysalis this morning. Another female—so we've produced three egg-laying monarchs that, we hope, will help keep our dwindling monarch population extant for another season. It has been a fascinating process throughout for many of us here.

But waiting and watching are not to everyone's enjoyment. I have noticed, over the weeks we have been watching the growth in our monarchs, that some of our residents are interested in every stage. They check every day to watch the tiny caterpillars chomp their way through milkweed leaves. They are disappointed if they are not in attendance when the caterpillar forms its chrysalis and are delighted to finally see the butterfly emerge. Then there are others who aren't eager to watch the "worms" as they call them, but enjoy seeing the beautiful chrysalis and its emerging butterfly. And then there are others who aren't interested at all in anything of the process and ignore it completely.

Even for those avid watchers, the time drags on and no one seems quite as excited about our third "birth" as they were for the first. Our attention spans dwindle and the phenomenon takes on ordinary character. But let's hope that our third butterfly somehow retains the will to live that will take her to her southern wintering grounds, with hope for another season.

We're counting on you, little one!

SEPTEMBER 22

Today I've been thinking about my mother. I don't know why, on this particular day, I can't get her out of my mind. Perhaps it has something to do with the fact that I will be celebrating a milestone birthday later this week. Perhaps that fact started me thinking about what lies ahead—the latter part of my life yet to be lived.

My mother was my beacon, although I would never have acknowledged that fact when I was in my teens. She truly was a positive force in my life and an example of how a life can be lived fully even through more than enough ups and downs. She lived to celebrate her 95th birthday. I have ten more years to go!

Will I be as gracious when giving up my freedoms as she was? Will I bow to illness and infirmities with as much forbearance as she? Will I continue to meet each day with good humor and grace? Will I be the kind of person I'm hoping to be, if and when illness comes?

All of life is a test of heart and soul. My mother passed her tests with flying colors. My brother is passing his tests with the good humor that has always been a special part of him. My husband bowed to Alzheimer's disease with stoic acceptance and grace. No amount of study will guarantee that I will be like them, but I keep hoping that will be the case.

Lord, help me.

SEPTEMBER 23

Such a beautiful picture outside my window today! Bright early fall sunshine, the bluest of blue water, the grass still summer-green and lush, red roses still blooming their hearts out for my neighbors across the pond. I must remember this picture because I know it won't last.

Already the tiny leaves of the locust are beginning to yellow and, one day soon, they will carpet the ground. Some morning the grass will be tinged with white as frost descends on the low spots. The roses will be put to bed for another season. We are reluctant to see fall approach, but know it happens every year. Still we wish to hold on to what we have right now.

Yet, when this same frost touches the maples and oaks we will again marvel at the beautiful colors and drive to find the most scenic spots in our area. Will it be as colorful as last year, or even more so? We compare the beauty of fall seasons just as we compare spring rains and winter snowfalls. It's part of the midwest psyche, I think, to test one season against another as if we had the power to do something about it.

Life seasons are like that, as well. Just about the time we get really comfortable and enjoy the age we are, another year rolls around. It's time to get used to another season, another test in the passage of life.

As if we had the power to do something about it.

SEPTEMBER 24

Marge, an old friend and former neighbor who now lives 100 miles away, called this morning to wish me a happy birthday. It was one of those unanticipated, but most welcome, calls that gave my day a delightful beginning. I haven't stopped smiling yet.

At one time, hardly a day would pass without Marge and me greeting each other with a "hello" wave or a shared cup of coffee or a choir rehearsal or any number of activities. Although our children were mostly grown and gone, we had plenty of interests in common and never lacked for topics of conversation. She and I were both more interested in talking about what was happening in the world than what went on in our neighbor's bedroom. A good neighbor to have and hold.

After 14 years of good-neighbor-liness, we moved away. They also moved away. Her husband died. My husband died. We still kept in touch, but mainly through Christmas greetings. I visited her twice in her new home but the drive began to loom as just a little too long.

Then came this morning's phone call. We played a quick "catch-up-with-family" but my primary delight was just in hearing her voice again. I could easily picture us sitting in their sunroom enjoying coffee and conversation, or playing bridge in the living room, or . . . the list could go on and on.

Should every day bring such morning blessings!

SEPTEMBER 25

This morning our retirement center's ground crew is in landscape mode, getting ready for a special weekend Fall Festival. At the same time, they are catching up on some much needed tree trimming. The trees on this nearly 15-year-old campus have been growing to the place where some are taking up more than their allotted space. So tree trimming, and replacing in certain places, is one of the priorities.

While watching the activity outside my window, I think about the space I have been occupying inside. There is need for some necessary trimming in my apartment as well. Where to start?? My computer desk, definitely. Too many papers in haphazard piles. The computer as well, where unnecessary files need to be banned to the trash bin. My bedside table that accumulates odds and ends too trivial to file away and too important (temporarily) to discard. The spice cabinet in my kitchen that houses too, too many outdated spices. Then there is always the clothes closet plus the storage bin downstairs.

There are places in my brain that could also use some housecleaning. Memories of old slights that should have been forgiven years ago and now it's too late. Old prejudices that linger even though I know better. Is there some sort of memory-trimmer that can lop off the unwanted, undesired thoughts as our ground crew is trimming branches? Let me know if you hear of one.

SEPTEMBER 26

Tomorrow is Bluffton's annual Fall Festival—a community celebration of life in this little corner of Ohio. It spills out from the center of town and incorporates the home where I live, and the Swiss Homestead where I will be spending nearly all my time tomorrow. More on that later. But now I must tell you of my evening walk down memory lane.

For the last few years our head maintenance man has organized an antique tractor show as part of the Fall Festival. Late this afternoon the old tractors started to arrive and now they are all lined up on display on our front lawn. Several red Farmalls (International Harvester), some green John Deeres, a couple of ancient Minneapolis Molines, an old Silver King, an orange Allis-Chalmers, others I didn't recognize readily. All well-seasoned, all the top of their line at one time but now just shined up for reminiscing. There is also, on display, one gigantic and shiny-new John Deere to show what the big farmers now use on their Ohio farms.

My father-in-law went into the farm implement business in 1908, when horses still supplied most of the farm power. As a young wife, I helped my husband and his father at the implement store when, by that time, the familiar bright red IH tractors were our store's showcase. So this evening's walk was a trip back to those times in the 1950s. Good memories will make for pleasant dreams tonight.

SEPTEMBER 27

It was a glorious fall day to be out on the farm, recalling earlier times when horses pulled the plows and fresh-baked bread with apple butter was a familiar anytime snack. I was there all day, greeting people of all ages as they came to visit our Swiss Community Historical Society's picturesque and beautifully restored 1843 homestead.

As one of the docents on duty, I was attired as a proper Mennonite grandmother—long black dress and white apron. Stationed upstairs in the four-bedroom house, I greeted children and explained to them how a rope bed worked and demonstrated the difference between a straw mattress and one filled with feathers. Women enjoyed watching needle-workers plying their craft. Men came to marvel at the rough-hewn rafters and nearly bumped their heads on the low-cut doorways.

Apple fritters, hot from the hearth, were a taste treat in the summer kitchen. Freshly-popped popcorn and hot soup were served from open fires on the lawn. Children climbed on straw bales and fished in the creek. Horse-drawn wagon rides, workshop demonstrations, farm-smoked Swiss cheese and music were all part of the day.

I delighted in watching the children as they explored the farm, experiencing something from another era. Equally as delightful were the heart-warming stories told by descendants of the original owners. At the end of the day I was exhausted but exhilarated. A wonderful way to enjoy the past while enlightening our future!

SEPTEMBER 28

On a scale of one to ten, today is a ten. In fact, today is one of a complete week of tens. The first week of fall, and one to remember. In our tendency to categorize much of our lives, we will probably remember this fall of 2014 as starting out with more than the usual ideal days—one for the history books. Just as last winter was one for the history books, although in the less than ideal category.

We humans enjoy comparisons. Comparisons help us to measure ourselves against whatever our ideal happens to be. We'd like to be better and, if we truly work at it, we can be. But somewhere along the line of getting better and obsessing over it is a middle ground. Sometimes we need to stop and assess where we are and where we still want to be.

I'm pretty content with my life right now. I still feel active in my community, although not as much as I was at an earlier age. I'm OK with that. I still feel aware of the needs around me, but am no longer driven to answer every call. I'm OK with that. But sometimes I wonder whether I'm enjoying my leisure too much. When does one get to the point of being completely satisfied with one's life? Maybe we never get there. Maybe we're never supposed to get there.

Maybe I'll just enjoy the rest of this beautiful day and be thankful.

SEPTEMBER 29

It was back to the Swiss Homestead this morning as four classrooms of first graders were scheduled for a guided tour. As one of the five volunteer docents, I was kept on my toes assisting them in learning how life on the farm was for children during the mid-1800s. Many of the children's questions and reactions were anticipated, but they often surprised with their perceptiveness.

A first grader is still a wide-open vessel, full of questions and eager to learn. This was evident as we looked for similarities and differences in the bedrooms of yesteryear, compared with theirs today. They visited the summer kitchen where all the cooking and baking were done in the hot season of the year. Touring a house from an earlier era gave the children a taste of something quite different from their modern-day world at home.

After the tours were over, some of the younger docents played old-time games on the front lawn with the children. I was content to watch. The children needed no fancy jungle gyms or swing sets to have fun. Their laughter rang out as they played games that their great-grandparents would have played at their one-room country schools many years ago.

All it took for a good morning was a busload of children and a few adults to take the time and effort to enjoy life with them on this pleasant fall morning. They won't forget, nor will I.

SEPTEMBER 30

There was a welcome sound coming from just outside my window this morning. No, it wasn't a beautiful bird song (although I have been known to wax poetic about such things). It was the sound of hammers.

We have been waiting all summer for construction to begin on a fishing pier and screen house at one end (my end) of the pond. The foundation for the project was poured late last fall and construction was expected to begin then, but winter set in too early and in earnest. By the time spring finally rolled around, our contractor was no longer interested nor could we find another contractor free to take on the project until fall. Naturally, we were disappointed.

But life went on, now it's fall, and construction began this morning. Yes, the hammers were a welcome sound. And the sight of young men climbing around on the new framing makes us feel that our long-awaited project is finally under way. Although we won't be able to make good use of this new facility before the cold weather chases us inside, we've lived long enough to realize that there will be another spring and many more opportunities to enjoy our screen house.

Life has taught us that next year is not nearly as far away as we used to think—back in the days when we were young. Fall and winter will pass and spring won't be far behind. We can wait.

October 1

I've been fascinated this afternoon, watching the roof dance outside my window. Not being particularly fond of heights, I can't imagine how anyone would willingly walk up a ladder, step onto a steep-sloping roof and walk around up there as if on level ground. Carrying on his shoulders a stack of shingles, as well.

I wonder how he felt, the first time he stood on a slanted roof. Was he always eager to climb, to try everything his mother deemed dangerous? Had he always given his parents cause for heart attacks as he dared to go higher? Or was he timid at first, feeling his way up and overcoming his fear little by little? I only know that today he's sure-footed and knows his job.

The world contains all sorts of us—the brave and the timid, the talker and the listener, the contemplative and the boaster, the provider and the user. We're all here together, rubbing shoulders and trying to make a life for ourselves in a world that accommodates us all. Still, it's often hard to accept that the person next to us can be so different from ourselves, one who can't understand our feelings, one with whom we have nothing in common.

And yet, that's what makes life interesting. You are different from me. I am different from you. We are not all the same and we need each other. Otherwise, the little screen house outside my window would have no roof.

OCTOBER 2

Today has been all about Alzheimer's disease. I took part in an all-day seminar focusing on the advances being made in research and awareness. Since Alzheimer's has suddenly come to the forefront of diseases that as yet have no cure, this was a timely topic and one near my heart.

When my husband Dean was diagnosed as having Alzheimer's a dozen years ago, it wasn't talked about much except in hushed tones. We weren't sure where to turn, but there was a new "early stage" support group starting in a nearby city. Dean was eager to go and find out just what it was we were dealing with. It was the beginning of our long-term association with the Alzheimer's Association.

Today, years after that first meeting, there is still no cure and none just around the corner. But I hang in there and lend a hand, or a voice, or a smile, where I can. Yesterday was my chance to lend a voice in support of the caregiver, a truly unsung hero in this struggle against the disease. Did I do any good? One never knows, but one keeps on.

That should be a goal for all of us—to keep on keeping on. Maybe we don't have a specific cause that drives us, but life itself should be enough cause to keep us going forward. Life is good. Life is precious. Life is not a gift to be tossed aside and wasted.

I intend to keep on keeping on.

OCTOBER 3

Today I went shopping, a rare event for me as shopping is not one of my favorite things to do. However necessity, plus bargains, sometimes push me out the door. Not only did I need some comfortable walking shoes for this winter, I also had a 20% off anything coupon. So off I went to the mall.

You have probably guessed that I came home with more than a pair of shoes. A purse sale (and I *did* need a decent black purse—really) plus a pair of dress slacks (again on sale) were the other finds. And then a carry-out soup and salad from Panera Bread topped off the afternoon's foray. Mission accomplished!

Why is it that some of us go shopping at the drop of a hat while others of us put it off as long as possible? I probably have a little of my mother's blood in me—she was not an avid shopper either. But while one of my daughters abhors shopping, another daughter loves it. So blood lines are definitely mixed in our family.

As I think about all the people around the world who have no hope of getting a new pair of shoes, or even a used pair, I feel a bit guilty bragging about my bargains. And yet some people would say that I was very restrained in my purchases. So, who's right? Who's wrong?

We are so blessed to have options.

OCTOBER 4

The tiny compound leaves of the locust tree outside my window have held on for dear life today as the wind has kept up an incessant assault. Usually, if there is a good wind blowing during the day, it lessens by late afternoon. That has not been the case today.

How is it that those tiny leaves can keep their hold in the face of such constant pressure? Even the leaves that have begun to turn yellow have hung on while the branches dance hither and yon. They have grown and developed there over the summer and will stay until something built into their nature allows the stems to come away from the branch. When it is time for the leaves to fall, they will fall. In the meantime, they remain where they are. In the same way, the locust tree is standing where it was planted. It cannot move from that place by any will of its own.

We humans are much more fortunate. We can move from place to place. We can find a sheltered spot when the wind becomes too strong. If we get tired of being buffeted around, we have the option to search for a more agreeable spot. Some of us are more willing to change location than others. Some of us prefer to stay put, even during adversity. But there are always options.

I love trees, but wouldn't want to be one. I prefer having options.

OCTOBER 5

It was a lazy Sunday afternoon filled with nothing more strenuous than a crossword puzzle and a good book. I had shed my "Sunday" clothes, put on an old pair of slacks and a sweatshirt, slippers on my feet, and was enjoying the quiet. Then came the phone call.

My niece, in town for a week visiting her parents, asked if I'd like to drive over and join them for dessert and conversation. Now, usually I'd be all for it—the dessert and conversation with family. But here I was, nearly in my "jammies" and not really in the mood for changing clothes and going out again. So I said, "No, thanks, not tonight. But have a good time."

And then the inner conversation kicked in.

You probably should have gone.

But I'd have to change clothes, get in the car and drive over there—besides, it's chilly outside.

Marty and Barry are only here for a few days.

But we've had a couple of good visits already and I'll see them tomorrow.

The inner conversation niggled for a while. Was I being too selfish? I'll try to make up for it tomorrow. Today was my day. Tomorrow I'll be ready for everyone else.

I'm slowly learning that once in a while it doesn't hurt to say "No, thanks."

OCTOBER 6

The heavens opened up this morning with a gigantic bucketful of rain rattling my window. It was an eye-opener, to say the least, and one that no one was expecting. Ohio doesn't get rains like that—sudden, extremely short, but with hurricane-like force. This surprise deluge, somewhat like the ice-bucket showers endured by winning coaches, also touched off the fire alarm system and attracted everyone's undivided attention.

And then the day suddenly went back to normal. The rest of the day was cloudy and a bit rainy, but more like Ohio is supposed to be at this time of year. Everything went back to being more predictable, more ho-hum.

We DO like the ho-hum, don't we? We don't like to be jolted by too many surprises. We may say we get tired of the predictable but, generally, we get upset if life confronts us with too much of the unexpected. It messes up our plans and, let's face it, most of us do like to plan ahead. And we want things to go according to plan.

How best can we order our lives so there is room for a little disorder? How can we plan ahead but still make room for a sudden change of plans? This is a thing that most of us struggle with most of our lives—how to embrace the unexpected while awaiting the expected.

My mother set the example for me, facing what life threw at her with grace. Thank you again, Mom!

OCTOBER 7

After a few sunny days of activity outside my window, as four carpenters hammered and measured to erect a screen house, the rains came. Today the sun is out but there is only one man at work. He is doing the slow, painstaking work of putting on the trim—measuring, sawing, fitting, adding the touches that are necessary to a job well done.

Watching this work in progress, I have been made much more aware of all the little things that have to happen to complete this job. The structure went up fast, the roof went on quickly, the windows were set in with ease. Now has come the exacting work of the trim, including small areas of siding. Work not suited to the impatient.

It reminds me of the days when I was sewing clothes for my children. My sewing machine could join the pieces together in next to no time. It was the finishing touches that took more effort. Buttons to sew on and buttonholes to make (yes, there were days before buttonholer attachments to sewing machines). Hems to do by hand. And then perhaps a bit of decorative embroidery on a dress. The finishing touches.

There is little glory, but a lot of satisfaction, in adding the finishing touches. And, especially, to do them right. Sweeping the sidewalk after mowing the lawn. Placing a sprig of parsley on the dinner plate. Writing a thank-you note.

Adding to someone else's pleasure can be reward enough.

OCTOBER 8

This evening I went to the nursing home just down the road to play piano for their weekly chapel service. Pastors from the community volunteer their time to provide leadership for this ecumenical service and, when they do not bring their own pianist, I am often asked to fill in.

Our small Ohio community is relatively homogeneous, settled primarily by central European immigrants who arrived in the mid-to-late 1800s. So we do not have a wide variety of faiths or nationalities represented here. Most of the nursing home's residents grew up singing the same hymns, even though they come from several different denominations.

The song books are large print, easy-to-handle, created especially for older folks. The hymns are ones that most of the residents remember from earlier days. Although their voices are weak and some of the minds are not as sharp as they used to be, they love to hold the song books and sing along as best they can.

When I was in elementary school, 70-plus years ago, my mother used to take my brother and me to the "old people's home" in town to play the piano and sing for the folks there. Back then, we were singing some of the same songs we sang tonight. Will it be that way for my grandchildren and great-grandchildren? I doubt it. But what will they sing? Will they even have a chapel service?

OCTOBER 9

Today I've been thinking often of my youngest daughter. Kay is the one whose husband died suddenly at the end of June, and who is facing their wedding anniversary tomorrow. They would have been married 33 years. Not long enough.

What does a mother say to her daughter at such a time? Words seem so empty, and distance does not allow us to physically touch. I know Kay will be kept busy, as she and two of her daughters plan to drive north to Bar Harbor and Acadia National Park for the weekend. Acadia is the place where she and Dan spent their honeymoon—a place that holds many fond, as well as poignant, memories.

There will be plenty of tears, I'm sure, but also times of peace and of laughter this weekend.. With her daughters beside her, Kay will relive both the good memories and the bad. And she will return home with another of this first-year's milestones behind her.

Each of life's milestones must be encountered, not shoved out of sight and mind, if we are to live full lives. We need to face each one, savor the memories, and go on with life as it presents itself. So, to Kay I say "I know you are hurting, and acknowledge that this will be a bitter-sweet weekend. But you are loved and prayed for, especially today. God go with you, and guide your path."

OCTOBER 10

This evening my friend and I went to a nearby Thai restaurant to enjoy some of our favorites, including their delicious fresh spring rolls. While there, a young couple came in to sit at a table nearby.

Just an ordinary couple, both of them more than a little overweight, dressed in their "grubbies" as many young couples do today. Probably someone from the neighborhood. Nobody in particular.

Still my attention kept being drawn to them. Why? Because they were obviously in love. Sitting across the table from each other, they held hands constantly until their food was served. Their faces were animated in conversation and the look in his eyes as they talked was telling of more than just friendship. It was refreshing to observe their actions.

Maybe this was an early courtship date, although I doubt it. Perhaps it was their wedding anniversary and this was the most they could afford to celebrate. Maybe one of their mothers was babysitting their children to let them have an evening out together. Maybe, maybe, maybe. I'll never know.

There is a lot we don't know about most of the people we encounter each day. We go about our business and don't pay a lot of attention to the unknown people that surround us. But once in a while it's fun to wonder—to wish to know the "rest of the story." Such was the case tonight. I wish them well, whoever they are, wherever they go.

OCTOBER 11

The clouds set the pond on fire tonight. At sunset the not-quite-clear sky was streaked with heavily-tinted clouds—slashes of brilliant pink tracing all across a sea of blue. The intense colors were reflected in the quiet pond outside my window. And then, as the sun settled to the horizon, the reds became much more intense until the glow pulsed with its radiation. Too soon the colors faded as night crept in. But what beauty while it lasted! I was fortunate to be here to take it in. It was a most impressive show.

In our everyday busyness, plus our inattention to things going on around us, we often miss out on natural happenings like this evening's sunset. Just as I missed the beautiful lunar eclipse a few mornings ago because I forgot and didn't get up in time. Perhaps it's all right we don't always notice—otherwise we might too soon become immune to the exceptional beauty around us.

In fact, sometimes it takes a stranger in our midst to point out beautiful things that happen every day. "Consider the lilies of the field, how they grow. They toil not, neither do they spin. Yet Solomon in all his glory was not arrayed like one of these."

There are no lilies in my garden, but there was a beautiful sunset just outside my window. It set the pond on fire and opened my eyes to enjoy one more evening blessing.

OCTOBER 12

There was a real flurry of activity in the tree outside my window this morning. Birds kept flying in and out—robins, sparrows, starlings, a blue jay. The reason? I really don't know. Perhaps it was because frost had come in the wee hours, whitening the rooftops and chilling the air. Perhaps the activity was due to the birds' anticipated migration further south. Perhaps there was a hawk in the vicinity. Perhaps I just happened to be sitting at the window at the right time to notice.

Now, two hours later, the activity in the tree has gone back to normal. The branches are, mainly, empty and still. Everything calm, including the pond. Sunday morning quiet.

Of course, if the birds had been looking at me through the window as I had with them, they would have seen a flurry of activity after breakfast as I got ready for church. Then they would have seen an empty apartment, still and waiting in Sunday morning quiet, followed by activity again as I returned home.

Life does seem to follow patterns of activity and quiet. We need those quiet times between the spurts of moving, going, doing. The older I get, the more precious are those quiet times for reflection. Quiet times to breathe, to relax, to refresh. As summer moves to fall, and fall to winter, let it be a life-giving renewal time for us all.

OCTOBER 13

My niece lives nearby on a farm in the country, in a large farmhouse that has seen more than one renovation over its years. The trees that were planted many years ago to shelter the house from the north winds have grown mature. They provide a beautiful background for the farm setting.

Yesterday when I stopped to visit, Carol and I sat at the big picture window that faces the garden, marveling at the beauty outdoors. As part of the buffer of trees behind their garden are two maples that are outdoing themselves in color this fall. One has completely turned from its summer green to a brilliant yellow-orange. The other is a strikingly beautiful combination of original dark green interspersed with bright red, orange and yellow. The rest of the trees have not as yet started their transformation.

The seasons come and go, and I have lived long enough to have seen plenty of Midwest seasons pass. The change from summer to fall, fall to winter and on to spring and summer again never fail to amaze. I may rail sometimes at an Ohio winter when it forces me to stay inside too long, or when summer days get uncomfortably hot. But this is home.

There's something about "home" that satisfies and soothes. I may travel to see my children and enjoy a change of weather, along with change of pace. But it's always good to arrive back home. May you feel the same, wherever "home" is for you.

OCTOBER 14

My great blue heron was back this morning, stalking the pond outside my window. What grace, what beauty in every step! Like a lighter-than-air ballet dancer, placing the feet just so, holding the body still while moving fluidly along the stones. All the while keeping an ever-intent watch on the surface of the water.

But there are other water-loving creatures without that beauty, without that grace. The frog, for example. Squat and square-ish, goggle-eyed and green. Also one of God's creatures. Also a thing of beauty, to a frog-lover. Also necessary to the health of our cycle of life. We need each other.

From childhood, if we are lucky, we are taught to respect all of nature. We learn to acknowledge the worth of both the ungainly frog and the graceful shorebird. However we soon discover that it's easier to accept differences when dealing with wildlife than with humans. Going to school, our attitudes are challenged when a person doesn't look, act, speak, or dress exactly as we expect. Yet we learn over time that, with humans, we don't just back away and say "ick." We need to learn to live with our neighbors, no matter how different.

Oh, we are a stubborn human race. We find all sorts of excuses to avoid dealing with differences, to keep to our own beautiful heron-selves and ignore the ugly, noisy frogs. We may live to regret it.

OCTOBER 15

One of my daughters-in-law is an artist with cloth. She is a quilter with a perceptive eye coupled with a creative spirit. I have written about Nancy and her work before, but now it's time to tell about her latest creation. I have only seen pictures, but those have impressed.

The quilt Nancy just finished is a gift to her recently-widowed sister-in-law, Kay, and was completed just in time to commemorate Kay and Dan's wedding anniversary. The colorful quilt, long and narrow, can be used as a table runner or as a decorative piece to lay across the end of a bed. The subject of the design is Dan's neckties.

Dan was a middle school history teacher who wore a different tie to work every day. The ties ranged from straightforward and formal to cartoons and caricatures, somber colors to fluorescent brights. The new quilt uses a combination of all of these, and more. The backing of the quilt is all about music, Kay's other love. Perhaps Kay will display the quilt's "tie" side some days and the reverse on other days. Her choice.

Nancy created a quilt for Dean and me for our 45th wedding anniversary—incorporating squares made by each of our six children. We used it on our bed in our travel trailer and enjoyed having "family" accompany us, and keep us warm, all across the country.

Memories can keep us warm, and keep us connected. Thank you, Nancy.

OCTOBER 16

A morning fog hung heavy over everything this morning—rooftops, trees, grass. As I ate my breakfast, I could barely distinguish the Canada geese grazing on the other side of the pond. The fall-yellow leaves of the locust were the only sights clearly visible. Now, two hours later, the fog has lifted somewhat, but there is still a whispery-silent feel in the air. Yes, it's fall.

Schools in the area had two-hour delays or outright cancellations this morning. Reprieve for those with homework due. But, for school administrators, the job of readjusting schedules and recording teaching time.

Thinking back, I don't remember having two-hour delays when I was in school. I grew up in rural Illinois when, in the early '40s, there was no such thing as a school bus to pick us "country kids" up. We either walked to school or someone drove us there. If there was fog, we either made our way through it or stayed home until it lifted. And yet, we learned and graduated. Then we went on with our lives, either joining the long list of "marrieds" or beginning college or a job.

My grandchildren, growing up in the city, really have no idea how much different their growing-up lives are than the one I remember. Nor how many more choices they have—how many more possibilities. And yet, I do not envy them all their advantages. Those advantages also spawn more responsibilities. There is always a price.

OCTOBER 17

It looks like a mass convention on the bank across the pond. I count three hundred geese, then stop counting. All of them facing the sun, their puffed-out breasts reflecting the bright sunlight. Most of them have their heads raised and sit, or stand, nearly motionless. None seem to be sleeping. Only a few move at a time, with nothing in particular to direct their movements, while the others stay still. Some are lined up on the stones at the water's edge, but most are on the grass.

They have spaced themselves out across the grass—none touches the other, no snuggling up. The ones standing on the stones above the water are nearly all in a straight line, about as close to the water as they can get without wetting their feet. The configurations seem almost precise, as if there were a reason for each goose to be in its particular space.

Off and on for three hours I watch the geese, fascinated at their behavior. They remain there, even after a cloud bank rises to obscure the sun. But as time goes by, more and more are drawn to the water's edge. They swim randomly back and forth, while others just stand at the edge and watch. Eventually there are more in or near the water than on the grass.

Nearing sunset, the geese finally begin to disperse. One group takes to the skies. Minutes later, another group. And another. Darkness comes. All is still.

OCTOBER 18

I caught the movement out of the corner of my eye. A flash of bright red landed on one of the topmost branches of the locust tree outside my window. A male cardinal! The sky was gray but he lit up the scene and focused my attention for the next several minutes. I drank it in.

Cardinals aren't that visible around here in summer, preferring more heavily wooded areas to the individual trees scattered around our building. So it was a nice surprise to see him pay a visit, and to stay a little while. Buffeted by the wind, his feathers ruffled as his body swayed with his perch. But his crest, the most identifying mark of the cardinal, stayed trim as if doused with hair spray.

The leaves are falling fast from my locust tree. Soon there will be nothing but bare branches to block my view. Some morning I will wake to see a skim of ice forming at the edges of the water. It is that time of year—a time of slowing down and getting ready for dormancy.

Although winter is not my favorite season, I know there is plenty of beauty to look forward to. I will watch the snow skitter over the ice on the pond, see the world turn white, and look for the red flash that tells me my cardinal has come to visit once again. Something new always awaits. I must watch for it.

OCTOBER 19

Over the last two weeks I have seen more people than usual on the sidewalk beneath my window. I'm sure most of it is driven by curiosity. They want to see the progress being made on the screen house and pier on the pond outside my window. I don't blame them—I enjoy watching it myself, as I've already written about more than once.

There's something about new construction that fascinates both young and old. This is a small project—no bulldozers and other heavy machinery making a lot of noise. Only hammering once in a while or an occasion buzz of a saw. Intermittent rain during these last weeks has definitely slowed progress. But evenings and over the weekend—both this one and last—walkers from the adjoining neighborhood have been passing by regularly and checking things out.

Many times they are walking their dogs, which gives their inspection trip a certain legitimacy for being here, on our sidewalks. It's not that they are forbidden to use the sidewalks—the walks are there for any and all. But some of the regular subdivision residents may feel that they are trespassing on property deemed only for us "old folks" in the retirement village.

We're happy to see them take an interest in what goes on here. We're proud to have them come around and check things out. Openness makes for good neighbors.

OCTOBER 20

I stopped at one of my favorite places this morning—the local public library. I took with me three books that, somehow, got devoured during the past week and I was ready to find more to take their place. It seems as if I am turning back into my elementary-school self, loving nothing more than sitting down with a good book.

If my mother was ever looking for me, she could usually find me in one of two places—in the barn playing with the kittens or curled up in the big wicker chair in the sunroom reading a book. I didn't discriminate much at that age. I just liked to read. Then, during high school and throughout college, I didn't read for pleasure but devoted my time to reading what was required. In the years following, reading still was not my top priority. I was more involved in music and its many rehearsals.

But now, with all those years of busyness behind me, books have once again grabbed my attention and my heart. Discrimination has also come to the fore. I don't care to read much of what grabs the headlines. I prefer meat to froth and a challenge rather than a formula. And it is particularly satisfying to find, once in a while, a book that I absolutely must tell my best friends about.

One of the blessings of getting older—spending an entire afternoon with a good book and not having to apologize.

OCTOBER 21

What a delightful morning! A class of university students came to interview more than a dozen of us "older folks" for a class project. It was a half hour filled with lively one-on-one conversations. I, for one, wouldn't have missed it for the world.

For me, the delight started when I saw the young man approaching. He had the facial features, and the demeanor, of one of my grandsons. As we shared stories I felt more and more as if he could be part of the family. He had a set of questions prepared ahead of time, but whether he kept to them or not, I don't know. I just know that our conversation time was too short. I look forward to our next meeting, a companion session to be held in two weeks.

Some of my friends who have grandchildren living nearby may not have been as refreshed as I, but I saw a lot of smiles as we headed to our apartments. Contact with a younger generation, particularly in one-on-one conversation, has a way of lifting spirits. It was good for all of us.

Wouldn't it have been fun to be a mouse in one of the cars going back to the university? To listen in to their conversations? How many of them were thinking of their own grandparents and comparing them to the persons they just interviewed? Did we help them, in that short time, understand a bit more about their own lives? I hope.

OCTOBER 22

Every small town has its gathering places for different times of the day. This morning I ventured into one of those places. I had taken my car to the garage for its twice-yearly check-over. The coffee shop was just a couple of blocks away so I stopped in for breakfast of hot chai and a muffin.

Dean and I had frequented that coffee shop quite often before his illness, but I almost never go there now as a single. But here I was, sitting alone at a table at 8 a.m. watching the passing scene. Some that came in may have wondered what in the world I was doing there, but didn't ask. Most didn't notice me at all.

There were two other women sitting at a nearby table discussing an ongoing project. Three men stood at the counter discussing whatever it is that men discuss when they get together in the morning. And there was a steady stream of singles, both men and women, stopping in for a quick carry-out. Four professors came in, prepared for a meeting of the minds at a corner table.

And so it went for the 45 minutes I sat there. A few people touching base with others, but most of us just occupying our allotted space for a short time, then moving on. I felt alone, not quite uncomfortable, but alone in that unaccustomed space. The chai was warming, the muffin was filling, but next time I'll come with a friend.

OCTOBER 23

Tonight was an evening of reminiscing through music—the big band style of music as presented in a concert at the university. Eleven instrumentalists, all at or near retirement age, plus two younger vocal soloists treated us to an evening of songs from an era I remember well. The musicians played and sang their hearts out as they dished out selection after selection of tunes we used to hear coming from the juke boxes for a nickel a play.

Thinking of those days brings back memories of the late '40's when my future husband and I sat at the Suzie-Q sipping cokes and listening to the same record over and over. We wanted to learn all the words to the song that became our personal theme song, Dean Martin's "Dreamer With A Penny." It is one of those songs that has long been lost from most memories, but for us it remained. The sentiment was one we cherished.

"I'd rather be a dreamer with a penny than a rich man with a worried mind. . ."

All of our children can readily verify that Dean and I sang that song for many years. Even after Alzheimer's crept in, he had no trouble remembering the words to that song, nor had he lost the ability to sing. That's one special thing about music—it has an effect that, many times, transcends time and adversity and incapacity.

Once more I give thanks for music—and memories.

OCTOBER 24

Sit for a moment and contemplate the backs of your hands. Do they look familiar? If you're as old as I am, you will likely see your grandparent's hands. I certainly see my grandmother's hands at the end of my arms. Skin getting thinner by the day, veins and tendons that used to be hidden now lying exposed.

Yes, I well remember my grandmother's hands. Since she and my grandfather had a home-based bakery, my memories of visiting their house centered around the heavenly scents that rose up to my bedroom long before I was ready to get out of bed in the morning. When I finally arrived downstairs, Grandma was busy shaping clover-leaf rolls to be popped into the oven after rising one more time. She and Grandpa had already baked all the pies that were standing on the table, ready to be delivered. It never entered my mind to be awed by the fact that they had risen long before dawn to have this all accomplished. It was just what happened at Grandpa and Grandma's house.

There is another, deeper remembrance of Grandma that has never left me—that of my grandmother's love. I can't recall any particular spoken words of affection, although she may have told me many times that she loved me. But I knew it with no words being spoken. She said it in her eyes, in her voice, in her actions.

May all our grandchildren's memories be as warm.

OCTOBER 25

At noon today Bluffton's Farmer's Market closed up shop for another year, not to return until the first Saturday in May. I, and many others, will miss those Saturday morning scavenger hunts. We've enjoyed all the seasonal offerings, from spring's rhubarb and asparagus to fall's squash and cider—plus mid-summer's cornucopia of fresh fruits and veggies. We'll miss the breakfast rolls and home-baked pies, but perhaps our bodies will be better off if we take a break.

There's just enough time, six weeks between now and Thanksgiving, to get ourselves ready for the season of eating more than we should of rich foods and sweets. Plenty of time to take brisk walks and drink in the beauty of fall while the grass is still green and the trees show off their finest colors. Time to take advantage of each sunny day for we know that our beautiful fall days will not last forever.

We must also acknowledge that our seasons of life do not last forever. I would not want to go back to my childhood days. Nor do I wish to repeat my years of guiding teenagers through their growing-up years. I would prefer to go back to our post-retirement traveling years but know that it, too, is impossible. So I will enjoy this season of life while it lasts and try to take advantage of all the opportunities that still come, even in my mid-80s.

Life can still be good.

OCTOBER 26

One fall, about five years ago, my across-the-hall neighbor Annie and I selected one maple tree on our campus to be the most beautiful of all. Every day as we took the stairs we could see it framed in the window, somewhat like a magic mirror answering our question "who is the fairest of them all?" In succeeding years that tree, although always especially colorful, was never quite as spectacular—until this fall.

The tree started to color early this year, but only a little bit at a time. A little yellow first appeared, then oranges and reds gradually took on new intensity as the weather turned cooler. Even today there is still a bit of green near the bottom. But most of the leaves have now turned to a more uniform russet-orange.

Over a lifetime we are witness to many changes—in the world around us as well as in ourselves. Just as with the trees, some years of our lives are more special, or more troublesome, than other years. At times we experience too much rain in our lives, or not enough. The winds of adversity sometimes come on too strong. But, just as with the tree, we must take what comes and weather another season.

For me, right now, this "autumn" of my life is most satisfying. To be in this place at this time is good enough.

OCTOBER 27

I was witness to a hit-and-run accident yesterday, so had to give a police report. The only damage was to a flower bed. But it was enough to warrant the police investigation. I don't know whether I'll hear any more about the incident, but for a time I was part of the process.

We are often caught in the web of someone else's action, not to the point of what I needed to do yesterday, but caught nevertheless. Actually, much of life is centered around dealing with what someone *else* has set in motion. We are not islands unto ourselves, but part of a community. And, for that, we need to answer when called.

In the senior living community where I live, I live independently yet I depend on the work of others in many ways. Before retirement, both my husband and I were involved in a network of job and volunteer responsibilities. We were responsible for our own work, but we definitely did not work alone. And, before that, I was caught in the web of caring for our children. In that position, there was plenty of community to deal with, as any parent will know.

We like our independence but, in actuality, our lives depend on a network of connections and dependencies. We may not always appreciate some situations we are put into, but it's all part of the process of living in community. And most of us really DO choose community.

OCTOBER 28

Weather can be fickle here in the Midwest. Beautiful one day, dark and rainy the next. For the record, yesterday was beautiful. Today is dark and rainy. Since my daughter-in-law Debi is visiting from North Carolina, I was hoping that most of our days together would be sunny and warm, but it seems that the cooler late-October days have decided to set in for the rest of her stay.

Yesterday Debi and I went to visit my brother Norm in the nursing home nearby. It was a delightful fall day—temperature in the 70s with bright sunshine. We took Norm in his wheelchair all around the home's campus, stopping often to drink in the beautiful golds and reds of the trees. It was probably the last really warm day we will see this fall so it was good that we were able to share that special time with my brother.

I remember doing the same with my mother, in her later years, and then with my husband. Each of them spent their last years in that same nursing home. Yesterday we followed the same paths, stopped at the same benches, enjoyed the same beautiful trees plus a few more that have been planted since. I would not be surprised if, some day, I will be the one to be wheeled along those same paths, under those same trees.

There is something special about constancy. About family and shared memories. Yesterday was one of those special days.

OCTOBER 29

As Halloween approaches, the television ads feature more and more images of the bizarre, the extra-weird, the zombies. What, at one time, was expected to be an evening of scary-fun for kids is gradually being usurped by adults, evolving into the eerily-grotesque costumes for the parents.

But this evening, at our church, our children were the focus and the costumes only secondary. In what has become a tradition, the children come dressed up in their favorite costumes but they also bring their talents with them. For a half-hour they entertained us with a program including some new songs they have learned as a choir, plus each of them performed a talent of some kind. We enjoyed listening to the offerings of several piano students, three violinists, a couple of poets. Each year we see their talents growing just as their bodies and minds are growing.

But the most interesting memory I brought home from this evening's Halloween concert was after it was all over and we were going home. One family, who had a boy and a girl in the program, was heading down the stairs to go out to the parking lot. The boy was trailing and being urged on by his mother. Why was he trailing? Because he was busy reading his book. It was a hard-back story book that he continued reading as he automatically walked down the steps and out the door. Completely engrossed in his book.

Surely a scholar in the making.

OCTOBER 30

The locust tree outside my window has finally lost all its leaves. And I think the Canada geese have finally gone as well. I say goodbye to both leaves and geese with a mixture of feelings.

I'll miss those tiny, compound locust leaves because they lend a green softness to the landscape that the bare branches cannot do. At the same time I know that those bare branches will look lovely with a coating of snow this winter. In addition, the winter birds will be much easier to spot and identify.

I'll miss watching the Canada geese come and go, especially since they finally learned to stay on "their side" of the pond as summer came to an end. It has been fun, and an education in bird behavior, to watch them assemble in such large numbers recently. Nature calls, they heed and begin their migration.

Every season has its own particular beauty and, for me, the changes exert a constant pull to the window. Even though winter is not my favorite, I look forward to seeing those first snowflakes as they turn the green lawn to white. I look forward to watching the snow skitter across the ice, letting the wind form patterns on the pond's surface. I look forward to watching the neighborhood children try out their sleds and saucers after the first good snowfall.

I look forward to it all.

OCTOBER 31

There is one Halloween evening that stands out in my memory as being the most special of all. It has nothing to do with costumes or scariness or anything else that we usually associate with Halloween. But it made a difference for me and, if you try it yourself sometime, it may make a difference for you.

We were retired and living in a small condo on a quiet street in town. I had been writing a monthly column for our town's weekly newspaper and, for the occasion, had written about Halloween. The gist of my column was the question, "Why do we send our children out to beg for candy when we should be sending them out to give, rather than to receive? What are we teaching them?"

So, in order to "put my money where my mouth is," I went to the florist shop, bought two dozen carnations, dressed as a farmer's wife and started walking. My husband stayed home to hand out peanuts on the porch while I spent the evening walking to our neighbors and handing each household a flower. Of course, the neighbors were surprised and pleased. But the greatest pleasure was all mine.

It was a simple thing to do, but I'll never forget that evening of giving rather than taking. One of my former neighbors, whenever she sees me, reminds me of that evening. "That was *so* special," she says. "I'll never forget."

Neither will I.

Musings at the Half

Why do I write? What is it that brings me to the computer at odd hours, sometimes on a true mission to get something written down RIGHT NOW, at other times a more studied approach? What is this exercise in writing "a reflection a day" doing to/for me? Because it really *is* for me, even though I write as if I want you to know. Well, I guess it's really for both of us—you and me. I want you to feel a little of what I feel—for you to catch a little of what I have just caught. A picture, a thought, a bit of excitement or a bit of sadness or whatever it is I'm feeling or remembering or wondering about.

Why is my goal to do this for a year? Because I need to go through all the seasons. Each season speaks to me differently. I think and react to the stimuli around me and, as the seasons change, I change as well. Although I usually write these reflections at home, I do travel once in a while. All that travel adds another layer to what I see and experience. When I've written my 365th one, will it be much like the first or will my writing and my outlook have changed? That is yet to be seen although, at almost the halfway point, I believe my thoughts and writings are basically tracking in the same direction.

Why am I considering putting this all into a book? Because I need to share some of my delight in discovering the "little things" that make a day special. So many times, as I write, I'm smiling. Perhaps a few of those smiles will come to your face, as well, as you read. There is so much in this world, right under our noses, that we fail to see. Or we see but don't comprehend. Or we comprehend but then we turn to something else and the moment is gone. I have enjoyed learning to take that fleeting moment, hold onto it and savor the experience. Then, in writing about it I savor it once again. And in reading it, I savor it once more. And maybe, next year, I'll read and remember these experiences all over again.

It's worth the effort.

November 1

They told us it was coming, and it came. Our first snowfall, on the first day of November. It wasn't really very much. The rooftops sported coats of mottled gray and white this morning. The grass was still green, with a scattering of snow on top. But the stuff we knew would be showing up—showed up.

The wind kept the pond moving, so there is no trace of ice on the surface this morning. But that, too, will happen one of these days. It's one of the facts of life if one decides to set roots in Ohio, or any state above (and sometimes below) the Mason-Dixon line. The snow will come and go, the ice will come and go, life will go on.

For those of us who are retired and have no regularly-set schedule, the snow is more a conversation piece than anything. We don't have to get out and shovel in order to get to work. But we can also empathize with the commuters, the school bus drivers, all those who have to clear their driveways before they can back the car out of the garage.

There is something about the change of seasons that I like. It's as if the earth needs a new wardrobe, desires a change of pace, wants to get away from what has become ordinary. So, along with Mother Nature, I get out my sweaters, adjust my schedule and look forward to the changing scene outside my window.

NOVEMBER 2

It has seemed awfully quiet around my apartment since my daughter-in-law Debi's visit came to an end. Oh, we weren't really that noisy, or that busy, but we were together each day and truly enjoyed each other's company. Debi has been a part of our Niswander family for more than 35 years, so we have had plenty of time to gather common remembrances.

I remember the first time Debi came to visit, before she and Rick were married. She had grown up in the West and this was her first time this far east—all the way to Ohio. Over Christmas vacation, no less! We had plenty of snow and cold while Debi was used to warm and sunny. It was not a good season to be introduced to the new family she was joining. But join she did, with a smile. Love helps in making good choices.

Each one of my daughters-and-sons-in-law has, I'm sure, gone through times of indecision. Is this really the person I want to choose? Is this family going to accept me as I am? In joining a new family there are many dynamics going on—holding on to old ideas while accepting new challenges. And we, as a family, face our own challenges as we learn to know each new family member and recognize them as a vital part of who we are, collectively.

Families are a special kind of love.

NOVEMBER 3

I have a tiny three-inch-long sculpture on my desk, one I've had for at least 20 years. It reminds me, every time I look at it, to not take myself too seriously. Four little globs of clay shaped into round faces with bulbous noses, open mouths and toothpick-hole eyes. They stick out their tongues and laugh their silent laughs at me. I can't help but smile whenever I look at them. They are there to keep reminding me that there is always a light side to life.

It was at a street fair where I found these little guys (they must be guys because no woman would go out in public with her hair looking as bad as theirs). The clay figures were offered in different sizes and, considering the prices were somewhat high, I picked the smallest. So glad I did, since what I have is just the right size to keep giving me a gentle reminder without shouting. A reminder to keep things in perspective and find something to smile—even laugh—about each day.

Life isn't always fun, or funny. But neither is it all gloom and seriousness. Life is, well, life. A little good, a little not so good, but never bad enough to lose perspective. So I enjoy what life has to offer and give thanks every day. There is always something to give me a lift. All I have to do is look at my gallery of goofy guys and smile.

NOVEMBER 4

The area around Bluffton and Pandora, Ohio where I live was settled in part by immigrants from Switzerland. There are people still living in this area who grew up in households where Swiss was spoken at home, around the table and in general conversation. In fact, some of our older residents did not learn to speak English at all until they went to public school. Today one rarely hears the Swiss dialect spoken except for occasional phrases now and then between some of the old timers.

But this afternoon, in our Family Room, two dozen people sat around tables with big smiles on their faces and Swiss conversation filling the room. Oh, there definitely weren't any youngsters in the group. Ages ranged from nearing 60 to over 90 years old. But nearly all of these were individuals who had grown up speaking Swiss as children and were now trying out their early language once more. As the afternoon progressed, the conversations increased in volume and vocabularies expanded as the almost forgotten language sparked memories of earlier days. The smiles on people's faces were enough proof that another day like this will be in the making.

And those plans are already taking shape. Next month they plan to get together again and bring friends who might have been too shy to attend this first time. It will be another celebration of memories coming alive once more.

There are many ways to exercise the mind while having fun.

NOVEMBER 5

The other day a friend showed me a lovely quilt, fashioned around several of her great-aunt's lace-and-embroidery handkerchiefs. A beautiful creation, put together to preserve something one seldom sees any more—a lady's handkerchief.

The world of Kleenex (and all the ensuing brands) has certainly saved the skin on our noses and has made the common cold more manageable, but at the price of some beautiful handiwork. Now we save our ancestor's delicate handkerchief in a picture frame, a quilt—or, most often, in a box in the attic.

I still remember the handkerchief dolls my mother used to make to keep me from fidgeting in church. I would sit next to her in the pew, watching the folding and rolling process, then spend the next few minutes mesmerized as I rocked my "baby" back and forth. Then I'd pull on the ends and make the baby disappear, only to watch my mother do the creation trick one more time. It kept me quiet.

This morning I tried to re-create one of those dolls, using a small square of soft cloth (no handkerchiefs in my house!). No luck. It's been too long since I have seen one of those handkerchief dolls, much less create one. Anyway, mothers (and grandmothers) don't need to make handkerchief dolls in church any more. Now, if the children attend church at all, there are all sorts of activities to keep the small fry occupied.

One more creative skill lost to progress!

NOVEMBER 6

Today is my oldest son's birthday—a good time to go back into memory to recall those early-parenting days. The days when my husband and I were just beginning to learn what raising a family is all about. And, like most every young couple, we had a lot to learn.

I was fresh out of college and really hadn't a clue about parenting. Oh yes, I had read all the books (Dr. Spock was the guru for those times). We had good friends that had already started their families, and Dean's sisters were having babies around the same time. But there's nothing like two greenhorns holding hands and marveling at the child they produced, while wondering how they'll ever get through the first night home.

With the help of two grandmas, one grandpa, several aunts and uncles and cousins, we made it through the first years—adding a few more children over those years. But I still can remember that first night at home (after the required two week stay in the hospital—yes, they kept mothers and babies there that long, back then!). I still can picture Dean and me standing at the bassinette, our first baby waiting to be changed, and both of us realizing how really clueless we were.

And yet, Rick grew and thrived and is thriving still. He loves his wife, loves his job, and is there for his Mom when she needs him. I guess we did all right.

NOVEMBER 7

There is something so soothing about waking up to sunshine, with a placid pond mirroring the blue sky outside my window. I never tire of the sight. The stillness ensures, for me, a good morning.

I think I've always relished quiet times, or at least I feel more attuned to all the other senses during those times. Even when growing up among the cornfields of Illinois, I sensed the wonder of quietness. One of the first real poems I ever wrote, when I was in 7th or 8th grade, spoke of the soothing night sounds I could hear from my window. I can still picture myself in that tiny upstairs bedroom, lying in bed and listening to the summer night sounds. Here are excerpts from that poem, which my mother saved for me:

"A drowsy cricket chirps . . . a lone car rushes past, seeking refuge from the darkness . . . a train cries faintly, sadly . . . a summer shower starts softly, gently, cooling the parched earth . . . eyes grow heavy, earthly things grow dim and sweet dreams replace them."

So much for early teen romanticism. But it's still there—that reaching out to the quiet space and relishing the stillness. Maybe that's one of the reasons why my television is seldom turned on and why, if the radio is on, it is tuned (quietly) to the classical station.

If you haven't heard silence lately, just listen.

NOVEMBER 8

With the change of seasons here in the Midwest there comes a gradual change of wardrobe. This morning I decided it was time to go through the summer clothes and put aside all those short sleeves and tank tops—things I won't need for the next several months—and replace them with more season-appropriate attire.

It's funny how, when summer is here, one can hardly imagine pulling on a heavy sweater. But gradually a light wrap feels good on a cool evening and then, before you turn around, the winter wardrobe beckons. That's one reason I like living where I do—there *is* a change of seasons; there *is* a reason to clean the closet.

I know, even those who live in summer-all-year follow the seasons with changes in color and texture, at least if they are financially able to do so. And there are advantages to being able to get appropriately dressed in the morning without checking the weather report first. But I'll still vote for a change of season.

In the seasons of life, it's the same. I'm grateful that I'm not a child anymore. I'm grateful that my children are grown and on their own, even if they live far away. And now, even in widowhood, this season of life is all right. I still look forward to every day and the challenges, and blessings, the day will bring.

May it keep on being so.

NOVEMBER 9

I arrived at the window soon enough to see it, but not soon enough to focus in. I just knew that the bird perched on the bare locust tree outside my window was a hawk. A red-tail? A Cooper's? It didn't stay long enough for me to verify. Besides, dusk was settling in—not a good time for positive bird identification but still enough light to know that what I saw was not the usual smaller denizens of that tree.

Bird watching became one of my most engrossing hobbies after we moved to a house in the woods, not far from Lake Erie and the seasonal bird fly-way. We had red-headed wood-peckers at the feeder, thrushes singing their haunting songs in the morning, and all varieties of warblers migrating through every spring and fall. We also learned to monitor bluebird boxes every spring. Each new experience, each new identifica-tion, was a delight.

After Dean retired, we did considerable traveling through-out the United States and, during those years, my birding life list lengthened. Now most of the birds I encounter are those that appear outside my window. So every heron that stalks the pond, every hawk that perches in the tree, every woodpecker that climbs the trunk, and every Canada goose that lands and takes off is noticed and (sometimes) appreciated.

I am thankful for eyes to see, for a mind to recognize, and for a heart to appreciate what is there—just outside my window.

NOVEMBER 10

Today was a day to watch youth at work. A day to see some of our surroundings transform under the hands of young men and women the ages of our grandchildren—or maybe even great-grandchildren. Some were from an established business and will be paid for their services. Some came from the university, offering their willing hands and youthful ingenuity with only a light supper as their payment. All of them were workers, set to a task.

In the morning came the tree service trucks, rolling in with equipment to take away several trees that had outgrown their space and replace them with trees of a different size and variety. The men went about their work with the machines, the skill, and the confidence of professionals. The job was done quickly and efficiently, while leaving the landscape clean and neat. A job well done.

In late afternoon came the students, none of them knowing exactly what they were supposed to do, but willing to do whatever task it was. They got busy stringing strands of outside lights along the front porch, through the bushes, over the bridge in back, everywhere that our Christmas tradition has set a precedent. When the last outdoor lights were in place, they gathered inside for their payment in kind—chicken sandwiches, chips, salad and brownies.

Two jobs well done, satisfaction all around. Another good day.

NOVEMBER 11

I thought they were gone for the winter, but evidently not all have taken the trip yet. After four days of no Canada geese gathering on "their" side of the pond, they appeared again this morning. Not as many as the day recently when I counted 300—perhaps only a third of that amount. And I must admit, they are beautiful in the bright sunlight that accentuates the striking white slash at the cheek and rump.

I guess it comes close to a draw—this love-hate relationship I have with the geese. "Oh no—they're back again" clashes with "but I'm fascinated by their beauty and their behavior." I hate their messy ways, but happy that they've learned to stay away from our sidewalks.

Nature never quite stops giving us these little enigmas— these challenges to living peaceably. What may give me joy might give you the shivers. I enjoy working with the wiggly monarch caterpillars every summer but our activities director wants nothing to do with them until they spin their beautiful chrysalis and emerge as butterflies. I've never been one to welcome pets into the house, but when my children were younger I had no choice but to bend to their wishes.

So, today I'll keep watch over the flock outside my window and puzzle over their structured behavior—while shooing them away when they sneak over to my side. I'll give them their space, as long as they honor mine.

NOVEMBER 12

A jumbled variety of thoughts and memories entered my mind as I picked up the kaleidoscope that has been standing on a table in my living room for a good many years. It has been such a part of the household landscape for so long that I seldom think about it. But today I picked it up, held it, rubbed it, shook it, peered through it as I turned it, and entered a memory world once more.

This kaleidoscope isn't of the brightly-colored cardboard toy variety. It was never designed for a toddler. It is a work of art, a decorative item, with an elegance all its own. Crafted of beautifully-grained walnut and polished satin-smooth, it is special even before you lift it to your eye and watch the colored crystals inside work their magic.

Try as I might, I can't remember where Dean and I purchased this beautiful souvenir. In our travels across the U.S. we usually found at least one special piece of art to bring home with us. I have a large envelope where I keep the information about each piece, but I find nothing in the envelope about this kaleidoscope.

Whose hand selected the crystals? What artist designed the piece to fit an adult hand so naturally? Who polished the wood to perfection? The glass at the end that holds the crystals is inscribed with a name and date: "Paretti '86." That's all I know.

Thank you, my nearly-unknown artist.

NOVEMBER 13

What serendipity! I walked to the window to check out a little snow flurry that was happening at the moment. But it wasn't the snow that stopped me in my tracks. Nor was it the gathering of about two hundred migrating Canada geese that had earlier landed on the pond. It was a pure white goose at the edge of the pond. It stood out from all the others, but was still a part of them. "An albino!" I thought.

But no. On second look I saw that the goose was not pure white. Its wingtips were black. And then I noticed two other geese nearby. Their coloring was more like the Canadas', but their heads were white and the wings mottled. We definitely had three geese with the flock that weren't Canada geese.

Out came the binoculars and the bird book. Soon I found and identified the strangers—one snow goose and two blue geese. They were easily identified because they looked just like their illustrations in the book. How exciting and how special to see them here in Ohio—passing through to wintering grounds!

Had those three geese been blown off their course? Their migration route is normally a little farther west. If they are off-course, where will they land to spend the winter? In Alabama rather than Texas? Will they stay with the Canada geese and find common winter quarters with them?

I'll never know. But I'll wonder.

NOVEMBER 14

It smells like fall in my kitchen this afternoon, this first-of-the-season vegetable soup day. This phenomenon will happen every so often for the next few months, every time my fridge needs cleaning out and I need a special winter pick-me-up. Homemade vegetable soup is one of those treats that conjures up a host of memories for me, as it probably does for you. It makes the house smell like "home."

Some odd combinations went into the soup today, as often happens. I had two small pieces of meat—chicken breast and bratwurst (a strange combination) plus a portion of a leftover hamburger/potatoes/peas casserole. Some needing-to-be-used celery, half an onion, corn and peas from the freezer, plus fresh green, yellow and red pepper chunks. It made a bright combination of veggies. I added a variety of herbs from the spice cabinet. The ensuing soup smells and tastes delicious.

But I'm not finished. After all this combination simmers a bit longer, I'll turn off the heat and let the soup rest a while. Then I'll take out just enough for my evening meal, add a little more water, bring it to a boil and add a handful or so of thin-cut noodles, then boil until the noodles are just the right softness. Devour.

Tomorrow evening, or the next, I might add rice instead of noodles. Or maybe small pasta shells. Or maybe nothing else at all. And the kitchen will continue to smell like "home."

NOVEMBER 15

Here we go again. Another reflection on my love-hate relationship with the Canada geese at the pond outside my window. This morning it was like standing at an airport window watching as the air traffic controllers work their magic with take-offs and landings.

There were 50-75 geese beneath my window when I first looked this morning. No big deal today—I no longer try to count how many. They were (choose your modifier) contentedly, greedily, fastidiously, hungrily eating the still-green grass near the pond. By the time I had finished breakfast they were all in the water, milling around and seemingly aimless. But the whole flock, for the most part, was facing the southwest.

Was there a signal? None that I could tell. But one small group of about twenty geese suddenly turned tail, faced northeast, and swam toward the middle of the pond. Then this group about-faced once again, now facing the southwest, and took off with loud squawks and a flurry of wings. Two or three minutes later, another group did the same thing. And then another until all were gone.

How do they know? What squawk-language tells them it's their turn for take-off? Who's the boss when they're airborne—to orchestrate when the flock's leaders change rotations? Is there a chief navigator in each flock that picks the route and decides when to take a lunch break? I wonder...

NOVEMBER 16

It was a sunny, chilly fall day. But it suddenly warmed for me when, in mid-afternoon, I chanced to be in the right place at the right time. How often does it happen that I walk from the computer to the living room and, perched on the locust tree outside, is a Cooper's hawk? Not often.

Big and beautiful, the hawk perched on that limb as if for a formal photograph. I eased as close to the window as I dared, not wanting to chase it away. Its back was to me. The body remained perfectly still but, as I watched, the hawk moved its head nearly all the way around. Probably looking for this intruder that it sensed was watching. The hawk stayed there long enough for me to drink in the rich brown streaking on its tail, the lighter-colored collar, the sharp, curved beak.

When my husband and I moved into this apartment, we left behind a lovely "window on wildlife" from which we could watch the birds at our feeder. Now, living in a second-level apartment, I no longer have a bird feeder, nor am I able to feast my eyes on feeding birds. But that's all right. Now, spotting birds is no longer commonplace but a gift. Any sighting is special, whether it be a bright red cardinal, a blue jay, a kingfisher, a flock of geese, an occasional hawk.

Thank you, Creator, for such gifts.

NOVEMBER 17

The room is set with round tables, decorated for fall. Around them sit a majority of our retirement village's residents, primed and ready for a party. The occasion? Our quarterly reception for new residents, and this time there is a large number to introduce and honor.

This quarterly gathering is somewhat like a block party—welcoming a new family that just moved into the neighborhood. We need to get to know them, they need to know something about us. We have to try each other out, get acquainted, find our common interests. For some, adjusting to this new situation is relatively easy. For others, it's a trial. Some of us have been the new kids on the block many times. For others of us, this may be the first time. But now we're here together, in this place, in this community.

One of our new residents plays the dulcimer so the group he plays with came to entertain us. Another new resident moved in just yesterday, but he is happy to take the microphone and tell a bit about himself. Another is more than happy to proclaim "I love it here!" A couple of others are a bit more shy, but pleased to be officially welcomed.

And so our ties to each other, here in this place, begin to be strengthened bit by bit. We're working together to make the most of this later-in-life adjustment to a new environment. We celebrate. Together.

NOVEMBER 18

It's a perfect Christmas card morning. A two-inch frosting of white lies over everything in sight. Every branch and twig of my locust tree holds as much as it can of the snow that came down overnight. Each evergreen presents a portrait of early winter. Oh, to be an artist on such a day!

But there is one blot at the edge of my picture. I want to let it go and not mention it, but I keep returning to the window to check. It's those Canada geese again. One in particular. The one with the broken wing. The one that keeps cropping up in these reflections every once in a while. It's that one goose I keep worrying over.

This morning, that goose is standing alone on the other side of the pond. But no, it is not alone. Another goose stands in the water not far away. Is it a mate? A disabled friend? They are definitely alone. Alone together. Does each have a problem it cannot solve alone?

The goose with the broken wing waddles to the water's edge, swims gracefully across to my side for a few minutes, then swims back. There the two stand—grooming, grooming, grooming. The water in the pond is completely open today. Not a trace of ice on the edges. But the temperature is predicted to stay below freezing all day, tonight, and into tomorrow. Where will they go? What will they do?

God of innocent things, be gracious.

NOVEMBER 19

I've been thinking today about mentors—those people who are special guides along our individual life paths. I have three mentors who stand out in memory, each of whom gave me direction when I most needed it. First, my college organ professor. Soft-spoken and gentle, he had faith in my abilities when I had no confidence. When faced with a challenging new organ sonata, he would say over my doubts, "yes, Miss Vercler, you can do it." And, since I didn't want to disappoint him, I always conquered it. He gave me the skills to lead, through music.

Second, an evening class writing instructor who encouraged me to write prose when I thought the only thing I could write was poetry. Her words of encouragement pushed me into a new medium and gave me confidence in what I could do. She opened my eyes to new ways of putting my ideas and feelings on paper.

Third, an art educator who, with a warm heart behind her perfectionist manner, cultivated in me a love for museums and art appreciation—this to someone who can't draw but who was looking for something new to conquer. She gave me, in middle age, a new outlook on the world of art.

And then, I wonder. Who have I mentored, when I least expected to? Is there someone who can say of me, "she set me on a special path?" I wonder...

NOVEMBER 20

Our pond, that beautiful beckoning expanse of water that draws my eye daily, is frozen this morning except for a space near the center where an aerator has kept the water moving. Yesterday there was only a thin skirt of ice at the edges because strong winds were chasing waves all across the pond. Overnight, the cold took over and caused this new slim ice covering. Snow is skating across the icy surface now, skittering here and there as the wind dictates.

It looks, and feels, like January. It should not be this cold in November! Not in Ohio! Not before Thanksgiving! This is an anomaly. Extreme cold and snow is not supposed to happen now. The weather channel is having a heyday. Plenty of news. Plenty of records being set across the country.

And then, amidst my complaining, I remember how fortunate I am to be living in this place and at this time. My basic needs are met, and more. I am not homeless, or destitute, or wondering where my next meal is coming from. I am among the most fortunate people on earth, with a solid roof over my head and all the amenities that make for comfortable living.

One of these days soon the sun will warm the air, the snow and ice will gradually go away, my world will come back to a more normal November. And I will forget my complaints. I hope I won't forget to offer thanks.

NOVEMBER 21

After our cold and snowy wake-up call at the beginning of the week, the sun is shining today. The wind has decided to rest for a while and the outside thermometer no longer has icicles hanging from the rim. And, just as the weather reverts back to what we expect at this time of year, we as creatures of habit do the same. We revert back to our regular activities. So what is there to talk about, now that life is slowly getting back to normal?

Ah, normal! So comforting. Dull, maybe, but comforting. The unusual makes for spirited conversation and speculation, but normal is where most of us spend the majority of our lives. The ever-present 24/7 news channels can make our blood pressure rise and fire us up, but most of our lives center around more mundane activities and less headline-grabbing news. Ho-hum is a necessary part of life.

So, how can we make the most of every-day life? How can we truly enjoy the mundane? By looking for the little things that make the heart sing, even in the midst of the ordinary. By paying attention to the small occurrences that don't shout but are there if only we'd take notice. That's what these daily "reflections" do for me. They make me stop and think rather than pass by and ignore what's going on under my nose.

There is so much more out there than we realize. We just have to pay attention.

NOVEMBER 22

It was like watching a host of third graders heading out for recess. But they came in a rush of wings, not legs and arms. Loud honks, not laughing voices. Another large flock of migrating geese came swooping down and took over our pond this afternoon—evidently a designated rest stop on their way south. They have been taking advantage of all the amenities available.

First, a refreshing bath in the center of the pond which continues to provide open water. The geese did not swim calmly around, in their usual way. They ducked and dipped and nearly did somersaults in the water as they cleaned their wings, then flapped them dry. Their loud honks were like cries of joy—what a great rest stop!

Next came a time of settling down, standing on the ice-covered edges of the pond or opting to occupy the grassy bank. Time to preen and re-oil the feathers. The geese quiet down now—no more exuberant squawks and honks. Nearly all of them have turned to face the same direction, holding their breasts to the sun.

Some of those on the bank nibble at the grass occasionally, but there is none of the frenzied activity that was going on half an hour ago. They've settled in to rest, I suppose. After all, flying requires strength and stamina. They still have a long way to go.

Two hours later, they quietly take off in groups. *Bon voyage!*

NOVEMBER 23

The Cooper's hawk came to call again this afternoon. Well, maybe he didn't just drop in for a visit, but he did drop down onto a branch of my leaf-bare locust tree at just about dusk. I was sitting at the table by the bay window, no lights turned on as yet, and saw movement outside—just at my eye level. There he was, facing me, his clean white breast heavily streaked with brown. Feathers rippling every-which-way as the wind was coming in strong gusts.

So there we both sat, face to face. He in the tree and I at my table, pondering what to do next. I dared not move or the hawk would have flown off in a flash. He turned his head from side to side, ever watchful. The wind gusts blew the feathers on his back to reveal white underneath. I just sat there, unmoving but deeply moved, and drank it all in. How often can one be this close to a hawk and not be spotted right away? It was a special, serendipitous sighting.

The magic must have lasted all of two minutes, then the hawk was gone. But now, sitting and writing about it, I see it all happening once more. The surprise landing, the almost instant identification, the long moments of silent admiration. And the gratitude that I happened to be at that place and at that time.

The memory is one I will savor again and again.

NOVEMBER 24

I went to an Alzheimer's support group meeting this afternoon—a monthly gathering of caregivers and ex-caregivers. I've been attending for the past ten years, even though my husband succumbed to the disease nearly five years ago. Why do I still go to those meetings? Because I have a need to give back and offer whatever help I can.

The support that was given to Dean and me when we were struggling to make sense of living with Alzheimer's disease was a valuable resource. The speakers, the discussions, the friendships shared at those meetings helped us to cope with an uncertain future. The monthly gatherings offered a safe place to ask questions, to learn, and sometimes to let off steam. Both of us looked forward to those monthly meetings.

Today there were six of us who shared joys and frustrations. We probed and learned together. Since Alzheimer's disease manifests itself differently in each person, I continue to gain new insights at each meeting. That's what keeps me going. That, and hope that some day there will be a cure.

Will I live to see that day? I doubt it very much. There is still so much unknown about the human brain and its workings, much less how to fix it. But that fact does not stop our Alzheimer's group, and other support groups across the country, from meeting and sharing. We truly need each other.

NOVEMBER 25

Menacing gray skies surrounded me when I woke this morning. Then rumbles of thunder in the distance. Suddenly, heavy rain was lashing the windows and strong winds whipped the columnar evergreen from side to side. Then, just as suddenly, the rain was gone only to come back with the same ferocity a few minutes later. When the rain finally stopped, water was standing in places where it seldom stands. Not a good day to go to town, which I had planned to do.

Now, a mere hour later, the sky is blue with only a few clouds, the sun is shining, the world has taken on a completely different face. It looks as if I will have a good do-as-previously-planned day after all.

This morning's changing weather reminds me of days when our children were small. I learned, early on, that children's storms come quickly and usually pass at the same speed. Separating two squabbling children and requiring them to sit on separate chairs for a period of time (that usually ended up to be however long it took *me* to calm down) often did the trick. It was not long before they were playing peaceably again.

Then the children grew up. Now they live many miles from each other and get together only occasionally. They have learned to adjust to the little idiosyncrasies they still see in their siblings or their in-laws. When we all got together this summer there was bonding, not squabbles. The sun still shines.

NOVEMBER 26

Today was a day for a memory trip. I was riding with good friends Dick and Corrinne. They were driving to visit family in central Illinois for Thanksgiving, and I would be visiting my son's family near Chicago. Corrinne and I both grew up in central Illinois, we both went to the same college in Ohio where we met our future husbands. Our families attended the same church, we sang together and played together. But we had never traveled to Illinois together before.

The memories flew as we drove west out of Ohio, all the way through Indiana and into Illinois. The roads and landscape were very familiar, as we had driven these same roads year after year as we paid visits to our parents and extended family. So, what did we talk about on this trip together? We swapped stories—stories of different "adventures" we had during those long driving trips—car troubles, winter weather, the dearth of amenities along the way. We pointed out familiar landmarks, remarking on things that had changed as well as all the things that had not changed.

How swiftly the time did go! Our combined memories enhanced this 21st century trip and the miles just melted away. Little did we know, fifty years ago, that the traveling memories we were storing up year after year would provide entertainment for us on this later-in-life trip.

Stored memories. Valuable and precious.

NOVEMBER 27

Thanksgiving Day gave me a look at two different worlds. The experience made me especially thankful for the world in which I usually live.

I was with son Tom and Nancy and family in suburban Chicago. Their church sponsors a meal a month for a homeless shelter in a neighboring town. This month their turn happened on Thanksgiving, so I accompanied them as we all helped prepare the special meal. Our family's responsibility was to provide a sweet potato casserole that has been a family favorite the last few years.

We parked at the shelter, outside of which were about fifty people waiting to be let in the doors at 9:00 a.m. It felt strange to walk past those waiting and enter the warm kitchen, but we did have work to do. We soon were busy peeling, then mashing, sweet potatoes for the expected 175 people. Brown sugar, butter and chopped nuts were added and it was not long until the casseroles were ready for the ovens. Another family came in to prepare the green beans, another family to cut the pumpkin and apple pies. Others would come later to serve the afternoon meal.

We then drove home to finish preparing for our own Thanksgiving feast. And yes, a feast it was. Our sweet potato casserole was just like the ones we had prepared for the shelter, but our circumstances and our surroundings were so much different.

We all were especially thankful.

NOVEMBER 28

Today was Black Friday for the world of shoppers. But that scenario was not for us on this day after Thanksgiving. Instead, we enjoyed a day for relaxation and renewal. For my college-age grandchildren it presented a morning to catch up on sleep. For my son Tom it was a day to tinker around at a few odd jobs. For Nancy and me it was time to put our brains to work with Scrabble. In the afternoon and evening it was football and hockey, with a few board games sandwiched in between. It was a great do-nearly-nothing day.

There is value in a day when nothing exceptional happens, no adventures beckon and no duties are heaped on anyone. A day to wake up to no particular schedule and let the day happen as it will. For Tom and his family this was truly a vacation day. Although my own daily schedule is almost always relaxed, for them this day offered a chance to breathe something other than work schedules and studies.

How often we pride ourselves in our busyness. We measure our worth by what we produce. We find it hard to let go, sit down and just let things happen. But that's what happened for us, on this quiet day after Thanksgiving. We let the day pass without all the musts and shoulds that usually niggle at our consciences.

Would that we could, more often, remember that the soul constantly needs refreshing, too.

NOVEMBER 29

The mini-vacation I enjoyed during this Thanksgiving week was a perfect getaway time. Time spent traveling with good friends, then time spent with family. One particular blessing was that I was able to have some short, but refreshing, one-on-one talks with my college-age grandchildren.

Teenagers, when they are still in high school, are usually hard to pin down for a quiet talk as they are either spending time with their studies or with their friends. But for this short holiday weekend my grandchildren, now in college, had left their books at school and seemed to have much more time just to relax and talk. They also seemed to be more attuned to sharing about future plans and dreams with their grandmother. I truly relished my time with them.

Was I as self-directed, when I was in college, as they are? Perhaps. I enjoyed my studies and earned good marks. Was I as career-oriented as my granddaughters seem to be? Definitely not. When I was in school, careers for women were limited in scope and variety. For most of us, marriage and family were still anticipated goals. Today, all of my grandchildren study with a definite career in mind. They might not know exactly what that first full-time job will be, but their awareness of the possibilities and the requirements necessary for success are much on their minds.

I wish them well, and breathe a prayer, as they reach for their dreams.

NOVEMBER 30

I have a quasi-love-affair with maps, stemming back to my days in elementary school when geography was my favorite subject. Although my family never traveled far from home, the world was out there for me to learn about. And I could dream.

Fortunately, I married a man who loved to travel. Over the course of more than 55 years we visited all fifty states, many of them numerous times, and a goodly number of other countries as well. Most of our travels in the States shunned the Interstates, giving us the opportunity to enjoy what author-traveler William Least Heat Moon dubbed the "blue highways." With Dean as driver and me as navigator, we took pleasure in finding the long way home and discovering out-of-the-way places.

Which brings me to ask the question of why we have, so quickly and heavily, fallen in love with the soothing voice of our GPS? Where have our road maps gone? Every state used to print vast quantities of maps and gave them out readily to anyone who asked. Now, maps are much harder to find. Stop at a roadside rest area and a map will probably be posted, but are there any available to take along? Not often. Road atlases have also nearly disappeared from view. What a loss!

If you are hankering to hold a road map once again, or take a peek at an old atlas from 60 years ago, stop in. Together we'll recall how it used to be.

December 1

Volunteers have descended on our community to decorate for Christmas in the lobbies and gathering rooms this afternoon. By evening our building will be all aglow for the holidays. We always look forward to see what magic the volunteers bring to our halls. And, in keeping with the day, many of us are also decorating our apartments.

Since I will be gone during much of December, I have only decorated outside my door for others to enjoy. For me, it's a music theme this year. A copy of Handel's *Messiah* stands in a niche by the door, with a gourd angel singing her heart out. Above hangs a framed batik of poinsettias, a long-ago gift from a friend who brought it to me from India. On the opposite wall hang five miniature needlework Christmas carols—work I had done many, many years ago.

Each of us has Christmas treasures that we bring out every year. They may show their age with chipped paint or an out-of-style look. But it is the memories that make Christmas, or any holiday, special. Memories that tag along with the paint chips and the wobbly Santas.

Each private apartment here will be decorated differently because we all come from families with somewhat-differing traditions. But in this primarily-Christian farming community, most of us living here hold to the same basic beliefs. We celebrate the birth of the Christ-child and pray once again for Peace on Earth. May it be so.

DECEMBER 2

It takes a bit of a push from someone, or something, to get me to sit down at the piano. It didn't used to be that way. I played nearly every day for my husband. Even after Alzheimer's disease put him pretty much in limbo for doing anything else for himself, he still enjoyed listening to me play. But after his death, the purpose and joy of sitting at the piano was no longer there. The piano stood silent. So I surprised myself yesterday afternoon by spending nearly an hour at the piano, enjoying every minute of it. The impetus? A few early Christmas elves.

I had headed toward the office to take care of a little bit of business. On the way, I saw that a group of volunteers had arrived to decorate the public rooms for the holidays. But it was so quiet! Our volunteers were talking together as they decorated, but where was the Christmas music? Well, maybe I needed to provide some. So I hurried back to my apartment, pulled out my most favorite book of holiday arrangements and sat down at the grand piano in the living room.

The next hour just flew by. I had forgotten how much fun it used to be, buying a couple of new Christmas books each season and entertaining myself (and my husband and anyone who wanted to listen) with interesting arrangements of the familiar Christmas hymns and carols.

Sometimes all we need is a wake-up call.

DECEMBER 3

The landscapers are working outside my window again today, this time with front-end loader, roto-tiller, spade and rake. Last week, while I was gone for Thanksgiving, they came to prepare flower beds and plant trees bordering our new Memory Garden. The two men here today are completing that work, focused now around the screen house. Their efficiency seems remarkable to me, as I watch them go about doing what they've obviously done many times before. No wasted effort—just get the job done. But, at the same time, do the job well. I'm constantly drawn to my window to watch the progress.

A certain curiosity is innate in all of us. We like to know what's going on under our noses as well as out in the world. Each time the workers come, some of our residents manage to take a casual sidewalk stroll, eager to see each transformation. Sidewalk superintendents, every one of us. But most, if not all, of us have reached the age where we no longer wish to volunteer our services for the physical labor involved.

So we appreciate the chance to see the landscape change, to anticipate using the screen house and deck next spring and summer. There's always something new to look forward to. That's what keeps life interesting, and makes for interesting lives.

Thank you, landscapers, for giving us reasons to hang around until spring!

DECEMBER 4

There were four men hard at work this morning, finishing the landscaping job begun yesterday. They were busy planting, fertilizing, and mulching the area around the screen house. All of it taking place just beneath my window. It was fascinating to watch as they firmed the ground around each plant, stomping with their heavy boots as if to press the life out of them. But it is really to make sure the roots are settled, the earth tight around them, so the plants can wait out the winter and flourish when the spring rains come.

Next came the edger, cutting a sinuous curved line between the grass and the beds, with a stiff barrier of edging put in place between the two. To top it all off, a thick blanket of black, black mulch was added. One man with a small bucket loader brought the mulch to the site while the other three worked the mulch around each plant, defining its place in the landscape. A job well done.

When the crew was giving the finishing touches to the job, just before noon, I decided that the best way for me to show my appreciation for my morning's entertainment was to go out to them and say, "Thank you." I think I surprised them with my appearance and my verbal thanks. I hope it made them feel good—I know it made me feel good.

I must do that more often.

DECEMBER 5

David Brooks, in his New York Times column today, wrote something that drew my attention. His theme was that of happiness. The title: "Why Elders Smile." So, being one of those elders he was talking about, I took notice. He went on to say that research shows that people who rate themselves highest on the happiness scale are ages 82 to 85. Hey, that's my age—85! And I'm smiling!

Yes, there are many, many things for me to smile about. I realize that a portion of my happiness quotient happens to have come from my mother, a quiet and resourceful optimist who planted that quality in me. A portion comes from my being in relatively good health. A portion comes from my financial circumstances which, though not tremendous, assure me a home for the future. And a portion comes from just plain good luck.

Now that I am heading toward the ages above 85, will it all be downhill? Am I going to turn into an old grouch? Not if I have anything to say about it! Living in a retirement area, I have learned to focus on the good examples of aging well, rather than dwell on those who see the dark side of life. I pick the friends whose outlooks are much like my own. There are plenty of good examples here.

So I look forward to 86, and 90, and beyond—and trust that my happiness doesn't expire before I do.

DECEMBER 6

Once upon a time (not that many years ago) I took a high school typing class on a regulation manual typewriter. It was wonderful, not having to write letters by hand any more! Not many years later I was corresponding with my college-age children via letters typed on a brand new electric typewriter that was light-years ahead! A few years later still, I was an overwhelmed owner of a new IBM computer, studying the manual to find out how to make the thing do what I wanted. Now, sitting at the computer every day comes so naturally, feels so commonplace. And all of that has happened in my lifetime!

Once upon a time (not that many years ago) I stood in my childhood home, turning the crank on our wall-mounted telephone to ring "central" and ask, verbally, to be connected to my friend in the next town. Not many years later, I called my friends with a phone on which I could dial the number myself. A few years later still, an answering machine could answer all my calls. Now my cell phone can do many more things than I ever need it to do. All of this in my lifetime!

To my grandchildren, I'm already far behind the times. I'm only good at certain things on the computer, but that's fine. My cell phone doesn't text or play games, but I really don't care. I have all I need to stay in touch.

It's good enough for me.

DECEMBER 7

The day started out just right. It was a perfect early-winter Sunday morning with bright sunshine after several cloudy days in a row. Morning frost painted the rooftops white. A thin skim of ice stilled the pond. Best of all, there was no wind. The air was still, everything quiet. Everything at peace, outside and in.

After church it remained a beautiful day. Frost gone but ice still evident on the quiet pond. Coat weather, but gloves not absolutely necessary. I drove out of town to meet a friend for lunch. Delightful conversation over good food. Back home for a short nap. Everything made for a perfect day.

And then the skies began to turn. A few clouds began to gather, but they enhanced what was already there. The lowering sun turned those white clouds to orange and pink, with a few random jet trails adding dramatic accents. My window provided the perfect frame for a winter sunset.

Then, when the skies grew dark, my neighbor's Christmas tree took over for a change of scene. And then another neighbor, across the pond, turned on an outside Christmas display. Soon another decorated window lit up. The landscape turned festive, adding another special touch to an already beautiful day.

All of it was provided, free of charge, for me as well as anyone who was open to see the blessings all around us. I am grateful for the gift.

DECEMBER 8

Today we headed for the hills—the hills of Kentucky, that is. My daughter Kay had flown from Maine to Ohio and we were now on our way to visit her daughter and family who had moved to central Kentucky in the fall. Although my husband and I had wandered over many roads throughout the entire United States during our life together, my recent travels have been mainly by plane. So this was a welcome change, this getting back "on the road again."

Abandoning the flat terrain of northwest Ohio, we began to encounter more hills as we neared Cincinnati (once termed the City on Seven Hills). Crossing the Ohio River into Kentucky, our road climbed to a higher plane and it wasn't long before we sighted a familiar landmark—the town of Florence's huge water tower rising above the interstate with the words "Florence Y'All" reminding us that we were now in the South.

Traveling the interstate highways, which are built to move traffic faster and more efficiently, makes one almost unaware of the undulating hills that are on all sides. But, when we finally left the interstate to travel approximately ten miles through the countryside to my granddaughter's home, we were introduced to the true Kentucky landscape. We drove the narrow roads winding this way and that, along streams and rolling hills, which finally brought us to our destination.

Excited shouts of "Grandma!" let us know we had arrived. Music to our ears.

DECEMBER 9

Sometimes the best-made plans go awry. Such was the case today. My granddaughter Sara and her four children, ages 2 to 11, planned to take us to Shaker Village, an hour's drive away. It would be a great educational day for the children (home-schooled), plus entertainment for the grandmothers.

We drove to the site and had already explored two of the buildings. But then, as we were mounting the steps of the next building, Sara tripped on a step and fell—breaking her arm. All of a sudden our plans for the day made an about-face. A quick run to get a wheelchair, a return to the car, and the drive to a hospital emergency room in Lexington suddenly were the orders of the day.

It was not long before we determined that big city hospital emergency rooms are not the place one desires to spend a vacation. But we did get served, the children were more patient than I ever dreamed they could be, and we arrived home that evening with a splinted arm and an appointment to return the next day for more X-rays and consultation.

And so, even though the day's original plans were shattered and, during the rest of our stay in Kentucky we will be doing things we had not expected to do, life continues on. We will do what has to be done and ask for special patience, and love, to carry us through.

That's what families do.

DECEMBER 10

There is one big thing that has been bothering me the last two days. Ever since my granddaughter Sara broke her arm. It niggles away and I try to make excuses for my judgmental attitude, but maybe I just need to get it off my chest.

My problem? People. Unconcerned people.

You see, when Sara fell on the steps at Shaker Village, there was no one else around to see it but us, her family. However, during the next 15 or 20 minutes as we tended to her, decided what to do, located a wheelchair, and walked to the car, there were probably at least twenty visitors that went in and out of the building (walking those same steps) or strolled by on the walkway. I did not see anyone official at the site, only visitors. But not one of those visitors stopped to ask if we needed help. NOT ONE.

That's my problem.

None of those folks were blind. They glanced. They saw that something was amiss. Even though my daughter and I were there helping Sara, don't you think there would have been at least one other person who might have come up to offer assistance? Were they all too afraid to get involved? Did any of them pass by with a guilty conscience? Or did the guilt come later, after they were safely home?

Who is my neighbor? "A man was going down from Jerusalem to Jericho, and he fell . . ."

DECEMBER 11

Today we celebrated Christ-giving Day—a combination of Thanksgiving and Christmas. The day began with home-made chocolate chip muffins for breakfast and ended in the evening with turkey and all the trimmings. Mark took the day off so we could all enjoy this special day together.

After breakfast we got out the ancient kitchen grinder—one that clamps to the side of the kitchen counter and grinds up the ingredients for our family's traditional cranberry salad. There were many hands eager to feed in the cranberries, apples and nuts and take turns at turning the crank. Add the crushed pineapple, sugar and jello, then pop the mixture into the refrigerator to cool and gel.

Next came the huge 20-pound Butterball turkey, thawed and ready to put in the roaster (dressing would be baked separately for this family feast). Later on, we washed and diced a big pot-full of white potatoes to be cooked and mashed to receive the wonderfully-rich turkey gravy. Cans of green beans finished off our menu for the day. We all decided that dessert would be unnecessary, with such a promised feast.

And feast we did, but not so much that we weren't able to sit around the table after dinner and sing Christmas carols. Each of us picked one—what a celebration in song! This special Christ-giving Day, with eight people representing four generations around the table! Certainly a day to put in our individual memory books.

DECEMBER 12

It was with reluctant hearts that Kay and I packed our bags and headed back toward Ohio. We would have preferred to stay and help longer, but duty called to both of us. So, over the weekend, Sara and Mark will need to assess their resources and carry on with life, even with a broken arm to hinder progress.

Life *is* a continual series of decisions, compromises, wrong turns (sometimes), adjustments. "If I had only…" "Maybe it's best if…" "What do we do now?" Mark and Sara will pray, listen to what they feel is God's voice in this situation, and put their trust in that decision. They are strong. They will survive this crisis and be stronger because of it.

As I look back on my own life, I see decidedly important turning points. Had I not changed my mind on where to go to college, I would not have met Dean and would probably have married someone else. Who? Where would I have lived, and would I have had any children? Or maybe I would have never married at all—which would mean that I certainly would not have been traveling to Kentucky with my daughter to see her daughter and family. Had we not gone to Shaker Village a few days ago, Sara's arm might have remained unbroken.

Decisions, decisions. We cannot dwell on what might have been but must live with the decisions we make daily. It's all a part of life.

DECEMBER 13

Oh, how dependent we are! We surround ourselves with things that make life comfortable for us, then we're lost when something goes wrong with one of our toys. In my case, the toy is my internet service. My modem, which I know is outdated, no longer performed its usual service last evening.

When I got home from our Kentucky trip, I tried to pull up the email that would have accumulated over the five days I had been gone. No service. What? No service? What will I do? Whatever email is there lies somewhere in the ether and not on the computer screen. So my computer life is in limbo for the entire weekend.

Somehow life *is* carrying on, even though I am also carrying on (at length) about it. Somehow I feel awfully deprived. Let's face it, I'm spoiled. I have gotten so used to having things at my fingertips when I need them that losing that privilege sets life awry. Although I have always thought of myself as a relatively patient individual, I've seen the other side today—and I don't like what I see.

So, I say to myself, take a deep breath, calm down a bit, and pick up a good book. Get yourself reading and thinking about something other than what you can't do anything about right now. The weekend will pass, you'll have your internet back in a couple of days and all will be well again.

Just cool it!

DECEMBER 14

What makes us individuals? What is it, really, that shapes our basic personalities? What makes me "me" and you "you?" I've been thinking about that recently, after my trip to Kentucky to visit my granddaughter and her family. Those four children are alike in many ways and yet so different. They all came from the same parentage, the same womb, and yet their personalities are definitely distinct.

One is patient, soft-spoken, filled with quiet abilities and strengths. Another is impetuous, noisy, happy-go-lucky. Another is creative, sensitive, still a bit unsure of himself. And the youngest—well, so far he is mainly a charmer. All of them with distinct personalities still in the making but with traits that will stay with them through life.

We compare and assess. "Oh, he looks just like his grandpa!" "Your mother was just like that when she was a little girl!" "He is so studious—just like his dad!" We see the similarities and compare with earlier generations, while picking out our favorite traits to brag on. We try to live a good example, mold where we can, point them in the right direction. And yet, each child has to find his/her own way. Each of them, eventually, has to find a particular niche in the family, in the community, in the world.

We, as parents, start them out on their path through life. We try to give them the best start we know how to provide. Then we pray.

DECEMBER 15

This morning as I walked down the hall, I saw three teen-age boys and a girl sprawled on the floor. Then I saw a few others farther down the hall, also lying on their bellies or on hands and knees. What was going on?

I soon discovered that it was a group of high school students volunteering their services to whatever needed to be done on our premises. Their job? Wipe down all the baseboards in the lengthy hallways here at Maple Crest. They seemed to be having a great time doing a job they probably would have complained mightily about if they had to do it at home, alone.

Isn't it funny that we can enjoy a job, or hate it, depending on where it is and with whom we are working? I remember how I hated the chore of dusting the dining room chairs at home when I was young. It seemed like an endless job, running the dust cloth over every rung, every chair back. Perhaps, if I had had a sister, we might have been able to make a game of it. But, as I had no one else to share my pain, it was a chore.

I'm sure that today's volunteers would not want to come day after day to do the work they did this morning. But a job done once, with friends, can be a satisfying experience. I hope they went home feeling good about themselves and what they accomplished. Together.

DECEMBER 16

This morning our Patio Room was filled with nearly a hundred fourth graders and their teachers, invited here for a special program. They were not here to put on a program for us (even though they did that, too) but to learn. To learn from John, one of our residents, what it is like to live and thrive, even with physical disabilities.

John was born with cerebral palsy and has lived a good and productive life despite his handicaps. His mother was a long-time teacher in the Bluffton school system where these children now learn, so John showed them pictures of the old, three-story brick school that predates the sprawling one-story building now in use. John's eyes shone as he recalled what it was like to go to school in his time—admitting there were some children who teased him and called him names. Those children, now adults, became some of John's closest friends. He showed the children pictures of his wife and children, plus a granddaughter just their age. He opened his life to them and they drank it all in.

After an enlightening question-and-answer session, the children entertained all of us with songs of the season, some of the carols performed on recorders. It was a time for celebration and sharing—young and old singing together "We Wish You A Merry Christmas!"

That's what this season is all about—learning, sharing, and opening our hearts.

DECEMBER 17

The words of Carl Sandburg, "The fog comes on little cat feet," came to mind this morning as I looked out my window. But it wasn't fog. The air was misty with the tiniest particles—not quite rain, not quite sleet, not quite snow. It didn't last long but, while it was here, the world changed appearance and brought that little poem to mind.

There are many times when some small occurrence can change our outlook, our perception of the world. But most times we are not aware, too busy with whatever we are busy with at the moment. Perhaps that's all right. Perhaps, if we concentrated on every little thing that happened around us, we'd be overwhelmed with trivia. And yet, if we don't snatch those quiet and thought-provoking moments, we find ourselves equally overwhelmed.

So, how to catch and hold on to those special moments? "It's easy for you to say," you tell me. "You're retired, nothing to do but write about distracting stuff like this. I don't have time for quiet moments." I agree—but only in part. Yes, I have time. I probably have many more quiet moments than you. But some of the moments that reach out to me are not quiet moments. They happen while life is going on all around me. I have begun to learn to catch those moments when they happen—something that has taken me a lifetime to discover.

You're never too old—or too young—to get started.

DECEMBER 18

The Christmas season is becoming more and more evident each day here in the retirement community. First it was the outdoor decorations, set alight Thanksgiving weekend during the town's annual Blaze of Lights celebration. Then the big tree was placed and decorated in the lobby, with smaller ones in each public space. Young carolers have come some evenings to walk down the halls and sing for those of us who open our doors. Tiny snowmen were placed at every door this year, compliments of a local church. All in celebration of a special season of the year.

Today a special community meal is planned, one that includes the residents who live in the villas and do not eat regularly in our dining room. This meal is a way to celebrate the season with members of our retirement family that we don't see as often. The cooks enjoy planning a special holiday meal which, this year, includes lamb chops with mint jelly, a treat for a number of us.

I am fortunate still to be able to travel, and so, next week, I will fly to be with my children in the West. But many of our residents are not so fortunate. Some may be alone over the holiday. But their feeling of alone-ness is alleviated today in our community celebration. We care about, and for, each other. So, during this special dinner today, there will be plenty of spirited conversation, lots of laughter and a festive feeling all around.

Good neighbors are family, too.

DECEMBER 19

Music has a healing touch. I've known that for a long time, ever since I read a paper on music therapy more than 65 years ago. I was a music major in college and considered going into that brand-new field, but decided against it. Still, music has proved to be my own therapy throughout life, as it was with my husband. When Dean was struggling with Alzheimer's, I played the piano for him almost every day. Even after he could no longer respond verbally, he would nod his head or clap his hands when I played. Music kept both of us going when the going got rough.

So it was interesting to me what happened this afternoon. It was getting toward dusk—a dark and cloudy day—and I was restless, a bit down. Nothing seemed to beckon me to get up off my chair. But then I thought of my Christmas music, sitting idle in the bookcase. "It's Christmas time," I said to myself. "Get that music out and play."

And I did. I found a free piano and, for the next hour, put it to use bringing my spirits up to their normal level. Some of the arrangements were relatively new, some time-worn but still lovely. Playing that music was just what I needed right then. The sun still didn't shine, but I began shining again on the inside.

What is it that brightens your day and fills your soul? Do it.

DECEMBER 20

An incipient trip always entails some early planning and mental packing. But today the actual packing occurs. Tomorrow morning I will be driving to the airport for a flight to Denver and, after a couple of days, to Santa Fe and Carlsbad, New Mexico. It's all part of the "Christmas in Santa Fe" that my three children who live in the West have been planning for some time. They graciously invited me to join them. What mother can pass up that offer?

Old-time family favorites will be part of our shared holiday this year. We will enjoy recipes that have been duplicated many times over the years in either my own family or in families of the in-laws. Our menus will vary, from German to Italian to Mexican to just plain American. With all the good cooks and bakers in this extended family, I'm sure we will not go hungry! And I am looking forward to experiencing the special Christmas traditions that Santa Fe has to offer.

So, for the next two weeks I will be writing from a different place, perhaps with a different angle, but always spilling from what my heart sees. I look forward to sharing a familiar holiday in a new location, to sing the same carols in a different setting, and to drink in the love and joy that will certainly be a part of this, another special Christmas season.

DECEMBER 21

It is a beautiful first-day-of-winter morning, sunny and relatively mild for Ohio. Right after church I leave for the Dayton airport, destination Denver. I park my car at the motel where I plan to stay overnight after my return flight. Everything going according to plan. I check my bag, sail through security, purchase a book I've been wanting to read, settle in at my assigned gate and start reading. All according to plan.

Announcement: 4:00 flight to Denver delayed until 5:00. I keep on reading. Announcement: 5:00 plane arrives but something wrong with it. Another plane to be flown in from Chicago. Estimated boarding time deferred until 9:35, to arrive Denver 10:40 (after midnight, Ohio time).

Groans from everyone, but panic for those expecting to catch a connecting flight at Denver tonight—they race to make flight changes. I call my son Mark in Denver. He has already heard the news, thanks to the ever-vigilant Internet. So I find a restaurant, enjoy a leisurely soup and sandwich supper, then get back to reading my book.

Replacement plane arrives from Chicago shortly after 9:00. We board and are finally airborne. Arrival at Denver according to plan, Mark waiting. Luggage arrives intact, airport traffic clears and we pull up to Mark's welcoming townhouse—but five hours later than expected.

All's well that ends well. And better if you don't sweat the middle.

DECEMBER 22

I am in Denver for only two nights—last night with my son Mark and tonight with my daughter Lee. Tomorrow we will head to Santa Fe for five days over Christmas, meeting daughter Jeanne and family there.

This afternoon, when Mark and Lee met to "pass Mom off to the next kid," Lee took me for a tour of the area of Denver where she and Dick plan to move next year. It is an old, well-established neighborhood undergoing the changes that happen in the city—property being transformed into a new kind of pocket community. They are downsizing, building a duplex for a new stage of life they will enter when their son goes off to college in the fall.

My grandson is definitely much less excited about seeing his parents moving to a new area of Denver. The large suburban home he has known for the past eight years will not be the home he comes back to for vacations. Although the family has moved before, he has few memories of his previous homes, nor of the friends he had as a child. And he cannot foresee that the new friends he makes in college will supersede many of the friendships he now embraces.

Our youngest daughter went through this type of grieving process when we moved from Michigan to Ohio after her sophomore year of high school. But she soon adapted and found her niche. We trust that history will repeat itself once again.

DECEMBER 23

Santa Fe, New Mexico. A picture-book place to spend a few days over the holidays. And here I am, with three of my six children (the ones who live in the West) and their families. We have foregone Christmas presents this year and have pooled our resources to rent a house in Santa Fe for five days. And what a house it has turned out to be! It is spacious, well equipped, all in a beautiful setting. I am grateful to be a part of this special Christmas celebration.

Since we will be preparing all but one of our meals here at the house, each car has arrived packed with fresh-baked Christmas cookies, special utensils and condiments necessary for our favorite holiday recipes, some special Christmas decorations, and plenty of food, food, food. Everything to make this home-away-from-home family time be a memorable time.

We discovered a few special amenities—a large recreation room complete with a pool/ping-pong table, a movie room, TVs in each of the five bedrooms, and a vast kitchen island big enough to accommodate all of our family's chefs and helpers. But the most special amenity is one that our rental fee cannot provide—family itself. That amenity we will provide, in full, along with our own special brand of laughter, music, stories, and plenty of love.

There are some things that money can't buy.

DECEMBER 24

Downtown Santa Fe is the place to be on the night of Christmas Eve, and we were there. Bundled in our warmest winter wear, we were fortunate to find a place to park near downtown, so we headed first to enjoy the lights on the city square. We sang carols with the trumpeter, had our group picture taken by a generous passer-by. We stood at the steps of the massive cathedral, its wall topped by paper-bag luminaries with memorial names written on each bag.

We then followed the crowd to Old Canyon Trail, a street lined with artisan's shops and especially illuminated for Christmas Eve. There were fire pits blazing to offer warmth to chillstiff hands, instrumentalists playing carols, everyone in a merry holiday spirit. At one point, our own family group stopped to stand around one of the fire pits to sing a few carols. All of it making for good memories.

Filled with the Christmas spirit, we came back "home" to a warming feast of black bean chili and special-recipe southwestern cornbread. All of it topped off with Christmas cookies, then singing carols around the table.

This year's Christmas Eve wasn't like ones when I was growing up. Nor was it like the ones our children experienced in their early years. Perhaps none of us together there in Santa Fe this season have experienced Christmas Eve quite like this before. A special Christmas Eve with our special Western families. Together.

DECEMBER 25

It is Christmas Day according to the calendar, but our Santa Fe gathering has postponed our celebration for two days until everyone can be here (one had to be at work today). Since there are no young children with us here, we had no need to concern ourselves with Santa's schedule, and the day was free to hike and explore the area. Tonight we celebrated with fondue—a tradition for some of us—and fare that lends itself to informality and sharing.

An old West Bend electric fondue pot, which my husband and I acquired back in the early '60s, heated the peanut oil for cooking cubes of beef tenderloin. A much newer pot kept the cheese fondue the right temperature for dipping fresh vegetables and bread cubes. It was a jolly evening of story-telling and laughter, with any formality quickly flying out the window. Nine of us shared the two cooking pots until we were stuffed. But there was more to come. For dessert, our newest melting pot kept chocolate hot for dipping squares of pound cake and apple slices.

Informal meals like this one, where everyone cooks his/her own food and dips from the same pot, presents a kind of togetherness that is missing from most "American" meals—at least the type of meal my mother would have served. And yet I know that there are people around the world to whom this way of dining is common.

Maybe we've been missing something all along.

DECEMBER 26

Some of Santa Fe's charm comes from its location, as it is situated on a high, 7,000 ft. plateau with much higher mountains in the distance. Piñon pines abound and the typical flat-roofed adobe houses create a picturesque setting worthy of magazine covers. The homes, as a general rule, do not shout "look at me" but stay nestled among the pines. However, one knows that beyond the plain adobe walls and black wrought iron gates there are many families much like our own—making a life in the place where they are planted.

Because of the overnight snow making the roads treacherous this morning, we postponed a planned trip north to Taos. By afternoon the sun had melted enough of the snow that Lee and I took a leisurely walk in the neighborhood. And that's when I realized how much of a flatlander I am. The altitude, which I had barely noticed before in mile-high Denver, sapped my breath when the sidewalk led us upward. We had to stop occasionally for "Mom to catch her breath." But it was still a lovely walk.

Santa Fe—a beautiful place to visit, especially with family and at Christmas. But I will also be happy to return to the flatlands, home and old friends when the holidays are over. Then, for the remainder of the winter, I can take these special memories out again and again. Whenever I wish.

DECEMBER 27

Our family's Christmas feast day started early with the day's cooks busy in the kitchen, preparing the traditional (for some of us) prime rib dinner. Potato casserole from one family, special green beans from another, cranberry/apple salad from one, layered lettuce salad from another, special home-baked dinner rolls from another—all prepared by many hands in our spacious rental-home kitchen in Santa Fe.

But, before any eating could be done, we eleven adults gathered together in front of the fireplace to sing carols for nearly half an hour, accompanied by guitar and keyboard. Everything from "O Come All Ye Faithful" to "Rudolph the Red-Nosed Reindeer" was on the song list. Then a picture-taking session in front of the fireplace. A perfect prelude to this year's Christmas dinner, served at noon.

And that was only the beginning of the day. In the afternoon we made pisellis, thin Italian pressed cookies baked in special irons, then dusted with powdered sugar. Then, to top off the day, we watched experts at work as my son-in-law John and his daughter Joanna made fat and delicious burritos worthy of any good Mexican restaurant.

A different holiday celebration than this Ohioan usually experiences but no less (maybe even more) special. I will remember, and give thanks, for this varied, talented, loving family where I answer to Mother, Mom, Grandma, G-ma, or anything else they want to call me. I love 'em all.

DECEMBER 28

It's time for our family to part ways and leave Santa Fe for our own homes. That means packing up all the special things we brought for use in the kitchen, dividing the remaining Christmas cookies and other leftovers, and leaving our home-away-from-home as we had found it five days ago. This time I am riding along with my daughter Jeanne and husband John to stay in their home in Carlsbad, New Mexico for a few days.

Driving almost straight south, heading to the other corner of New Mexico, we soon drop down in altitude, leaving the snowy piñon forests for the diminished vegetation of the high desert. Roads are smooth and traffic is sparse, so different from Ohio's heavy truck traffic and bumpy frost heaves.

This is spare, desolate country. One wonders how the pioneers survived their lonely journeys across this vast continent, with mile after mile after mile of nothingness interrupted by an occasional river, then a series of mountains in the distance. I'm sure they were hardier than I, or at least more desperate.

Eventually we reach more people-and-industry-friendly country, then arrive at Carlsbad, our destination. For me, a familiar place since I have visited Jeanne and John several times before. It's always good for a mother's heart to visit her children in their established homes. That's part of what this journey has been about—seeing and experiencing with family and knowing that all is well.

DECEMBER 29

A woodpecker landed on the trunk of a huge pecan tree in my daughter's back yard, just a few feet from their patio. The bird soon moved around the trunk and out of sight and my thoughts turned instead to the deeply-scarred trunk of that massive old tree. "How old?" I ask John. He tells me that his parents planted that tree about 60 years ago when they built this house.

There are many pecan trees in this Carlsbad area, some planted for shade in individual yards but most of them planted in groves as a cash crop. There is a saying here: "If you take care of a pecan grove for seven years, it will take care of you for the rest of your life."

This pecan tree's most recent scars are the result of two almost back-to-back events. Three years ago, a local farmer brought his tractor and equipment to shake the pecans from the massive tree. This rough shaking tore off some of the bark, leaving random rust-colored scars. A year later, a lightning strike burned a deep fissure from the top of the tree down a main branch to the trunk, then to the ground. But the tree still stands, firmly anchored, with scars that will remain and, over time, become part of the landscape.

All of us, too, bear scars. Some are obvious, others hidden. This old tree is still living and producing, despite the scars. I hope I can do as well.

DECEMBER 30

On the road during this holiday season I have been treated to a variety of special Christmas celebrations, starting with home lighting extravaganzas in suburban Denver, rooftop luminaries in Santa Fe and now, lights along the river in Carlsbad. Since their house is located on the Pecos River, Jeanne and John are involved each December with "Christmas on the Pecos," a tradition begun there 20 years ago. Homes on each side of the river are specially decorated from Thanksgiving weekend through New Year's Eve. So each year my Carlsbad family is busy setting up large lighted decorations on the slope leading down to the water. Standing at the window, looking toward the river, offers a delightful panorama of color and light.

Last year, when I was visiting here at Thanksgiving, I was treated to a boat ride to view all the lights along the Pecos. What a delightful trip! There was a definite nip in the air but not as cold as Ohio. The lights reflecting in the water kept everyone in a festive mood, as the boat's captain narrated stories and answered questions.

Not every town has a river to decorate and show off to a crowd. But every vital community needs some creative way to demonstrate its community pride. For Carlsbad, it's "Christmas on the Pecos." For my town of Bluffton it's the "Blaze of Lights" with no river but plenty of lights. People come from all around to help celebrate.

"Bah, humbug" is not spoken here!

DECEMBER 31

It is interesting to note how differently we look at, and celebrate, the arrival of a new year—much of it depending on what age we happen to be.

When we were children, most of us looked eagerly to the time when we were allowed to stay up until midnight on New Year's Eve. This was "grown-up" stuff that we wanted to be allowed to experience. Not many years later, we were old enough to take responsibility for how we celebrated the coming of the new year. Some of us learned lessons the hard way and paid the price for too much celebration. Then, as we were raising children of our own, we felt a new challenge and an added responsibility to a younger generation. And finally we get to the age where we are happy to celebrate the coming of the new year at home and at whatever time pleases us most (generally early in the evening).

This year, in Carlsbad with my daughter and son-in-law, we three watched the ball drop at Times Square via television—at the much more preferred time of 10 p.m. Mountain Time. After a toast and a few hugs we three were off to bed, knowing that the new year would eventually get to New Mexico whether we stayed awake to greet it or not.

Sometimes we get smarter as we get older. We learn, over the years, that "everyone's doing it" doesn't necessarily mean *everyone.*

January 1

Please forgive my complaining on this first day of the new year, but 2015 has begun on a less-than-desired trajectory. It really started yesterday when I was informed that the forecast for freezing rain cancelled my anticipated flight home today—rescheduled for tomorrow. Then, a bit later, I got another call telling me I cannot fly out until Monday. I am at the mercy of the airlines and the nasty weather. So be it.

But then an even bigger challenge occurred this afternoon when we noticed water on the floor by the back door. Quickly gathering up old towels, we started mopping. But the water flow did not stop—it kept coming and we kept on mopping. John finally went outside and turned the water off at the main so no water could feed into the house anywhere. We finally got all the water mopped up, called the plumber (not at home, of course) and left a message.

Now—what to do? No water in the house and night coming on. We finally decided to book two motel rooms, move out and make the best of it. As John said, "When life gives you lemons…let's make a party of it. " So we three gathered up some extra clothes, went out for dinner and got situated in our motel rooms. We will wait until morning, hoping the plumber comes and can find out what's wrong.

One step at a time.

JANUARY 2

After yesterday's plumbing disaster and abandoning the house last night, Jeanne, John and I enjoy a leisurely breakfast at the motel and are faced with the hardest thing of all—sitting and waiting. We Americans are not geared to waiting. We want action. We want answers. We want, we want. Today I am one of those wanters.

So I sit and write, and wait, and wonder what's happening with the plumber and the leak. I wonder when the weather will change and my flight complications will be resolved. I feel like I am in limbo, just breathing and passing time until someone, somewhere, gives the green light and life can resume in a more normal pattern.

When schedules get messed up some people fume, some pace, some watch television, some play with their phones. I sit and write, and think, and pray. Pray for patience. And ponder on all the people in this world who have no means to stay at a motel when their home's water is turned off. Or those who have been evicted from their homes for not paying their rent. Or for those who never knew a home and family. Oh, the list can go on and on.

How fortunate, how truly fortunate I am to lead what is, usually, a boringly normal life. How fortunate I am to have a family that cares for me. How fortunate that I have options, plus a mind to process those options.

Once again, I give thanks.

JANUARY 3

Overnight this area of far southeast New Mexico was blessed with about two inches of snow. In Ohio, that much snow is normally ignored. But here in the desert southwest, snowfall is an occasion. Any amount of moisture is a blessing, despite the slippery roads.

Here, drivers are not accustomed to icy roads. Most vehicles are not equipped for ice and snow. By noon the highways are only wet, but all side roads are a mess of sloppy slush. Children in the neighborhood take advantage of the overnight snowfall, saucers flying down any shaded slopes available. The air is cold enough to hold the snow in its clutches in the shade, but rivulets of water pour from every sunny spot.

Being a Midwesterner, I am not accustomed to what a warm winter sun can do in the desert, turning snow quickly into puddles but leaving all shaded areas nearly untouched for days. I am fascinated by the steady drip, drip, drip off the sunny side of the garage roof, while the north side loses not a drop. Street intersections sport snowmelt in huge puddles, drainage nearly nonexistent since this much water all at once is highly unusual.

And so I have gained a bit more insight into the diversity of climate over this vast country of ours. Now, when my daughter calls to tell me school has been cancelled because of two inches of snow, I won't chuckle. I'll understand.

JANUARY 4

Every part of the country has some distinctive way of commemorating the beginning of a new year with a special kind of food. In my corner of northwest Ohio, in a community largely of central European descent, we always turn to sauerkraut and sausage as good luck charms for a New Year's Day meal. Here in my daughter's home, there is a different tradition. She is married to a man of Italian descent who has lived in the desert southwest nearly all his life, so ham hocks with black-eyed peas and cornbread are the specialty foods for the day.

We are preparing our postponed New Year's Day meal today. The ham hocks, already cooked a few days ago, are waiting in the refrigerator. We get out the recipe for the most wonderfully-delicious Mexican cornbread, open a couple of cans of black-eyed peas to go with the ham, and prepare for our belated good luck feast.

Yes, good luck and good fortune are things we are eager for right now, back from our necessary exile because of a water leak. We look forward to more ho-hum, ordinary days with few or no complications. Tomorrow I will finally head for home in Ohio and Jeanne and John can get back to their own schedules rather than playing host to Mother for more days than they expected.

It has been a wonderful trip, enjoying precious days with family, but it's time to go home.

JANUARY 5

Today was people-watching day. I didn't plan it that way, but that's how it turned out. The morning started very early as we drove to Roswell for me to meet a 6:40 a.m. flight to Dallas-Ft. Worth. Fog, thick as the proverbial pea soup, delayed my flight and hung on the entire morning. My flight finally took off more than five hours late. Needless to say, I missed my connection at Dallas and spent another five hours in that airport, finally arriving in Dayton around midnight.

So, when schedules suddenly went out the window, I decided to make the best of the situation and take note of my surroundings. A vast panorama of people gave me food for speculation.

The small Roswell airport played host to a wide variety of folks, from a tiny Texas grandma with a sparkle in her eyes to a restless young couple playing with their internet toys to a smattering of field workers in work clothes. I don't think there was one shirt-and-tie gentleman in the entire waiting room. Then, in the vast and sprawling Dallas-Ft. Worth airport I saw, again, almost all casual dress. But there were a few style-conscious young women who walked the long concourse in stiletto heels—perhaps about one in every 50 female passers-by. Ouch!

But then, who am I to pass judgment? One who, six decades ago, also felt the need to look stylish rather than be comfortable. They'll learn.

JANUARY 6

Almost home, but not quite. Because of my good sense, plus fading eyesight at night, I had planned from the beginning of my trip to stay overnight at a motel near the Dayton airport before driving home. The comfortable room and a good bed were most welcome. But the view outside my window this morning was not so welcome. Snow, six inches of it, had fallen overnight. My car, parked outside for the last two weeks, was covered with the stuff. My 85-year-old brain, on high alert, told me to be doubly careful before venturing out.

But the sun, as well as good fortune, shone once more. By the time I finished breakfast, traffic on the Interstate was moving normally and I went forward with my plans to drive the hour-and-a-half trip home. But I still needed to get to my buried car. For a little pocket money, the cheery desk clerk was happy to go out, clean all the snow off the car, then get it started and warmed up. She had no problem with any of it. By early afternoon I was home. A welcome sight.

When I think back on this winter trip, fraught with glitches but also filled with a carload of good memories, I know the good memories will win out over all the rest. And, by the time the next trip rolls around (when the weather promises to be better) I'll be ready to go once more. My suitcase stands at the ready.

JANUARY 7

Ah, it's good to be back. Even though a glance out the window brings a picture of snow and bitter cold, it feels good to be home. Such is the way with travelers—we love to go away and experience something different but are happy to see the familiar when we finally return home.

This morning the sky is blue, blue, blue. The sun is trying its best to melt snow from the rooftops, but the air says otherwise. It's an almost-zero Ohio morning, pretty as a picture but extremely cold. I have no need to venture outside so am happy to be inside, looking out. Now that my traveling plans are non-existent for the next few months, I will sit back and enjoy what is outside my window. The familiar landscape is one that I love, whether it's dressed in its green summer garb or in the whiteness of winter.

The older I get, the more comfortable I feel in whatever situation I find myself. It felt good to be with my children in several settings out West. I enjoyed the adjustment to noise and activity, laughing at anything, and eating wonderful Christmas fare. I was even content to sit in the airport and wait for my aborted flights—since I had a good book to enjoy all the while. Now, it feels good to be back home in my silent apartment, enjoying the view.

I wish for you the contentment that I feel.

JANUARY 8

It amazes me that the human body and mind can adapt to changes so readily. At least, my perception of my own body and mind tell me that all the ups and downs of the past two weeks have already become stories for me to remember and relate, not horrors to forget. And my experiences were only inconveniences, not tragedies. Sometimes I wonder what I would have done, had I lived through the time of the Inquisition, the Civil War, the Holocaust. Would I have helped, or hindered?

Although I have never experienced them, I read of the horrors of war and imprisonment, of injustices and enmities, and marvel at the strength that is often in evidence. I have not seen the movie *Unbroken* but have read the book and cannot help but be amazed at how one person can survive, much less end up forgiving. May I never be put to that test!

And so here I am, warm and comfortable in my chosen home. At my age, I do not expect to change the world nor do anything spectacular. In my financial circumstances, I cannot expect to underwrite a cure for Alzheimer's Disease, which took over my husband's life. But I can give what I can to that charity and others. And, here at home, I can volunteer my talents and help make living better for those around me.

It's never too late in the year to make resolutions.

JANUARY 9

The clouds tonight are winter-cold. Undefined, muted gray, mimicking smoke but warning of snow on the way. The sun, already below the horizon but still tinting the western sky, leaves no warmth in its wake. Another below-zero night expected.

Such is the view from my window. And yet, inside, I am warm and secure in that warmth. I heat a bowl of corn chowder, the remainder from last night's supper, and look forward to an evening of quiet music from my Bose and a good book in my hand. What a way to spend a winter evening!

Each of us has our own favorite way of relaxing. And that way usually changes over time. At one time, a long time ago, my idea of a great evening was to get together with some of my friends and just gab, have a talk-fest. Later, it was getting a baby-sitter and going out for an evening with my husband—anywhere—just to get out of the house. Still later, after the nest was empty, it was still fun to get out to a movie or a concert. But eventually we got to the place where it was just more relaxing to stay at home, turn on the music and read. And now, even though I am alone, a quiet evening with a good book and beautiful music is my favorite kind of evening.

Hats off to cold winter nights!

JANUARY 10

Tonight the western sky is on fire. Directly overhead there is nothing but cloudless blue, but toward the setting sun there are clouds on the horizon that are bursting with color. Vivid orange just a minute ago, now a glowing red which is slowly darkening to purple as I watch. I drink it in and try to remember.

Were I an artist, I would paint this word picture with much more precision. I would know the proper names of each hue and be able to describe the intensity of the colors. I would know how to put it all down on canvas for you to see.

And yet, an artist might have as much frustration as I, since there are some pictures in nature that defy imitation. How do you really describe, in word or in paint, the coldness of a winter landscape? How best to depict a misty morning in April or a heat wave in mid-July? Sometimes one just has to be there to appreciate (or not appreciate) the experience.

So tomorrow evening, just about sunset, look toward the west and perhaps there will be a similar, or even more spectacular, sky out there to be savored. It doesn't happen every night but, when it does, give thanks. A beautiful sunset is one of nature's free gifts.

JANUARY 11

My bookcase has accumulated more than enough books. I must go through them and let someone else enjoy the reading. I've done this before, this weeding out, and am always pleased when I see a neater bookcase. But there is another side of me that says "I'll just read this one more time." Then I turn to another task and forget about my intentions.

There are some books that have a special meaning only to me. Books that I used when working on family genealogies. Books that were gifts and I don't want to insult the giver. The French language books I studied 30 years ago and can't quite relinquish (I might study them again???) Books that hold a special memory, harkening back to childhood, such as *A Child's Garden of Verses* and *Why the Chimes Rang*. I'm saving those for—what? For my children to throw out when I'm gone? I don't know, but I can't give them up.

I very seldom purchase a book any more, even though Amazon is tempting. Our public library has more than enough new and old ones for me to enjoy—free. I find gems there every time I stop in. And if I'm looking for a particular book, interlibrary loan is a great resource too.

So here I am once again, pondering over which of my "friends" to let go. Maybe I'll just read this one more time . . .

JANUARY 12

Everything is white, white, white this morning with no defining line separating the snow-covered rooftops from the sky above. The overnight-into-afternoon snowfall has created a studies-free day for school children, a headache for working parents and, for me and my colleagues here at the retirement community, a day of remembering how it used to be.

Many of my female neighbors today were at-home mothers back then, as was I. It was not until my children were all in school that I took a job away from home. That was the way it was in the '50s, before a combination of necessity and wants turned most households into two-parent breadwinners. I'm happy I had the opportunity to be at home to see the children off to school and, on occasion, fill the house with more than enough clutter and noise on snowy days.

Back in those days of being a stay-at-home mom, the snowy days passed in this fashion. First, listen to the radio to see if school was cancelled for the day. Then check to see what was in the pantry to provide lunch, dinner and snacks for the home-from-school crowd and their friends. Then lay some ground rules for the day's schedule, including light chores for the kids before they headed out to play in the snow. And, finally, call a neighbor and see if she'd like to come over for coffee and a chat while the children are outside.

It was hectic then, but the good memories linger.

JANUARY 13

I'm not an avid sports fan, nor do I have the capabilities of watching ESPN on my small apartment TV, but last night I sat with friends and watched the first national collegiate football championship game until after midnight—to the very end. The Ohio State Buckeyes were playing. I live in Ohio. And so I should keep up with what's in my own back yard. Right?

There were just a few of us sitting on the couches in the family room, watching on the big-screen TV there. I'm sure there were plenty of others wide awake in their apartments, wearing their favorite red OSU sweat shirts while watching their beloved Buckeyes. All of us gathered around our television sets were hoping to witness a victory for this team that was not expected to win. After all, a Heisman trophy-winning quarterback pitted against an earlier-in-the-year third-stringer?

Well, David met Goliath and pulled out a decisive victory. Everyone will have plenty to talk about in the dining room this noon. Even those of us who don't usually follow football closely can enter into the conversation today. We'll savor our victory and then put it in our memory banks, ready to take it out a few years later to remind our great-grandkids that "we were there" to witness that very first collegiate football championship game.

Bragging rights will be allowed today.

JANUARY 14

The starlings are having a heyday this morning, flitting from branch to branch on a nearby ornamental pear tree, then flying off and circling back. Are they reveling in the bright morning sunshine? Perhaps. Do they know something I don't know? Probably. Will they stay? Not for long.

That's the way with birds. They go about freely, taking off at will, disappearing on the horizon. In the time it took for me to sit at the computer and write this first paragraph, they were gone. Every last one, gone to who-knows-where. The pear tree, and every other tree within my sight, is devoid of birds. They probably won't be back any time soon.

Perhaps that is one reason I have always been fascinated with birds. They appear, then disappear. They are hard to study because they are so elusive. Just when I have my binoculars zeroed in on one, it flies off. I must let it go and hope for another chance, soon, to see it again. To learn its behavior, to learn to recognize it without referring to the bird book. That education takes time and persistence.

I have forgotten a lot of what I learned 40 years ago when I really worked at spotting and identifying birds. But I have not forgotten the thrill of learning to recognize the vast number of migrating warblers when they came through in the spring. Or learning to identify the various water birds along the Gulf. It was time well spent.

JANUARY 15

"This morning, as I came awake..." are the opening lines to a song I learned back in college. They rushed to mind today as I looked out my window. A combination of a thin coat of ice topped by feathery hoarfrost was on every limb, every branch, every twig of every tree within sight. Coupled with yesterday's new snow, it created a vision of white. I reveled in the sight as I enjoyed my breakfast tea and toast at the table by the window. The air was frigid enough to preserve that visual treat until well after lunch, so I had ample time to enjoy the view and formulate my thoughts. What a morning to write about!

But words to describe the scene and the feelings that came with it do not come easily. How to bring that vision, those sensations, to someone who has never experienced hoarfrost? A winter scene like this is not an everyday occurrence even to those of us who live in snow country. How do I describe that to someone not here to see and experience?

I went to the office and asked the secretary to bring her camera and take pictures. You know the saying, "a picture is worth . . ." The camera did its work and the ensuing photos are beautiful. But the breathtaking awe that I felt when I first looked out my window is something no photograph can duplicate.

Sometimes, you just need to be there.

JANUARY 16

Today I spent a good deal of time in our small library, weeding out some of the older dog-eared books to find space for new books that have been donated. When new books come in, there are always hard decisions to be made. What do we keep and what do we send to the used bookstore?

Each of us living here has a different idea of what a "good" book is. What I will snatch up in a minute someone else will have no interest in. Some new biographies came in recently—we'll have to see whether they are picked up. The Amish books are quite popular now so they take up a whole shelf where, a couple of years ago, we might have had only one or two. Some readers want only paperbacks—the hardbacks are too heavy to hold. Then there are those who can read only the large print books, so those shelves are well used.

But isn't it great that we have a library! On those shelves we can find reading material that can take us, for a time, out of this world into a different one. A story that can change our mood. An article that can challenge us with a new idea. A book to help us remember the "good old days" and another book to take our thoughts to another country.

Thank you, writers, who enrich our lives with books!

JANUARY 17

Visual language. This is a new term that has just entered my vocabulary, one I read about in a museum magazine recently. But I now realize that visual language has been a part of my unconscious vocabulary for some time. For 14 years I was a docent at the Toledo Museum of Art. It was there that I learned how to be a visual language teacher every time I gave a museum tour. I learned there, at the museum, to see more fully what was there in front of my eyes and then to interpret those discoveries to others. It was a learning experience that has been invaluable ever since. I just never recognized how valuable.

For the past several months, as I write a new reflection each day, I have been honing not only my writing skills but my visual language skills as well. I have learned to look at my environment in a new way, to ponder it all, then take that discovery to a new level as I transfer that experience into words on paper. Words that I hope will convey my feelings and thoughts to you, the reader. Language made visible.

How often we see and do not recognize. How often we experience but do not learn. How often we hear but have not listened. How often we fail to take time to be fully attentive.

I give thanks for eyes to see, a mind to grasp, and words to tell.

JANUARY 18

After a week of snow and bitter cold, last night's temperatures rose above the freezing mark. With that rise came a winter thaw that presented an entirely new face to the world when I woke this morning. Rooftops bare, sidewalks clear, ice on the pond softening, grass once more in evidence. Was this the usual January thaw or just an illusion for a day or two? No matter what we call it, this was a welcome respite from the below-zero temps and icy conditions of the past week.

But the sun was completely absent today, so everything showed itself as dark and decidedly winter-dreary. During the week there had been some cloudy days but, since snow covered nearly everything, the world outside my window was very white. Today it was all decidedly gray. A dismal gray.

So, what does one do on a dismal, gray day? For me, it started with church (it's Sunday), then lunch and conversation with a good friend. Later, I had a pleasant visit with my sister-in-law, plus another friend in the nursing home. Then a stimulating late afternoon meeting at the church. Later I enjoyed phone conversations with two of my daughters before curling up on the couch with a good book.

The dreary weather outside was forgotten during this very good day. Good people, good conversation and good books will do that every time.

JANUARY 19

On this Martin Luther King Day, I've been pondering a bit about my life and how I seem to have lived on the edges of history-making times. I look back at the many things that were going on around me and, although I was aware, I was definitely not in the middle of things.

Born at the beginning of the Great Depression, I was not affected by it because we lived on a farm. We had food and shelter and love—what need had I for anything else at that time? I was not yet in my teens when the U.S. entered World War II, so was not personally consumed by what was happening. I saw men from the community go to serve, but that was in the grown-up world.

By the time I entered college, it was the time of the GI Bill. I rubbed shoulders with veterans of color returning to school, not going to war. When my husband and I were married, the armed services were no longer drafting married men. During the time of the Freedom Rides and Martin Luther King's messages, I was knee deep in diapers and getting children off to school. By the time my children were off to college, other things were on my agenda, as well as on theirs.

Had I been born ten years later, would I have been a protester? Would I have marched? What are my regrets, if any? Hmm.

JANUARY 20

Living alone, I have options on how to spend my evenings. I could watch television, but I don't. I could play cards with my neighbors, but I don't. Most evenings you will find me listening to classical music and reading a good book. What do I refer to as a good book? That varies, but I draw the line at pulp fiction, most science fiction, blatant romances, and prolific writers whose names are too familiar. In other words, there's a lot of stuff I don't read, but also plenty that I will read. Sometimes I am pleasantly surprised, sometimes not.

If I find one with a title that intrigues, fiction or nonfiction, I'll read the notes on the flyleaf to get an inkling of what's inside. If I find nothing there I want, I just roam the shelves and, sometimes, rediscover an old friend.

I'm in two book clubs—one a more formal and intense Great Books discussion group and the other offering a casual oleo of books chosen periodically by the group. Both groups fill a need for me to read and discuss on different levels. And then, there are all the other books I read in between. Sometimes I think I will read myself to blindness. If that happens, I'll subscribe to Talking Books and keep reading.

JANUARY 21

Twenty-five years ago, after retirement, my husband and I traveled all over the United States as volunteer Alumni Ambassadors to meet with former students of our alma mater, Bluffton College (now Bluffton University). It was work, but rewarding work, and through it we touched base personally with more than a thousand alumni over a five year span. Now, a quarter of a century later, reminders of those trips and those alumni visits still come regularly.

Through an email today I learned that one alumnus we visited is retiring after 25 years as administrator at a Michigan college. The article, which included his picture, took me back to the day many years ago when we sat together in his office talking about the challenges he was facing in this new position. Although we had never met him before, we were impressed at the time with his demeanor and his ability to express the dreams he had for this new challenge. Today's news, that he held that position for 25 years, speaks well for the job he did there.

I intend to send my congratulations to him and tell him that I still remember sitting in his office many years ago. He may not remember that day as well as I, but I'm sure he will appreciate knowing that someone met him once, for only a short time, but still remembers.

JANUARY 22

It was another gray day today—much like yesterday and the day before and the day before that. Here in Ohio, particularly during January and February, there are many gray days. It often makes me wonder "why am I here?" And yet I stay. This is my home, a good place to be.

This town of Bluffton is where my husband grew up, where I came to college, where we had our children, where we made good friends and stored up memories. Although jobs moved us to other locations and extensive travel after retirement gave us the whole continent to consider, Bluffton continued to beckon. We settled back in, almost as if we had never left. And I'm still here, in the gray Ohio winter, looking toward the green Ohio spring, the warm Ohio summer, and the colorful Ohio fall.

I'm quite sure that none of my children intend to move back to their home state. They learned early on that there are many desirable places to live and work. They have found their niches elsewhere, and that's all right with me. They come to visit, I go to visit them. Between times, I have a great community in which to live and good friends to keep me company.

Tomorrow the sun might be shining but, if not, it will still be a good day. I have good things to look forward to and much to be thankful for. We should all be so fortunate.

JANUARY 23

It is easy to put off doing undesirable tasks, but sometimes one has to knuckle down and get started. This afternoon I pulled out an accounting pad and the checkbook to begin working on taxes. I am fortunate. My oldest son is a CPA and does all the real work on my tax return. But the initial job, putting the year's figures together, is still mine to do.

I married a man with a business degree. He truly enjoyed taking care of our finances for many, many years. Although we always worked at tax things together (he wanted me to understand what was going on) the nitty-gritty at tax season was still his job. When Alzheimer's played havoc with his mental abilities, our son took over filling out the tax forms. But I continue to do the preliminary work, and that is what has been occupying my mind all afternoon.

Now I'm ready to sit down and do something else, like write my daily reflection—this time complaining about how much I really don't enjoy what I've been doing all afternoon. On the other hand, I appreciate the fact that, at age 85, I am still able to do the initial accounting work, then send all those figures to my son who will take care of the rest. Some year I will need to turn everything over to him, but for now I'll just give thanks for small favors.

JANUARY 24

I just received an invitation that is hard to refuse—to visit my daughter in Denver the first part of March. A special concert has presented the impetus, but it would be special enough just to spend some time with Lee and her family, plus my son Mark who lives there. So here I sit, looking out the window at an overcast sky, much like the ones I have complained about recently, and think about the plentiful blue skies over Denver. Hmmm. Tempting.

After the problems I experienced while flying during the Christmas holidays, it does give me pause. "Wait a minute—do you really want to brave the airline traffic in early March? The weather could still cause problems." And yet, the other side of me says, "Go while you can. If you don't, you'll regret it." Which side should I heed? I'll have to sleep on it.

In a sense, all of life is a quandary. Should I do this . . . or shouldn't I? Is this a wise move? Sometimes we don't know until we try. Sometimes we fail, sometimes we prosper. Some of us make decisions quickly and easily, others of us worry over every little decision, as well as big ones. Some of us are risk-takers, some of us are avoiders. Even at my age, I am still more of a risk-taker (unless it's on icy sidewalks).

I think I know what my answer will be.

JANUARY 25

The snow is ever-so-fine today. It began this noon as nearly infinitesimal airborne beings. One had to strain to see that what was accumulating on the ground was really coming from the sky. Now, a few hours later, we can see that the weather forecast for a clipper coming through is true. The wind buffets every flake around in little whirlwinds, promising that the country roads will be treacherous tonight.

Watching this all from the warmth of my apartment, I give thanks for the hardy folk who face these storms stoically as they drive their snowplows down the roads, keeping them open for any drivers daring, or foolish, enough to get out. Thanks to emergency workers everywhere who need to get in to work their shift, no matter what the weather. And to the loyal staff here at Maple Crest, my home, who keep all of us warm and well-cared for.

It is so easy to take for granted all the workers that keep the extra amenities open for those of us who need them, plus those of us who don't really need them but think we do. Those of us who phone in for pizza to be delivered in the midst of a snowstorm, and then don't even leave a tip. For those of us who will complain when tomorrow morning's newspaper doesn't arrive on our doorstep at the usual time.

We have much to be thankful for—each and every day. May we not forget.

JANUARY 26

The pond outside my window has changed faces numerous times over the last two days. A well-functioning aerator keeps a spot of open water moving constantly, but snow-blanketed ice covers the remainder of the pond.

Yesterday, when blustery winds kept the snowflakes dancing furiously, there was a larger-than-usual circle of open water moving in waves. Even with below-freezing temperatures, the ice had retreated to let the water do its dance. In the center there was a dark blue circle of moving water. This was surrounded by lighter blue snow-dusted ice, in turn surrounded by more deeply snow-covered ice, then pure white snow at the shore.

This morning, after lessening wind and temperatures in single digits, the circle of open water had shrunk to giant teacup size. The gradations of color in the ice appeared again, ranging from dark blue to lighter shades. But then there was an added circle of soft aqua before the water reached the white snow-covered shore.

Now it is noon. The sun has come out and it shines brightly on all the surfaces of the pond. The sun's warmth has widened the circle of open water but the edges have retained their lovely colors. Had I been born with artistic talent, I would have already gotten out my colored chalk or paints. However, my artistically-challenged hands search for words through the keyboard. They are woefully inadequate, but all I have to offer.

Perhaps that is enough.

JANUARY 27

In this day of instant communication through computer, email and cell phone, it is a rare day when I find a personal letter in my mail box. Wonder of wonders, today I received TWO personal letters by "snail mail" and it has set my heart to singing, literally. One letter from a soprano, one from an alto. Both good friends from two different eras of my life. And both have the same given name although they spell it differently. Ann and Anne.

I met Ann when we lived in Michigan. She and her husband, both musicians, became very close friends with my husband and me. That friendship has lasted nearly 50 years, even though now we live miles and miles apart. Although we communicate only sporadically, each time is as if we had never stopped the conversation. May it continue to be so.

Anne lives here in the retirement community, so we have the opportunity to see each other regularly. She moved to Ohio from out of state some seven or eight years ago and we "hit it off" from the first meeting. Our conversations lift my spirits. Right now Anne is visiting her daughter in Arizona so she sent me a letter just to keep in touch and let me know everything is going fine with her. I look forward to her return when the warmer weather beckons.

Two special letters. Two special friends. The sun is shining. All's well.

JANUARY 28

The pond was a-glitter with diamonds this morning, the result of a combination of a coating of snow, near-zero temperatures, and a bright morning sun. I drank in the view during breakfast, marveling again at what nature offers each day to any of us who have the time and inclination to sit long enough to notice.

All of a sudden there were seven puffed-up robins at the top of the locust tree outside. Red breasts all facing the sun, they remained nearly motionless for at least five minutes—until long after I had finished eating. Then four of them took off for who-knows-where, joined by two others a short time later. One stayed.

Another fifteen minutes later, the lone robin was still there, although he had shifted positions. Not much later he was joined by two other robins—friends from the earlier bunch, perhaps? After a few minutes, all three vacated my locust tree and disappeared into the blue.

Chance encounters, these little episodes. Not worthy of news. Yet, for me, memories linger and create something special enough to think about and write about. This morning's pondering takes me back to grade school days. My mother saved a picture I had drawn of robin red-breast sitting on a crooked branch. At that time, I thought all robins went south in the winter. Now I know that some of them stay to give us food for thought on cold, snowy days.

JANUARY 29

The skies were gray when I opened my eyes this morning, which gave me little motivation to get out of bed. So I lay there, half awake and half drifting. Just letting thoughts roll lazily around in my head. For some reason, through this morning haze, a phrase of the hymn "Great Is Thy Faithfulness" came to mind:

"Morning by morning new mercies I see."

That phrase suddenly got my brain in gear and, shortly after, my body in motion. "Yes," I told myself, "it happens like that!" Morning by morning, or sometimes evening by evening, new insights come to mind that feed ideas for these daily reflections. It has become so much easier, after these months of writing about what I see and experience, to recognize a blessing when it comes my way. My eyes and ears—really, all of me—have become more attuned to the little things happening around me.

I've been at this daily exercise for nine months now—the time it takes for a child to form in the womb. But this "baby" has another three months to go to reach my goal of one full year. Last May I had no idea whether I could sustain a project of this scope. Now I know it is possible. And then comes the question: "What next?" Will I stop at a year, or will I continue? Perhaps this is only the beginning.

"New mercies I see" every day, and give thanks.

JANUARY 30

We've all seen pictures of planet earth as viewed from outer space. That's what the pond reminds me of this morning as I look down from my window. It's as if I'm an astronaut viewing our planet from a porthole. The circle of open water created by the aerator is the center—Earth—and the surrounding multi-hued ice is the atmosphere The sun shines brightly on the ice-and-snow-covered surface and the blue sky above is reflected in multiple colors, depending on the thickness of ice and the pockets of snow lying on top. Beautiful!

Scientists tell us that traits of our physical world can be found copied in various living forms. Certain parts of the human body resemble certain parts of plants. When we build, we copy forms that are already familiar to us in animate objects. We take the familiar and incorporate it into something we call "new," but that new creation holds echoes of what came before. When I saw the pond this morning, it brought to mind a larger part of our universe.

In family history, we remark on resemblances to our ancestors. I think of our children, all unique individuals but holding some characteristics of their parents and grandparents. Pop's gray hair, Aunt Cassie's blue eyes, Grandma's hands. We are part of what was, and what will be.

May my life be worthy of reflection.

JANUARY 31

Music from around the world has been circling my mind ever since Thursday night's exciting Bluffton University artist series concert presented by Cantus, a professional men's vocal ensemble. So many songs, so many languages, so many beautiful sounds came from those nine voices. I marvel at their talent, their stamina, their enthusiasm, their professionalism. The concert was a gift.

Part of that gift was the gift of universality. The entire program was made up of traditional songs—but songs gleaned from nearly two dozen different nations and traditions. From the Far East, the Middle East, Europe, Africa, and even a few songs from the Americas. The men sang those songs in at least a dozen languages and presented sounds and rhythms different from what we Americans are used to hearing. The concert was an education.

The audience, made up of our regular middle-to-upper-age season ticket holders plus university students, loved it when we got to chime in with the familiar round "Row, Row, Row Your Boat" as well as watching the singers' antics in a Balinese monkey chant. There was something for everyone. The concert was eye-opening and fun.

Some folks get their enjoyment through sports. Some are tuned in to gardening. Some travel. For me, music has always been a very special part of life. Music provided an education and a lifetime gift. I am truly thankful.

February 1

It's Super Bowl Sunday, which doesn't hold any particular importance to me since I'm not an avid football fan. However, every year there is a party held here at the retirement community for any of our residents who wish to come and watch the game together. I attend for the snacks and the camaraderie more than for watching the game itself. And part of the fun of the whole evening includes watching the watchers.

The men are usually the first ones there—wanting to get the prime seats. But we also have some avid female fans who love the front row. The rest of us filter in and find places closer to the sidelines where we can kibitz without spoiling the fun for the real fans. There is usually a puzzle page handed out, including fill-in-the-blank questions about the better-known players (at which I fail miserably). There are prizes as well—the top prize being an authentic Super Bowl football. Since all of the Super Bowl footballs are produced in Ada, Ohio, just a few miles away, we have easy access.

In a few minutes I will head down to the Patio Room to join the crowd. I'll have a good time, but I don't expect to come back with any prizes. In fact, I'd probably be apologetic and not take a prize if I did win one by accident.

Unless it's the football. I'm sure one of my grandchildren would be happy to take that off my hands.

FEBRUARY 2

Bright sunshine and clear blue skies can put a different face on a lot of things, including the world outside my window. Yesterday's skies were filled with heavy clouds. The day-long snowfall blanketed roofs, grass, everything. Traffic going past was minimal. Two young boys brought their saucers, leaving footprints and slide marks along the pond's banks.

This morning the footprints have completely disappeared. Last night's wind has covered them all and, in their place, left drifts and wind-waves accented by the low morning sun's deep shadows. Tiny icicles hang from the branches of my locust tree, evidence that last night's forecast for a mix of snow and rain came to pass. School is cancelled for the day, so I expect to see the boys return to play in the snow sometime later today. I will look for them.

And so I greet another winter morning with gratitude. To me, it's a beautiful day and well worth the wait through yesterday's gray. Winter in the Midwest is fickle. One day clouds, another day clear. One day warm sun, another day bitter wind. Certainly not everyone's taste in weather. And yet, I stay. There is still something about the change of seasons that, evidently, fits my life. I enjoy visiting other places but, all in all, I'd rather just visit a while and then come home again.

I'm thankful that, at 85, I still have the opportunity.

FEBRUARY 3

My monthly jig-saw puzzle has arrived and I'm eager to get started on it. In case I hadn't mentioned it before, for the past five years my children have gifted me a 1,000 piece puzzle every month. It is so much fun to see what challenge they have selected for me. And yes, it is always a challenge.

The February puzzle is a "Madalene's Hearts" puzzle (just in time for Valentine's Day). I know it will be difficult to put together because they have sent two other puzzles from this series before. The beautiful heart pictures are crafted from flowers, seeds, other things of nature plus everyday objects. Delightful to look at, but putting the puzzle together will take some time. However it should keep me from complaining about the February snow and cold outside my window.

Puzzles, both jigsaw and crossword, are an important part of each day for me. They give me a challenge and keep me thinking. I know there are many people who enjoy neither of these pastimes—including my husband. He was not a puzzle guy. He was happy working with numbers and figures (plus sports on the side), things I had little interest in.

But isn't it great that we aren't all the same—that we have different interests and abilities? If we all loved jigsaw puzzles, when would we ever get anything else done?

FEBRUARY 4

Books, books, books! A kind benefactor just brought in a bag full of books to add to our community library. Since I'm the one who tries to keep the library stocked and in order, I got the first peek at them and am I excited!

So many times when books are donated to our library they are yellowed and dog-eared, having been on someone's shelves for years. These books are not. Most of them are very obviously new, and I have a feeling that some of them have never been read at all. Books that caught the eye at a bookstore but were set aside to read "another day" that never came.

None of these books have best-seller titles, and all but three of them are by authors with less-than-famous names. Neither do any of them resemble the pulp fiction that rolls off the presses at a dime a dozen (well, probably a bit more than that in today's market). I'm eager to get started reading them, and then to recommend some of these books to my friends who enjoy something new and different.

This gift of books has come at an ideal time, a cold and snowy week in February. There is very little on my calendar and plenty of time to read, read, read. Some of the things I had thought about doing will have to wait until a later date. Right now, I have a date with Olive Kitteridge (she's quite a character, I'm told).

FEBRUARY 5

This afternoon, as I was looking for something in the bookcase, I picked up the little red-leather-covered five-year diary that I got for Christmas when I was nine years old. It has been there for a long time, waiting for me to pick it up again, so I sat down and began leafing through the pages. I have done this before, this reminiscing, but not in the last several years. Today the diary entries spoke to me in a different way, perhaps because writing these daily reflections has taught me to look at fleeting things with a different eye and heart.

A small five-year diary doesn't allow a lot of room to chronicle a day's activities, but neither does a nine-year-old have a lot to write about. I didn't learn much about myself and my childhood thoughts, if I had any, but only a little about school or who came to visit. However the entries in the diary did tell a bit about the days before my father died of leukemia in March of 1939, and mentioned the many people who came to stay with my mother in what must have been trying days before and after his death.

Is it typical of a nine-year-old to write only facts and not feelings? I suppose. Particularly for an unsophisticated farm girl living three-quarters of a century ago. Except for photographs, that little red diary is the only material evidence I have of that nine-year-old girl.

That little bit must suffice.

FEBRUARY 6

It's a bitter-sweet day today, February 6, my husband's birthday. If he were alive, he would be 87 years old. It has been a little more than five years since his death which, at times, seems like a very short time. At other times it feels like forever.

That is the way with time, and memories, and all things held dear. We hold on, yet we forget. We commemorate, we reminisce, yet we keep looking ahead. Life goes on with or without our acknowledgement. Life is the way it is, the way it has to be. We cannot live completely in the past nor in the future. Now is where we are.

And so, what will I do today, on this anniversary? I will shower and dress, then have breakfast at my table overlooking the pond. I will move to the computer to check the morning news before opening Word to a new, blank page. And then I will begin to write "It's a bitter-sweet day today," a phrase that came to mind while I was still in bed. While I was still feeling sorry for myself.

It's not ideal, this being alone. But my life is so much better than what many in this world can only dream of. I have a home, a loving family, my health, my mind, a purpose in life. So it's time to get up and get going, out into the life that's waiting just outside the door.

Now is where I must be.

FEBRUARY 7

I'm thinking today of "community"—that nebulous term for a collection of people. But the word encompasses much more than numbers. Roget's thesaurus is filled with words partially defining the term. Today I'm thinking of community in terms of the places in which I have lived and how those places have, in one way or another, formed how I think and act.

I grew up on a farm with a father, mother, and one brother. We four constituted a very small community, a safe and secure place for a small child. School did not expand my community a great deal, since even my high school was in a small town. College was, again, a very small community of less than 300 students at the time. I was, I'll admit, pretty sheltered. But my horizons continued to expand with each community in which my husband and I lived during our 59 years together. Each move to a new community was an important step in learning about and adapting to a new world.

Today I live in a retirement complex of one hundred residents at the edge of a small town. Many residents have lived in this area all their lives. Others, like myself, have traveled extensively but have chosen this town in which to retire. We blend into a new community. Over a noon meal we share stories, experiences, a bit of ourselves.

I'm heading to Koffee Klatch right now. Would you like to join us?

FEBRUARY 8

Outside my window lies a different world this morning. Yesterday's warmer temperatures, plus more thawing overnight, has melted away the white rooftops, while clouds turn the leftover snow a dull gray-white. But the pond, that body of water that I love to watch in all seasons, has come to life in an entirely new way.

The snow cover that has insulated the ice is disappearing and, in its place, beautiful colors are reflected. There is still a border of pure white along the edges of the pond, plus streaks of white where the snow still lies thick on the ice, but much of the surface has turned to intense shades of turquoise. Water is displacing the snow and, in the process, creating a new landscape. I can hardly believe the amount of change that has happened overnight, while I was sleeping.

Ah, that culprit—sleep. No, not our regular nighttime sleep, but the sleep of not noticing. Had I been in a rush and too busy to sit down at the window for breakfast, I would not have noticed. I would have missed a good thing. I have probably missed many, many good things because of inattention.

But now, at this moment, I am in awe. In awe of the many miracles of nature that happen right under my nose. And I thank my Creator for giving me eyes to see and enough sense to sit and take notice once in a while.

FEBRUARY 9

This afternoon I got a phone call from my daughter in Colorado. A casual call to check on Mom and catch up on the latest news. Later, I made a phone call to my daughter who lives in New Mexico and we chatted for a good many minutes, catching up on the latest with her. No big deal, those calls. Just keeping in touch. So easy.

My grandchildren and great-grandchildren, growing up in this digital age, have no concept of "how it used to be." How we seldom made phone calls to someone outside of our area because of the cost for each call. And then we called only after the night rates went into effect. Anyone getting a long-distance phone call during the day was braced to receive tragic news. Such was life before cell phones.

I'm still pretty much back in the Dark Ages. My ancient, but still very reliable, cell phone does not accommodate texting or any of the other necessities. It is one of those basic "grandma" phones that is, for my purposes, just fine. If it rings, I answer. If not, I don't check it every 15 minutes. I do not carry it with me, except when I venture out of town which is seldom. If someone needs to get in touch with me, let them leave a call-back message.

I may be out of touch with the times, but I'm in touch with who I am. That's good enough for now.

FEBRUARY 10

I felt a little like a school kid this afternoon—one who has been waiting for recess and the class has finally been excused. This breaking-out-of-jail feeling marks the end of my week-long hibernation, self-imposed because of all the snow and ice that has made going out a hazardous adventure. For the past week I made no attempt to get out in the kind of weather that makes for good sledding but tough driving and walking. Finally the roads and sidewalks are clear and my exile is over.

Thinking back to my younger years, I would never have had the luxury of (or the interest in) staying home for a week without getting out of the house. Going to a job, running my children to where they needed to be, a multitude of "musts" and "shoulds" kept me on the go. I would not have wanted it to be any different. But now I am a bit more cautious, more content to let the world go by without me. It all has to do with age and the benefits thereof.

That said, it was a freeing feeling to walk outside and take in the sunshine and not quite so frigid temperatures, while not needing to dodge the icy spots. It felt good to take in a deep breath of air that didn't freeze the hairs in my nose. It felt good to get back to normal living.

Winter is not completely over, I know. But spring is getting closer.

FEBRUARY 11

At last, another winter chore is nearly finished. I just mailed my tax return materials to my son. Rick will now take the figures and do his magic with them. Will I get money back or will I have to send some in? I don't know as yet, but I'm prepared for either. And I'm not leafing through catalogs deciding what I'll buy if I get a refund. No use counting chickens...

But I think there are plenty of folks who are counting their chickens early, already using their credit cards to get everything on their tax return wish list. And there are others who are grumbling mightily about how much Uncle Sam is getting. We want to keep it all for ourselves, ignoring the fact that many of the services we as citizens expect to receive have to be paid for somehow.

I remember something my husband Dean used to say to our children when tax season rolled around. "Just be thankful you are able to pay taxes," he would say. "Some folks don't have that privilege." And so, if I owe Uncle Sam a little extra this year, I'll remember those words, pay all that is required, and be thankful that I am able. Although I am not rich, I truly *am* privileged.

I must never forget.

FEBRUARY 12

Today is Abraham Lincoln's birthday, a day that is no longer noted on that specific date. Instead we have taken his birthday plus George Washington's birthday, on February 22, and lumped them together to provide February with a patriotic reason to have a long weekend off. Now President's Day lands somewhere in the middle of those two dates. It all seems a bit heavy-handed, this manipulating birthdays to please our calendars. I'll bet that George's mother would "tut-tut" over the whole thing.

When I was in grade school, many years ago, we paid tribute to both Lincoln and Washington by remembering their births on their true birthdays. Their portraits were in evidence on our walls during the entire month of February. Each year we heard the stories about Lincoln growing up in a log cabin and his studying every night by firelight. We had our first lessons on honesty with the story of George Washington and his 'fessing up about cutting down the cherry tree. Lincoln and Washington were our national heroes and they each deserved a day for celebration.

In another hundred years, I wonder who of our country's leaders will make it onto our yearly calendar. At the rate we're going now, we may have found so many flaws in our country's leaders that we'll have none at all worthy of remembering.

Let's hope that's not the case.

FEBRUARY 13

Oh, we had fun this afternoon! I was asked to present a Valentine program at the nursing home in town. I had done something similar last year, and didn't want to repeat what we had done then (even though most of them may not have remembered, or would not have minded a repeat). This year I made a new list of familiar love songs to have a sing-a-long, plus I prepared a few short piano solos that they might enjoy listening to while catching their breath for more songs.

About 75 residents were brought to the gathering room, walking or in their wheelchairs. And did they ever sing! We started with "Let Me Call You Sweetheart" and I don't think there was anyone without a smile in the room. Heads were up, eyes brightened, the singing was great (although there was one dear woman who was either ahead of us or lagging behind during the whole song—but she sang every word, very lustily).

I think that people who plan and give programs for the ill and elderly often think these folks can't do anything—they can't sing, they can't remember, they can't…

Or else they think the only thing that old folks want to hear are songs from a hymn book. Instead of asking them to participate in a little fun, they expect their audience just to listen and not participate.

Today we had participation, smiles and fun. A very good day.

FEBRUARY 14

Another day of hearts and flowers and all things centered on love. This afternoon we had our Valentine's Day party at the retirement community, replete with a combo playing quiet music for listening and dancing. Also on the program was our tradition of crowning a king and queen plus a Ms. or Mr. Congeniality. Even though the winter winds were blowing snow against the windows, the atmosphere inside was anything but cold.

A beautiful but bittersweet thing happened after the king and queen were named and crowned. They are a married couple, younger than most of us living here, but he is disabled with a rare malady that affects his motor skills. As the musicians played a love song, our queen rose, wheeled her husband to the dance floor and proceeded to lead him in a quiet dance to the music.

Watching this couple on the floor took me back to eight years ago when my husband and I were selected king and queen. At that time, he also was in a wheelchair and I danced with him at the Valentine's Day party just as the couple did today.

I know they will also remember this day and their dancing to beautiful music with their friends all watching. It was their testimonial to the fact that, even though life gives us obstacles that challenge, there are things like love and music and friendships that help us through each day. May it continue to be so.

FEBRUARY 15

I am embarrassed. I did a generational boo-boo that, I realize, will be forgiven but probably not forgotten. I forgot a grandchild! Here's how it happened.

Yesterday, Valentine's Day, I sent an e-mail Valentine greeting to all my computer-literate family. On that greeting I listed everyone—the children and spouses first, then my grandchildren, then the great-grandchildren. I checked the list several times, more than even Santa does, and sent it over the ether to all the names on my computer's "family" list.

This morning when I checked my e-mail there was a quick note from my daughter in Denver. She informed me that, somehow, I had missed listing Elliott, her son, my youngest grandchild. Oh, no!!! How could I have done that? Forgetfulness is an excuse, especially for anyone over 80, but a very poor excuse to forget to list a grandchild! Really, really bad!

So, first, I picked up the phone to call Elliott and record my apology on their answering machine. Then I sent another email—not just to my grandson to ask forgiveness, but to everyone on that "family" list. I'm sure most of them are chuckling over my omission, and nodding their heads in chorus, agreeing that "grandma's getting to that age, you know." And now I write this third and most public mea culpa. Please forgive.

FEBRUARY 16

The pond has put on a new face this morning, just as it does occasionally when the weather changes suddenly. Two days ago, when the temperatures were cold but more moderate, the pond aerator kept open a hole in the ice at least 25 feet across. This morning, with temperatures below zero, that circle of open water is only washtub size at best. Surrounding that circle of moving water are shimmering white balls—water drops that froze in the air and came down as small ice balls. To a jeweler they must look like diamonds in the sun. In a kitchen lover's vernacular, they look more like sugar sprinkled on a pie crust.

But there is more! Leading out from the liquid center, concentric circles are outlined in the ice that indicate how the ice closed in overnight—very similar to what one sees when counting growth rings on a tree. The rings mark a pattern over time, a clue to reading what nature presents to us. I can see in those rings that, hour by hour over the nighttime, the colder air halted the flow of water except in the still-bubbling center.

Now, at noon, the cold is gradually loosening its grip. The sun warms the edges and the moving water slowly melts away some of the ice. It is an ongoing process, one that will reverse itself once the sun goes down and takes the temperatures with it. I look forward to seeing what tomorrow will bring.

FEBRUARY 17

I knew something must have been amiss because the robins were flying in and out of the tree by the pond, then around the corner to the tree with the feeder, then back again. They seemed more agitated than hungry at that moment. Then I saw the hawk cruising by. I say "cruising" because he seemed to not be in a hurry at all. Flying in a horizontal line, not diving. Just checking out the neighborhood, and probably planning another fly-by soon.

It wasn't long after the hawk flew by that the robins were back on the ground, feeding calmly under the tree. They seemed to sense that the danger had passed and it was safe once again to settle down to a late afternoon feast. And so I wonder—do the birds select a look-out to warn them when danger is near? While most of them are feeding, are there others that are especially assigned to be on guard duty? Do they give a warning cry, or do they just sense that it's time to get away from whatever is the menace of the moment?

There is so much I don't know about birds, even though I've been a bird-watcher for years. Much about animal behavior is a mystery as well. How is it that the creatures we flippantly term as "dumb animals" can be so smart? The entire world of nature is, really, a wonderful mystery.

Of course, there's us, too. Humans. An even bigger mystery.

FEBRUARY 18

Winter is the time for soup—the thick and hearty home-made kind that warms the innards and brightens the outlook. So each winter, our retirement community plans an event designed particularly for all soup lovers. Tomorrow is the night for it—our annual Soup Cook-Off.

Eight local restaurants have been invited to vie for prizes. Each person attending gets a small cup of each soup (which ultimately adds up to be a quite a feast) and we have a chance to vote for our favorite. The three top vote getters go home with not only prize money but free advertising. Even the losers get plenty of free advertising. And all of us go home with our bellies full and with smiles on our faces. It's a big win-win all around.

This year we anticipate some of the perennial favorites like tomato-basil, baked potato, and Italian wedding. Then there are some new combinations such as cream cheese chicken chili, cheeseburger, and Hispanic chicken. And, of course, each restaurant offering will have its own special seasoning and garnish. They go all-out.

With snow on the ground and temperatures hovering around zero with wind chills added to that, the crowd might be a little slimmer this time around. But I have a notion the weather won't stop most people from coming. They know from earlier years that there's a treat in store.

And, after a snowy January and a frigid February, it's high time for a party.

FEBRUARY 19

Exercise class. Such an interruption into a perfectly good morning! I'd rather just keep writing at my computer, but when Monday, Wednesday and Friday mornings come, I'm usually downstairs with the exercise bunch. I know it's good for me, both physically and mentally, so I'm usually there. It's just that it's an interruption to the flow of the day.

My life used to be filled with interruptions. In fact, raising a family is nothing BUT interruptions—check on the baby, stop fixing dinner to help with homework, get in the car to pick up a child at school, run downstairs to put the clothes in the dryer. I was multi-tasking long before I ever knew the term.

Once the children were gone from home, I had more time to myself and got used to that wondrous ability to set my own schedule. And, during our delicious retirement years, Dean and I relished being able to come and go at will, whenever and wherever we wanted. Now I have the best of both worlds. Living in a retirement community, most of my physical needs are met and I am free to do the things I enjoy doing.

But, along with that freedom to enjoy life, I am still obligated to do what is necessary to keep my mind and body functioning. So I'll keep going to exercise class, take a long walk every day, and try to eat right.

That's another way of giving thanks.

FEBRUARY 20

It just grew like Topsy. One minute, the hall was quiet with only one woman sitting and reading outside her apartment while the girls were doing the semi-weekly cleaning. I happened to be passing, getting my daily "walk the halls" exercise, so I stopped and took a nearby chair to chat with her for a minute—the exercise could wait. A few minutes later, her husband came out of their apartment and we three settled in for a longer visit.

It wasn't long before another resident happened by and was drawn into our conversation. And then another, bringing his own chair since we, by that time, had run out of seating options. The five of us sat there for well over an hour with never a lull in the conversation and plenty of laughter to draw the attention of, and comments from, any number of people passing by.

We were reminded, on this cold winter day, that our impromptu gathering was much like our summer "porch people" afternoons. Until now, we didn't realize how much we missed those informal, unplanned get-togethers that we had on the big front porch on hot summer days. And we speculated whether our new screen house by the pond will turn out to be another popular gathering place to sit and chat with friends.

All of us need places to gather and exchange ideas, whether it is over the garden fence, on the porch, or even in the middle of the hall.

FEBRUARY 21

There's a snow-globe scene happening just outside my window. I am enjoying one of those picture-perfect snow-falls with huge snowflakes coming straight down. No wind to cause drifting and no place I have to go. The television set isn't turned on so the Weather Channel can't intrude on the picture outside the window. I am just enjoying the scene as it unfolds.

Two days ago I was less than enamored with the fore-cast—snow once again for the weekend. But the weather people didn't announce that this afternoon's snow would come down as a Currier and Ives painting rather than a near-blizzard. I did not anticipate that the world would turn white with such quiet gentleness today. But it has, and still is.

If I were 10 years old, I would be outside with my head lifted, my mouth open and tongue out, catching that fluffy white stuff on the way down. Or I would be holding out my mitten to examine every huge snowflake, then blow on it to watch it melt. And then I'd be eager to start rolling balls to build a snowman, especially if my big brother was out there to help. That would be pure contentment, kid-style.

But today I'll just be happy to sit by the window with good music on the stereo, a good book in my hand, and let the snowy picture roll quietly past (pure contentment, old-style). Good enough for me.

FEBRUARY 22

On the top shelf of my tall bookcase stands a miniature tandem bicycle, the proverbial "bicycle built for two" of story and song. It is a reminder of the days when Dean and I took many wonderful day trips along country roads on our tandem bike. We bought it when we lived in Michigan and put plenty of miles on the odometer before we moved to Ohio and added to our mileage record. It was our recreation-of-choice in the summers after the children were grown and we had time for roaming.

There's something special about traveling the slow lane and discovering the little things one would not notice while driving past in the car. Things like where the bittersweet grows on the fence-rows. Or spotting a good place to find milkweed pods. Or knowing what roads to avoid because of the bicycle-chasing dogs. And there's nothing like stopping for an afternoon snack beneath a mulberry tree, staining your hands with the juice that drips from the sweet fruit.

Of course, there is also the memory of the day we had a flat tire much too far from home. And the time we signed up for a 50-mile biking fund-raiser and it happened to be a terribly windy day—great for going one direction, but a real bruiser on the return.

But good memories don't all have to be sweet and painless to be worthwhile. They are all part of a vast storehouse to treasure on cold winter days.

FEBRUARY 23

Beware! I'm about to complain. The view outside my window is simply beautiful this morning—clear blue skies with the sun shining brightly on pure, clean, undisturbed white snow. BUT I'm getting tired of sun on beautiful white snow. I'm getting tired of beautiful white snow on gray, cloudy days as well. I'm just getting tired of it all. I'm definitely ready for spring.

Yes, this winter is dragging on again, as it usually seems to about this time of year. What we first enjoy as a change of season becomes the same old, same old. Each February we eagerly look to March as the beginning of spring—new growth and balmier air. It happens to us again in late summer when the August days become too hot, too humid, too long. We look ahead to change and forget that even the change becomes tedious after a while.

Last summer, when I complained about the Canada geese and their persistent habitation of MY space, I never thought I'd be ready to see them again, leading their little goslings to the edge of the pond. But, right now, I would welcome a peek at open water and fresh spring grass that brings the geese to our neighborhood.

I know, I could move to southern California and get out of all this winter stuff. But then I wouldn't have anything to complain about anymore. Or—would I?

FEBRUARY 24

Something I've been expecting to happen, happened to-day. My car battery died. The combination of age and too many frigid mornings finally did it in. So I called our small but dependable neighborhood garage. Mine isn't the only car with battery problems this morning, they say. But they'll come out and pick up the car, take it in for a new battery and bring it back later today.

Such is life in a small town. When you need help, it's there. I can leave the garage door open for them to come, they'll help themselves to the car, fix it right and bring it back the same day. I can stop in at the garage and pay them later, next time I'm in town. No rush.

Of course, living in a small town has some disadvantages as well. No longer are there clothing stores on Main Street, although at one time there were two. I have little need for new clothes, anyway. There's no Wal-Mart, but that's fine with me since I never did like huge find-everything-you-need-plus-all-you-don't-need stores. All I need are a few groceries now and then, but the grocery we have in town is sufficient for that.

So I'm content where I am planted. I'm happy to travel to visit my children once in a while and get a touch of city life, but it's always good to be home.

FEBRUARY 25

I'm packing my luggage again. Tomorrow I'm off to Denver for a nine-day visit with my daughter Lee and my son Mark. They have been hoping for plenty of sunshine during my visit, but the forecast calls for cold and snow. Well, I've been in snow and cold before—like, right now in Ohio.

Actually, my reason for accepting Lee's offer has little to do with weather. It mainly has to do with getting together with family and enjoying our time together. I know that, one of these years, I'll not be able to pack up and fly to wherever one of my children lives. So, as my friends and neighbors tell me, "Go while you can." Their admonition gets more important every year.

Since I live in a retirement complex, I see every day the effects of aging in the bodies of my friends. I see it in the mirror as well, and feel it when I get out of bed in the morning. I don't have the strength and agility I once had, nor many other physical abilities that start to fade away as we get older. But I'm still able to drive to the airport, walk the long airport passageways and get myself to the right gate. When I can't do that anymore, that will be all right, too.

While I'm gone, I will continue to write my reflections on what I see and feel in Colorado. Come along. We will enjoy the trip together.

FEBRUARY 26

I doubt that there is anyone who looks forward to a change of plans or an upside-down schedule. Yet most of us face them at one time or another. A snow storm, a sudden illness—we all experience them, but our reactions vary.

Today I flew to Denver for a ten-day visit with my daughter and her husband and son. My trip to the airport went according to schedule but then as often happens, my scheduled flight was delayed two hours. For me, all I had to do was call Lee and she adjusted her schedule to meet me. But for other passengers it created additional problems. The waiting passengers reacted in a variety of ways.

The girl next to me was in a dither because she would miss her connection for the next leg of her trip. Panic was obvious—in her voice and body language. A man whose destination was Denver, like my own, gave the panicked woman some quiet advice which soothed her anxiety. Across the aisle another lost-connection customer took the problem much more in stride and quietly got on her cell phone to rearrange her schedule. The man behind me, with a voice and manner obviously used to commanding, made the entire area well aware that he was in control of everything. No problem.

In life we each have our own way of dealing with problems, large or small. I hope I can keep my cool when the time comes.

FEBRUARY 27

As I've said many times before, you're never too old to learn. Or start to understand, or experience something new. Today I finally understood the meaning of the term "powder snow."

I was with my daughter Lee and her husband Dick, driving north to Boulder where they had a scheduled meeting. Last night's snow was heavy on the trees and, the closer we got to the mountains, the more snow we saw. By the time we were in the city, snow was piled high on every tree. What I was seeing was the powder snow all ski resorts brag about. Snow so light that six inches can evaporate into almost nothing, just as a meringue can melt in your mouth.

At this altitude and dry climate, very little water comes with the snow—the accumulating flakes are pure fluff. The trees were piled high with it and, though branches were bent, there was not enough weight to make them break as they would have in Ohio. Tomorrow much of this will have evaporated away, going into the atmosphere rather than filtering down into the ground. So even though the scene is more spectacular than what I might see at home, it is not as nourishing to the earth. This was a new concept to get my head around—pure beauty but not much substance.

Of course, in Colorado and many other places in this world, any moisture is far better than none at all.

FEBRUARY 28

Anyone who has a computer is, in one way or another, computer literate. That said, there are many levels of that literacy. I would class myself as, perhaps, in lower elementary school. My age-old, well-practiced typing skills are excellent, my familiarity with Microsoft Word is adequate, I'm okay with emails, but most everything else is far beyond my ken. My literacy is one-dimensional.

In a few days I am going to be involved in a video conference with a committee I'm on—something I know absolutely nothing about. My son-in-law has just made arrangements with the committee chair, in Ohio, to plug me in to that meeting via the computer. It took those two only a couple of minutes of chat time to set it all up. It's all Greek to me, but I'm trusting in more computer-literate people to get it right for me.

So, just like so many things in life, I expect that everything will go well on Tuesday evening when the committee meets in Bluffton and I sit in Denver listening, and perhaps contributing, to the conversation. It will be a "first" for me and, as such, I look forward to it with a bit of trepidation as one does with something new. At the same time, another side of me is pleased to be able to experience this technology in action and be a part of it.

You're never too old.

FEBRUARY 29—LEAP DAY

It's February 29, a day that comes around every four years. A day inserted into the calendar to make the earth's internal clock and our calendars coincide. A day to allow children born on February 29 to celebrate a birthday on the actual date, but only every four years. For the rest of us, February 29 is just an added day in the month, in a year, in a lifetime. Most of us just let it happen.

The calendar is really a pretty amazing thing when you start to think about it. How the ancient astronomers and off-the-wall thinkers figured out how all these wonderful new discoveries work together. How we move from day to day, season to season, over a regulated period of time.

When I was working on family genealogies, searching ancient papers and posting dates, I would sometimes bump into a confusion of birth/death dates of early ancestors. This calendar-manipulating change began in 1522 when Pope Gregory XIII decreed that the old Nicaen calendar, set back in 325, be revised. (I just looked this up on Wikipedia and my mind is already boggled, so if you wish to research further, you're on your own).

Anyway, wherever we are on this earth, we live with the present calendar we have. Considering it has been in use for almost five centuries and still is amazingly accurate, that's a pretty good record. My checkbook can't claim that much accuracy.

March 1

We went to a high school basketball game today, something I have not done since my own children were in high school. But my grandson Elliott is a high school senior and his school's team was involved in a tournament game. Although the team wasn't able to pull out a win, they most definitely tried. Today we were part of the many families that follow their high school team, no matter what or where.

One of the things that impressed me was the large student pep team that kept one end of the gym rocking throughout the game (my grandson was part of it). Led by a very energetic cheerleading squad, the students never flagged in keeping the noise level up the entire game. We parents and grandparents on the sidelines could not help but be impressed with the school spirit displayed.

I know, there used to be a lot of school spirit even back in my school days, but I think today's teens, at least those who really want to be involved, throw themselves into it all with more abandon. They are also very creative in their chants and cheers.

Today, the cheerleaders' outfits might be a bit skimpier, their cheers different from the old "rah-rah-sis-boom-bah" days, the loud speakers considerably more powerful. But it's the same special school spirit that leads them on. I have a feeling that the world's still all right.

MARCH 2

My daughter Lee and I drove to the Colorado state capitol building today, right in the middle of downtown Denver. One of Lee's post-doctoral students is highly involved in advocacy for medical research funding so she envisioned and planned this event. Lee went both as speaker at the event and cheerleader for her student's project. I was privileged to watch it all from the sidelines.

The Colorado statehouse is similar to many of the older state capitols—massive, built to impress with plenty of marble and polished woodwork. Behind the tall door to the room we were assigned, four members of Colorado's higher education committee, plus several aides and a handful of onlookers, came to this "Lunch and Learn" session. Over sandwiches and veggies, the legislators listened to five scientists/lecturers give an illustrated overview of current medical research being done in the state's universities. Questions were fielded from the committee members and good discussion occurred.

Lee's student was pleased that her brainchild had gone so well. As we drove home, Lee and I talked about the value of this venture to her student. Contacts were made, awareness was raised, and the need for additional research funding was addressed. The seed was planted but now the hard work of cultivation has just begun.

Lee knows her student as one who is not easily discouraged. Today she found fulfillment in this initial project and is excited to continue with her "Lunch and Learn" idea. More power to her!

MARCH 3

It was a special celebratory night to commemorate Dick's birthday as well as celebrate the signing of a contract for a new Denver home for Lee and Dick. Since Elliott is heading off to college in the fall, they will be empty-nesters. They have decided to downsize and, at the same time, live a little closer to their work. So in honor of this special day we went to a very popular sushi restaurant for dinner.

Now, I have eaten sushi before but it is not something I seek out, primarily since I don't live near a large metropolitan area where sushi is served. Nor did I grow up eating raw fish and rice. It is an acquired taste, but one I have learned to enjoy.

The four of us stuffed ourselves with a variety of fresh fish and vegetable delicacies. While they are deft at manipulating chopsticks, I merely managed to get the food to my mouth. But no one laughed, I got plenty to eat, the food was delicious, and it was a great "family" time.

That's what makes for life memories—family times around the table whether it is all-American comfort food like pot roast and apple pie or a more exotic meal of sushi and green tea ice cream. It's being together and eating, talking, laughing, remembering. I hope I never get too old to embrace the new and different as I did tonight. Nor do I want to forget this special family time together.

MARCH 4

My daughter has been bemoaning the fact that the weather has not cooperated with my visit. During the time I have been here, it has been colder than usual for Denver (Ohio was colder than usual, too). We have seen very little sunshine and Lee's beloved Colorado blue sky has been noticeably absent (we have many cloudy days in Ohio, too). The snow has lingered because of the below freezing temps (nothing I haven't experienced elsewhere). I tell her not to fret. "That's all right— I'm just happy to be here with you!"

Lee's concern is typical, of course. We like to be good hosts to our guests. We plan things to do and places to go, with our guest's pleasure in mind. We want them to see our home and surroundings in the best possible light. We want our guests to have a good time and leave feeling that the visit was something special.

Of course, my visit has been all of the above and more. How could it not be? Lee and Dick have gone out of their way to plan some special things to do while I am here—I've written about some of those already. And there is even more to come before my plane takes off on Saturday.

And, when I do leave for home, I will take with me more than enough special memories to last until the next visit.

MARCH 5

I'm having great fun watching birds at the back yard feeder while here in Colorado. Located in the rolling foothills south of Denver, my daughter's bird feeder invites a wide variety of birds while her picture window offers a perfect view of all the activity. This morning I started a list of those birds I could readily identify, then turned to their western bird book to identify the strangers.

Some at the feeder are familiar to my area of Ohio, like the junco, song sparrow, blue jay, flicker, English sparrow and house finch. But there are others that stay in the West, so I can only enjoy them when I come to visit.

On this trip, I have reacquainted myself with the all-blue mountain bluebird, its color electrifying in the sun, and the western bluebird with coloring somewhat similar to its Ohio sibling's, yet different. The bold western and Stellar's jays come often to the feeder. The western towhee, with its rusty side contrasting with the white and black, is also a frequent visitor. And then there are the big and flashy magpies flying back and forth, stunning in their black and white coloring but pesky bullies to all the other birds.

This bird-watching makes me hungry for spring. I'm looking forward to the time when I can take my binoculars to the nearby nature preserve and greet the birds as they return from their winter resorts. Spring, come soon this year!

MARCH 6

Once in a while, if we're fortunate, we are able to witness the growth of someone with a special talent. This evening I was privileged to be a part of that process. It was a violin recital presented by an extremely gifted young woman. But the story begins earlier.

Several summers ago, I was on Cape Cod with my daughter Lee and grandson Elliott. During that time we were invited to the summer home of one of Lee's colleagues. Their high school age daughter was present also and, after everyone had come back from the beach, she got out her violin and played one of Bach's unaccompanied partitas for us. I was blown away—such talent, such musical maturity from a high school musician!

Now, four years later, that girl is a junior at university, majoring in music. She presented a pre-recital concert for about two dozen of her parents' friends, and we were included in the audience. Again, I was more than impressed with her ever-growing talent, her maturity, and her charming personality. She is someone blessed with a very special gift—one who is taking that talent to an ever-rising level. She credits her university professor for (and I quote from her program) "his gentle guidance, patience, and continued willingness to foster creativity and curiosity."

My violinist is on the way to making a difference in this world that needs, so much, the healing touch of music. May she continue to grow in grace.

MARCH 7

My last day in Denver: bright sunshine and, finally, warming temperatures. I stayed with my son Mark last night since he lives near the airport and was more than willing to see that I got on my flight home. Mark and his partner Mike are moving to Arizona (in part to get away from the snows) and are in the process right now of getting their town house ready to sell and to move all their belongings to another location.

Their many beautiful pictures are mostly off the walls and wrapped in bubble wrap. They have sold some of their excess furniture. My bedroom was empty except for the essentials—a welcoming bed, a bench on which to open my suitcase, and one chair. But the hospitality and warm feeling of being wanted and cared for was still very much present in that home.

Sometimes we feel we cannot entertain guests unless everything is perfect. Sometimes we feel that we need to do something very special to make our guests feel welcome. Sometimes we fail to understand that it's not perfect surroundings that are of highest importance, but the feeling of welcome that pervades.

So I'm thankful for the small blessings of a good night's sleep on a cozy bed, warm oatmeal with cranberries for breakfast, and an experienced escort through the maze of waiting lines at a very busy airport. Thank you, Mark!

MARCH 8

Home again—a good feeling. I love to go, I love to come back. So, what has happened since I've been gone?

I look out my window to the pond, my favorite looking-glass to the world. I spot a pair of mallard ducks. They have discovered enough open water to enjoy a little swim, plus a bit of courtship, this afternoon. They swim and dip with exuberance, as if let out for recess. They finally take off to wherever they have been keeping themselves warm. They will be back.

Yes, it *is* about time for the ice to begin disappearing. We've all been waiting for the warmer spell that came in over the weekend and is forecasted to stay for a few days. That's how it is when March comes. Our love of winter, if we ever had any, has long since faded. We watch for any sign of spring that might come along. The mallards are the sign for me today.

It seems like ages since our first snow—last fall when a smattering of snow whitened the ground, somewhat. That snow soon melted while we still had plenty of beautiful colored leaves to "ooh" and "aah" about. Once the snow came down in earnest, we were more muted in our response. Now we're beginning to see patches of lawn again and, even though the grass is a dull brown, there is hope.

One of these days…

MARCH 9

Our Bluffton Writer's Group meets every month and, usually we challenge ourselves with some topic to write about. For March, suggestions were to write on St. Patrick's Day, the Ides of March, the coming of spring—or whatever we wish. Reading the assignment, I got to thinking about the Ides of March. Hmmm. The March of Ides. Hmmm. The March of I'ds. Double hmmm. Here is the result (my fun for the day):

THE MARCH OF I'Ds

I'd do that in a minute.
I'd rather be safe than sorry.
I'd never in a million years!
I'd say that's a winner!
I'd go along with that.
I'd be happy to do it.
I'd never be caught dead in that outfit!
I'd have been there, but…
I'd be a fool to try that.
I'd be careful if I were you!

MARCH 10

Sometimes I wonder why I am so fortunate. What did I do, or not do, that has brought me safely to this time and place? Many others my age (if they have lived this long) endure chronic illnesses, multiple problems, debilitating worries. Yet here I am, relatively flexible, able, solvent, enjoying life each day and looking forward to many more tomorrows.

Is it my genes? That's a mixed bag. My father died of leukemia at age 41, but my mother lived until she was 96. Did growing up on a farm, drinking fresh-from-the-cow milk and eating carrots right out of the garden make me healthier, even now? Did going to church every Sunday give me immunity to ulcers or diabetes or cancer? What did my husband and I do to make our children and grandchildren all turn out healthy and caring, productive citizens?

Yes, I am fortunate. Little did I realize, at age 15, what life was all about. Now, 70 years later, I marvel at the fact that life's ups and downs (yes, there definitely have been both) have brought me, relatively intact, to this stage of life and this state of mind.

Tomorrow, or next week, or ten years from now, I may be telling a different story. My life picture may turn dark any day. But now, today, I count my blessings and look with anticipation to whatever future is waiting for me. The adventure continues.

MARCH 11

I have three wooden organ pipes hanging on my living room wall. They are part of a church pipe organ I first played 65 years ago. You might not recognize them for what they are, since the hundreds of pipes making up a pipe organ are usually hidden behind screens. Unless you are an organist, or really interested in pipe organs, you never see the inner workings that make pipe organ music happen.

When my church purchased a newer pipe organ—and even that happened about 45 years ago—the old organ pipes were auctioned off. Dean and I were there to bid on a few. We came home with the set of three I have on the wall (G, G# and A on the traverse flute stop) plus two large wooden bass pipes (they'll literally take your breath away if you try to blow a note through them) and an octave of tiny lead pipes (really high notes). Over the years, we have had fun with the pipes. We decorated one wall of our screened porch with the big ones at one time. I've used the tiny pipes to illustrate several children's stories in church. And the medium sized ones are a perfect wall decoration.

Today, pipe organs are becoming things of the past and classical organists (those who make music with their feet as well as their hands) are hard to find. Has our fascination with electronics made it too easy to make music, meanwhile losing our ear for the special sounds coming from the pipes?

Perhaps I have become obsolete as well.

MARCH 12

It's noon and the fog has still not lifted. The world outside is gray, although the air is much warmer than it was a few days ago. Of course, that is the reason for the persistent fog—warm air above, frozen ground beneath. Despite the fog, my mallard pair is standing at the edge of the pond's ice, probably trying to decide where to build their nest this year. A sign of spring.

Although the snow is receding to reveal bare patches on the lawns, and the ice on the pond is melting slowly, spring will still take its time arriving. We always get a bit too eager when the first really warm day comes. We know (down deep) that it's only a teaser but we wish the promise were more substantive. Our fingers itch to feel earth again. Our eyes long to spot a crocus or a snow drop poking out of the ground. And so we wait.

On days like this—the gray days—I wish for a quicker reprieve. I'd like an instant spring. I want the ice to quickly disappear from the pond. I want the rest of the snow to go speedily away. But if I get my wish, the creek will flood and the fields will become a soggy mess. Sometimes spring comes that way and we, in turn, complain. We can't have it both ways.

Both ways—so tempting.

MARCH 13

Over the years I have accumulated quite a few books that I have filled with my version of a daily journal. My ruminations start about the time that my husband retired and we moved back to his home town of Bluffton. They have extended through today.

At first those journals were plain spiral-bound notebooks, a dime-a-dozen at the local pharmacy. Later on I decided to use some of the lovely books my children would give me at Christmas—those beautifully-decorated journals that were intended to prompt me to keep writing, but that I hesitated to fill with nothing but my daily scribblings. Now I have used all of those lovely gift books—except one, the most beautiful of all. Can I bear to touch those pages with a mere ballpoint pen? And fill them with my getting-worse-all-the-time handwriting?

I remind myself of the "little old ladies" whose dresser drawers are filled with beautiful silky underwear, gifts that have never been worn because "they're too pretty to wear." So I open to the first page, put my pen to paper and write.

As I turn each day to another beautiful sketch, I will be reminded that beauty can be everywhere, in everything. Perhaps even in my writings. I will be inspired and, in turn, hope to be an inspiration to anyone who might, sometime, read my words. The book's artist has shared. Now it is my turn.

MARCH 14

I had a most interesting conversation over lunch today. It was with a college student whom I met today for the first time. He is the recipient of a scholarship that my husband and I had established some years ago at our alma mater, Bluffton University. Dean and I had tried to make a point of meeting with "our" assigned student each year. I intend to keep up that tradition as long as I am able.

This year's student and I met over lunch. There seemed to be a special rapport between us from the very first handshake. I would have been happy to claim him as a grandson, had he not had grandparents of his own. Handsome, outgoing, articulate and with a sparkle in his eyes, he has a wide variety of interests. We sat for more than an hour with never a lull in conversation.

It has been interesting, over the years, to meet these student scholarship recipients and follow their paths. Some have struggled, but persevered. Others have sailed through all four years with no apparent (at least, to us) problems. We have never, as yet, had a student that has not received his/her degree.

With no grandchildren living nearby, this is one way of keeping in touch with that younger generation in my own community. As my own youngest grandchild goes off to college this fall, I will still have a surrogate grandson right here in town.

Welcome to the family, Michael!

MARCH 15

Today we celebrated my brother's 90th birthday, a definite milestone. Norm is in a nursing home here in town, quite debilitated with Parkinson's disease, but we were able to wheel him to the chapel where his wife and daughters had planned a short program, with refreshments afterward. Two of the daughters were here with their families. The other daughter who lives in Canada was with us visually and vocally, via the newest in technologies. Naturally, it was a special family time.

As we watched a short video of family pictures depicting Norm's 90 years, there were plenty of chuckles as the candid shots triggered fond memories. Sweet baby pictures, photos of our families in their gawkiest stages, wedding parties, mugging for the camera (which Norm was wont to do on more than one occasion).

It does not seem possible that so many years have flown by since Norm and I were living on our childhood farm in Illinois, pushing the lawn mower through the tough grass, milking cows, picking green beans. Pictures help to bring those early years back into focus and remind us that, yes, it has been a long time. But they were good times, memorable times.

And it makes me realize that it's time for me to get out my boxes of old photos and put them in order—while I still can. It takes more than just good intentions to make for good memories.

MARCH 16

My family has just increased by one, with the arrival yesterday evening of little great-granddaughter Abigail. By this morning there were already nearly a dozen pictures of her, sent from Maine via internet. Her sisters and brothers, each of them, were pictured holding the new baby and, of course, mommy and daddy and grandma each had their pictures included as well. In a day or two, Abigail will be home and life will get back to what is normal for them.

My, what a difference from when I had my children, over half a century ago! There were telephones, but nobody saw a picture of a new baby until long after the birth. At that time new mothers stayed at least a week in the hospital—usually two. Younger brothers and sisters might be able to peek through the high window into the hospital nursery where the babies were displayed in their all-in-a-row cribs, but were certainly NOT allowed to be in the same room as the baby. Heaven forbid!

Back then, I was pleased to have a vacation from home and family chores. I did not chafe at the doctor's orders to stay two weeks. We women were, still, thought of as the "weaker sex" even though we knew we were strong enough to juggle a household and all that it entailed. Back then, I did not hesitate to enjoy my vacation time. I would be plenty busy soon enough.

I think I had a pretty good deal!

MARCH 17

Oh, for words! How can I describe the sky tonight? Every color—from gray to gold, orange to purple, blue to infinity. Every form—from ripples to streaks, from waves to straight lines. Every intensity from brilliant to dark, from muted to indescribable. All there in the western sky outside my windows.

I have been writing these few lines while running from window to window. I need to stop and drink in the scene during the short, short time it is here. But the sunset colors and intensity keep changing! If I don't write these words down immediately, the images and sensations will disappear, never to be remembered quite the same way.

During the last few minutes the scene has shifted from a calm and beautiful, mainly pastel, picture to the most intense orange-red I think I have ever seen in an Ohio sunset sky. It takes the breath away. I have written about sunsets before, but I do not think I have ever seen one so brilliant or intense as tonight. And, once again, as soon as I have written these words the sky has turned to an even more intense red, a ruby red that will soon become as blood before night engulfs the whole.

Will my words mean anything by tomorrow morning? Will they still evoke a response? Perhaps, but not the awe I felt while it was happening. Some things should stay in the moment. Tonight's sunset was one of those.

MARCH 18

Ever since last fall, when Canada geese gathered by the hundreds to bask along the far side of our pond, that bank has been empty. But I expect to see the geese return some day soon. No, we're not eager to see them come and befoul our sidewalks, but we expect it to happen. So far, there have been only two geese to pay a visit to the pond. Where are all the rest?

Perhaps I should not ask, for to ask is often to receive. It may be that the Canadas raise their babies at the larger Nature Preserve pond nearby, then wait to bring them over here until the grass is greener and more tender. If so, they won't be here for a while, but we'd better get prepared.

I've been rolling an idea around in my head—not a complete solution to our goose proliferation problem, but it could help. Last year, a few of our residents worked very hard to keep our sidewalks clear of goose droppings—by chasing the geese away whenever they got close to the walks. Their efforts really made a difference. Maybe this year more of us should take it upon ourselves to be vigilantes on a regular basis. Have a sign-up sheet: Volunteers Needed! Keep Our Sidewalks Clean! Be a Goose-Chaser! Lawn Chairs Provided! Ice Cream at the End of Your Shift!

It might be worth a try.

MARCH 19

The skies were gray but the air was about average for early spring in Ohio—chilly but not biting. I was inside, feeling a bit sorry for myself, so decided to go for a short walk to climb out of the doldrums. I am so glad I did.

My walk took me past the new screen house by the pond, so inviting but a bit too cold on a cloudy day like today. I noticed, while passing one of the villas, that snow drops were in bloom and a couple of daffodils were beginning to open their yellow faces to the world. And then I walked past my raised garden—the garden that will, later on, be overrun with milkweed but which is now at rest.

Ah, but that garden is NOT at rest. Things are happening both beneath and above the soil. My clump of chives is starting to send out new shoots and soon will be a bright green mound. My scattering of baby hyacinths is a cushion of new green leaves, soon to sprout with bright blue blossoms. And there are three small perennials—identification forgotten at the moment—that will tell me what they are when they finally burst into bloom later on.

So there was a new spring in my step, in more ways than one, as I returned from that short walk. Yes, the world brightened during that afternoon walk. Spring definitely is on its way.

MARCH 20

Today is "Dine and Shop" day for residents of our retirement community. It's a monthly excursion to one of the large shopping centers fifteen miles away. For those of our residents who no longer drive or who don't have family members living close by, this trip is very popular and important to them. But it is also special to those residents who just like to go places and do things, no matter where.

It was fun to see the bus-full of residents gathering this morning, smiling and chatting away like school children ready for a field trip. And it *is* like a field trip—leaving the same daily routine for something new. This is not an everyday occurrence. The trip provides fresh air for the body and a lift to the spirits, especially on this rainy, chilly March day.

I had forgotten how it was for my mother when she was older and no longer able to get out on her own. My brother and I visited her regularly and spent quality time with her. But she particularly looked forward to little trips to the ice cream store or a drive out in the country on a sunny day. I wish now that I had taken time to do that with her more often—simple things that don't take a lot of time but are important in the life of someone else.

What a shame we have to get older before we realize the time we have wasted.

MARCH 21

The first day of spring!

So, what do I see outside my window this morning? You should have asked me that a week ago. Then I could have answered, "Blue sky, warm sunshine, snow and ice disappearing, birds doing cartwheels, a wonderful day, etc., etc." But today I say, "Cloudy, a couple of degrees above freezing, birds holed up somewhere else."

And so it's not a great first day of spring here in northwest Ohio. But the ice *has* disappeared from the pond. The grass *is* starting to green up in sheltered areas. The spring menus *are* in effect in the dining room. And I know the birds *are* around—they're just not singing and doing flip-flops this morning. Neither am I, but I'm still alive and well and looking forward to a good day, even if it's not spectacular.

We've all seen enough springs to know that it doesn't all happen at once. Spring comes in fits and starts, teasing us to check the garden for new shoots even when we know it's too early, to shed our winter jackets while they're still needed. It's all part of the earth's yearly ritual of wakening.

And the wakening will happen. In its own time, not ours. At its own pace, not ours. No matter how smart we get, no matter how much we try to alter the rhythms of nature, there are some things we just can't control. There is some comfort in that.

MARCH 22

The aroma was tempting so I investigated. Fresh cinnamon rolls, just out of the oven, were the treat of the morning for Saturday morning coffee klatch. It's a weekly get-together open to all residents of our complex. The coffee klatch beckons to a mix of residents, from long-time main building regulars to some of the newest arrivals to our villas. It's a great way to get acquainted and acclimated to retirement living.

At one time, we all sat around one big table in our Family Room. Then, as popularity grew, late-comers had to fill in at a smaller table in the room. This eventually evolved into a men's table-women's table division, which has pretty much held sway for the last few years.

There are differences in the conversations at the two tables. One of our villa residents (a male) sometimes brings one of his collection of wooden puzzles and toys for the men to check over. The women generally talk more about their families and general community goings-on. There might be some women who are interested in the men's conversations, or vice versa, but the seating arrangements basically stay as the unwritten protocol indicates at present.

I don't usually attend this Saturday morning ritual any more, although my husband and I used to be there regularly. Instead, I'm often at my computer as I am now, writing away at this and that. That's my way of enjoying a Saturday morning.

MARCH 23

It is March 23, three full days into spring. And yes, it is snowing. It has happened before—this "snow on the crocuses" occasion. In fact, it happens nearly every year. But that does not mean that everyone's happy about it. I don't even think our first graders are all that excited about it, much less the rest of us. But that's what happens in early spring, here in Ohio as well as many other places at this latitude. We get our hopes up that spring is really here and, once again, we are fooled. It goes with the territory.

I look back to last fall. November 1, to be exact. I began my daily reflection that morning with these words: "They told us it was coming, and it came. Our first snowfall—on the first day of November." It didn't last, that first snowfall of the winter season. And this one won't last, either—this (dare-we-say) last snowfall of the season. Predictions are for a possible one to three inches. But we know from experience that whatever comes down today will probably disappear by sometime tomorrow. One of the blessings of spring.

So my grape hyacinth leaves will need to snuggle under their white blanket for a time. My garden chives will slow their growth a bit. The rabbits will snuggle down in their holes and wait it out. Change is coming, certainly, but it may take a bit longer than we hoped.

We can wait.

MARCH 24

The earth is snowy-white and still this morning, the pond is rippling except at the edges where a skim of ice has formed, the mallard pair swims slowly across the water as if it's summer, but the air is still below the freezing mark. Yes, I love to check out the pond each morning to see what's happening outside my window.

At the same time, I also tune to the television news each morning to check on the rest of the world, to see if I missed anything overnight. I like to know what's going on outside my door as well and, in this 21st century, there is news at my fingertips any time of the day. Twenty-four-seven, in modern terminology.

This habit of needing to know everything from everywhere, at any and all hours of the day, is a newly-acquired affliction that has infected us all, even those of us who came to it reluctantly. We feel secure in the knowledge that we now have—well—knowledge. We want to *know.* We accumulate opinions on anything and everything, announcing those opinions to everyone we meet.

I confess, this reflection is an opinion piece. My opinion. And yes, I did turn on the television this morning to check on the world at large. But now I'll turn back to my small window on life here at home and be content. At least until the nightly news.

Mustn't get left out of the loop!

MARCH 25

Waiting is always hard to do. Whether it is awaiting the birth of a baby, anticipating Christmas, yearning for spring, or even waiting for a death. This week, my sister-in-law, my niece and I have been watching and waiting for my brother to succumb to death via Parkinson's disease. It has not been easy, this death watch, even though every one of us has come to terms with the inevitability and are at peace.

No one wants to live beyond their time—beyond their alive-ness. Knowing Norm, I'm sure he would not have wanted this, either. But he is no longer able to tell us that, or do anything about it, so he continues to keep breathing. His caregivers are very gentle with him. And so we wait, and watch, and keep him as comfortable as we can while making funeral plans. That is the chore that we, the living, are assigned.

I went through a similar vigil when my husband died with Alzheimer's disease five years ago. It was not an easy time. Then, last June, I experienced a different kind of death, with the sudden death of my son-in-law. It, also, was not an easy time. Whether expected or sudden, death comes and we need to deal with it, each in our own way.

Go in peace, Norm. We love you.

MARCH 26

Eleven months ago I initiated a project. Did I really know what I was getting into, that morning when I put my first "reflection" on paper? Absolutely not! How could I have thought it possible to write one short essay per day—for an entire year? Was I out of my mind? Maybe, but here I am, still writing away with only one month to go until a year has passed. It has been a very special, very rewarding year.

It has been fun, challenging, exhilarating, exasperating, and most any other adjective you can name. But I think the best way to describe it is to say this year has been eye-opening and consciousness-raising. Little did I realize, when I began, that I was missing so much around me—so many little things that aren't really little at all. Small pleasures that become big pleasures just by noticing them. Daily blessings out of ordinary happenings.

Oh yes, there have been frustrations—days with little to inspire, gloomy weather prompting gloomy moods, unwelcome news. But then a beautiful sunset appears or someone comes along to remind me that life is good. Through it all I have tried to keep writing, keep thinking, keep looking positively at life even when things weren't always positive. The process has kept my mind sharpened, my eyes observing, my imagination working and my computer skills up to date.

At age 85, that's more than enough to keep me thankful.

MARCH 27

What a difference the sun can make! After a dark and cloudy day, with cold rain coming down, the sun appeared this evening and is once again doing one of its evening specials—a sunset worth taking in. Although not spectacular, this sunset has given my spirits a lift. The third lift of the day.

Often, on cloudy days, we need a spirit-lift—something to get us on a positive track. It might be a phone call from a friend that can make a difference, or some familiar song on the radio that gets the mind going in a different direction. At this time of the year, as winter slowly turns to spring, we get eager to have it all at once and are disappointed when our days aren't all sunshine.

So yes, my day started with a "downer" as I woke to a dark, dark sky. But things brightened considerably when I made a phone call to my great-granddaughter in Maine who is turning eight years old tomorrow. Who can resist the giggles and enthusiasm of an eight-year-old dynamo—or her younger brother who just wanted to say "hello" to Grandma Niswander? A special meeting this afternoon brought the day even more into clearer focus. And now, with the sun appearing and creating another special sunset, the day has come around to, yes, a very good day.

Sometimes we just have to wait and expect and—*voila!*—the world comes right again.

MARCH 28

Easter eggs and bunny rabbits were not on my mind this morning when I drove over to visit my recently bereaved sister-in-law, Mary Lou. But as I neared the parking lot, I remembered seeing the sign earlier this week EASTER EGG HUNT, 10:00 SATURDAY, RAIN OR SHINE. Everyone was descending at once, for a mission different from mine.

The sun was shining, although the grass was a bit frosty and the air nippy. That did not deter the children who, with parents in tow, crowded in through the front door with bags and baskets in hand. This Easter egg hunt is an annual tradition, held on the extensive grounds of our local nursing home. The young families of the community turn out *en masse* for the event.

I made my way through the crowd, up to Mary Lou's apartment, where we watched from her window as the tiny tots gathered up the bright plastic eggs that had been scattered liberally in the enclosed sycamore garden. The older children were then let loose to race over the more expansive grounds outside the enclosure. It was not long until all the eggs found owners and the children enjoyed refreshments.

We reminisced about earlier Easter egg hunts with real hard-boiled eggs—about the packets of Paas dyes, decals, and dipping wands—before plastic eggs were introduced. We soon decided that Easter eggs are for the young. Now we're content just to watch.

MARCH 29

My granddaughter Erika is celebrating her 20th birthday today. I've been thinking about her especially today, this day-she-moves-out-of-her-teens. Has she been looking forward to this day especially, or will it be just another day? Is it age 21 that she's really looking toward—another year from now? What does it all mean to her, this leaping into the next decade of life?

Back in the fall of 1949, when I turned 20, I was beginning my junior year of college, not having much of a clue as to where this college education would lead but just drinking in the experience. I know that Erika has done much more serious planning of her career than I did at that age, partly because women now have so many more expectations and career choices than I did. She is studying to be a teacher, something I did not aspire to be. But she has a love for children, a creative mind, and a sensitive spirit. She will be good in her chosen field.

Was I good in my chosen field—music? Perhaps not, because I never made it a career—a livelihood. Fortunately I did not have to, but could enjoy music as an avocation. However, music laid the foundation for my marriage, for our family, and is the glue that still holds us together. How does one measure worth like that?

Erika, I wish you so much on this, your 20th birthday. May you find a special happiness in looking toward this next year, this next decade. Go, and be a blessing.

MARCH 30

Every morning, about the time I'm eating my breakfast, he's there. Swimming slowly in the pond outside my window. I don't know how long he stays. I get busy with other things and forget about him. And then, by the time I remember him again, he has already left. Where does he go and why do I always see him just in the morning?

At first, it was a pair—a male and a female mallard duck swimming and dunking together in the water, even before the ice was completely gone from the pond. I wrote about them one morning when they were especially active—almost childlike in their frolicking in the still-cold water. Then the female disappeared and, for about two mornings, there were two male mallards swimming in the same area. Now, for the last several days, it has been the single male swimming alone. Is his mate sitting on a clutch of eggs, hidden away in the bushes nearby? Will we be privileged to spot some ducklings one of these days?

I'm curious, but not curious enough to search too far. Sometimes it's best just to let nature's creatures live their own lives, unhampered by snooping humans. Sometimes, through our own inquisitiveness and ineptness, we interfere too much and upset the balance. So, I'll keep watching the morning ritual while trying hard not to pry. I'll still watch out my window, but try to let them live their lives in peace.

MARCH 31

Spring fever must have arrived because I see my neighbor outside his villa, bucket and trimmer in hand, ready to clean up his flower beds. He's been ready ever since we had that warm spell two weeks ago but then the cold weather came back and chased him inside. I'm sure he jumped at the chance this morning to get out and make sure everything is ready for his roses to send out new sprouts.

It's good to have neighbors who take pride in their surroundings. And I'm fortunate to be living in a place where the administrator is very much interested in the landscape. He makes sure that bushes are trimmed, flowers are tended regularly, and the general environment is pleasant to the eye. An attractive, clean neighborhood is good for everyone's spirits.

These surroundings are also the impetus for my daily reflections. Would I have started this series of daily writings if the pond and the birds outside my window were not there to inspire? The kingfisher, the Cooper's hawk, the great blue heron, even the Canada geese have given me cause to marvel. The sunsets, the snow, the changing seasons provide much food for thought. My human neighbors bring the necessary camaraderie to keep life interesting.

Thank you, neighbors all, for brightening my little corner of the world.

April 1

April Fool's Day. The day I used to dread, but have long since made my peace and can take it all in stride (I think).

It was my brother who introduced me to the ignominy of the title "April Fool." Being four years older than I, and a natural tease on top of that, he always had a zinger or two ready to spring on me, his unsuspecting little sister. So I knew about April Fool's Day long before I went to school and was introduced to the big league of jokers. In those early school years I nearly always got caught and learned to dread going to school on April Fool's Day. But all that finally passed and, by the time I had a family, I knew all the tricks and could fake an innocence when my children tried their elementary jokes on their mother.

Now, it seems, no one tries to catch me in an April Fool's trick any more. Do they think I'm too old? Are they afraid they'll hurt my sensibilities, or that I won't understand what the joke is all about?

Of course, I'd rather not be part of some malicious-minded April Fool's joke. But if someone tries to pull a "Hey, you dropped your Kleenex!" trick today, I think I'll just stop, look on the floor all around me, pick up an imaginary tissue and say, "Oh, thank you so much," and go on with a smile. That'll fix 'em.

APRIL 2

There have been times throughout my life when I have thought myself relatively self-sufficient, able and willing to solve most any problem. Then, at other times I have discovered how wrong I have been and need to ask for help. The older I get, the more often these cycles of dependence occur.

This morning was one of those times when I appreciated someone else's expertise to solve a problem. My problem was, naturally, with my computer. This very necessary accessory to my writing is sometimes the bane of my existence—an inanimate object that reminds me again and again that there is much that I don't and will never know.

This time I feared that my computer had eaten an entire month's worth of these daily reflections. The file just wasn't there! It wasn't long before my problem-solver found the missing month and brought it back into its proper file. He then made sure I had everything automatically backed up so I can be panic-free the next time I slip up. Worries addressed and taken care of. I'm thankful that someone had the time, the ability, and the patience to take a senior citizen's problem and solve it with ease.

When you think of it, isn't that we're all here on this earth to do? To help our neighbors, wherever they may be, however we can, whenever we can? I'll help you, you help me, we're in this together.

APRIL 3

Our female mallard has evidently found her place to nest—a rather unusual place by my calculations, but then I'm not a duck. All day she has been sitting calmly along the foundation of our new screen house, all very visible from my window. She has made her nest in the new, dark mulch of the surrounding flower bed, so she is hard to spot. But there are no bushes or other foliage nearby. So I fear for her safety. Will someone walking by scare her away, either inadvertently or intentionally? Will a predator find her there, in such a vulnerable spot?

In checking the Internet, I find that incubation takes about 28 days. I don't know if I can stand the suspense that long—looking out my window to check on her every time she comes to mind. I would rather she were somewhere not quite so obvious, not quite so out-in-the-open, not right under my nose. But then again, she must have her reasons for selecting this spot.

As the weather turns warmer and the sidewalks begin getting used more regularly by our residents here, I'm sure there will be many others than myself watching and waiting, curious about our incipient mother and strolling by to check on her progress. Will too many passers-by scare her off?

I sound like an old mother hen myself, don't I? Clucking over someone else's behavior. I'd better get back to work at something more productive.

APRIL 4

Last evening as it was just turning dusk, I came home from a meeting and was walking from my garage into the building when my ears picked up a sound I had not heard for some time. It was a robin, singing its evening time-for-bed song. It then occurred to me that I had not heard that song since last summer. A song forgotten, then suddenly recalled.

Sometimes we don't realize what we've missed until after we experience it once again, later. That's how I felt when I heard the robin. It took me by surprise, that once-familiar sound that I had not heard all winter. The winter air has its sounds, and not the ones we hear in springtime and summer. We get familiar with the season we're in and, as the season moves on, we settle into the rhythm of that particular time and place. We forget how it was before, until the cycle comes round once more.

This robin's evening song has gotten me eager to hear the other sounds that are particularly summer—birds, frogs, children playing, maybe even lawn mowers (although that will only entrance the first time it happens this spring). New sounds mean that everything is waking up again.

Is there anything new that I should be doing, or saying, or thinking—now that spring is here? I must also celebrate this new season of life. It's a new day, a new season, another new beginning.

APRIL 5

A couple of days ago, Brahms' *Requiem* was the subject of my favorite morning radio program. I haven't been able to get the music out of my head since that time, nor do I wish to. The music brings back very special memories.

Throughout our married life, wherever we lived, Dean and I were singing—as a duo, in small groups, in large choirs. When we lived in Michigan we were part of a special group of sixteen, the Steiner Chorale. We studied and performed some of the more complex choral works, one of which was Brahms' *Requiem*. In fact, we sang the Brahms two different times. The second performance was presented following the death of our director, Bill Steiner, and dedicated to his memory.

The memorial concert was a fitting tribute to our director because the entire message of the work is that death is not the answer. Each movement contains two parts—a slow, darkly somber and meditative passage followed by an uplifting "and yet" moment of reassurance and joy. Sadness countered by hope. A universal message.

In our everyday lives as well, it is necessary that we recognize all the big and little "and yet" moments. "It's raining today, *and yet* the forecast is for sunny weather tomorrow." "This has been a terrible year, *and yet* my new job holds promise."

The yin and yang of life. Two sides.

APRIL 6

Bird watchers are known to travel hundreds of miles and spend a good bit of money to add one particular bird to their life list. I've never been quite that avid, but today when I heard of a new sighting in our area, it didn't take long until I was in the car driving to the site.

It was a great blue heron rookery, a communal nesting site high in the trees, just a couple of miles west of Bluffton. This is a new location, quite distant from any significant body of water. The Lake Erie shoreline is dotted with such nesting enclaves, but we are located at least an hour's drive from that popular area and with no larger body of water than a creek nearby. What has brought the herons here?

I have heard that many residents near the Lake Erie shoreline do not appreciate the herons nesting there—that the birds are extremely noisy and messy. I suppose they are. A big bird, a large makeshift nest high in the trees, duplicated by a bunch of rowdy friends (multiple nests in a grove of tall trees) makes for a noisy neighborhood. Perhaps the humans along the lake have taken steps to rid their area of the birds and so the herons have decided to relocate farther south—to someone else's (our) neighborhood.

If that is the case, we'll probably soon hear some complaining about the rowdy new kids on the block. That's how it is.

APRIL 7

Mission accomplished! Our library bookshelves are once again exhibiting some sort of order. Two days of sorting, clearing and reorganizing have brought a kind of serenity once more to the shelves. It's a never-ending job, this renewal of tidiness to the shelves of a growing library. Although I never studied library science, I love books. So I watch over this little library as if it is my own, keeping things relatively in order.

When this retirement community opened more than 15 years ago, there was space for a library but no budget for books. So the library grew only through donations of books from the community. Books from residents just moving in, donations of discarded books from the local library, newer books purchased and read by residents and then given to the library. Over the years we have seen many scholarly books fill the shelves as well as plenty of read-once-and-throw-away paperbacks.

It's not easy to discard a book, but with new ones coming in and no extra space, we have no choice. Books that never leave the shelves are not bringing enjoyment to anyone, so sometimes it's best to send them to new owners. I hope we're adding to someone else's enjoyment while making room for new volumes on our shelves.

This morning I found an interesting-looking book in a corner, hidden away and out of place. So now it's time to sit down, put up my feet and check it out. A good way to spend the remainder of today.

APRIL 8

Today was Volunteer Appreciation Day for our retirement complex here in Bluffton—a time to thank the many, many people who give time and talent to serve this special community of older citizens. In some ways we are saying "thank you" to ourselves, because many of the volunteers that were honored with a special meal today are our own residents. Senior citizens who learned long ago that giving of one's time to others is both rewarding and satisfying. And so, even in retirement, we keep on volunteering and doing something to benefit our neighbors.

Small communities tend to foster giving communities—at least I have seen that in the small communities where I have lived. There is little chance to be impersonal in a small community. We know our neighbors, at least most of them, and most of us are not reluctant to lend a helping hand when needed. We tend to look after each other.

At this point in their lives, my children live in much larger communities than where they were born. They live where their jobs have taken them and are happy in their chosen communities. But they have carried a bit of their earlier small-town upbringing with them as they find places in their communities to be of service. They all know how to give of their time and talents, to be a good neighbor, and to concern themselves with others. I hope they never forget.

APRIL 9

Our mallard pair has settled into a routine of sorts. At least, it seems like a routine. Every morning I see the male swimming back and forth in the pond, not for a long period of time but at least he shows up. The female, who is sitting on the nest at the other side of our screen house, does not join him at that time. Nor have I ever seen him come to the nest.

However, later this afternoon the female covered her eggs with down and left the nest for feeding and whatever else she had on her agenda. The pair evidently had a rendezvous today because this evening I saw the pair of them fly in from the east and land on the pond. Immediately the female proceeded to take her version of a shower, ducking her body up and down in the water. She then climbed out and, after preening her feathers for a short time, flew back to her nest. The male swam around a bit longer, then took off to wherever he spends his evenings.

This is the first time I have been able to watch this nesting procedure. Perhaps all of this is old news for the experts but, for me, it has been another learning experience that I did not seek, or expect to witness. That makes it all the better—no expectations, no test, no grade. I can just enjoy watching the story unfold.

Let's hope for a happy ending.

APRIL 10

It happens every spring. We wait. We wait some more. After the cold days of winter we are so eager for spring to arrive that we watch for every sign. I wax poetic about birdsong, the first blades of new green grass, the mallards nesting nearby, the first daffodils and snow drops. When the thermometer finally reaches 60 degrees we're out on the sidewalks once more, talking about how nice it will be to sit out on the porch again. We keep waiting.

Today is one of those "teaser" days. The forecast is for temps topping 70 degrees but with heavy thunderstorms accompanying the warmth. So we want to be out, but the storms will keep us in. Tomorrow the landscape will be greener because of the rain. The daffodils will be reaching for the sky. But, as usually happens, the temperatures will drop overnight and jackets will rule the day tomorrow.

But oh, how dull it would be to have sunshine and ideal temperatures every day! What would we have to complain about? What would stir us out of our complacency, our ho-hum-ness? Wouldn't we tire of sameness, day after day? It would be like getting our childhood wish for a dish of ice cream every meal. After a while, we would want something different.

Maybe the Creator got it right, giving us a whole world of options. We have choices—then we must do our best with what we have.

APRIL 11

Now I know spring is here. The early magnolias are beginning to open their pink faces to the sun. Along with the new spring-green grass, the bright yellow daffodils that are blooming their hearts out and the blue, blue hyacinths adding another shade to our palette, spring is definitely taking shape all around us. Today was a good day to get out and breathe in the fresh spring air and sunshine once again.

Our maintenance crew got in the spirit yesterday, bringing out all the porch chairs and rockers once again. The umbrella tables have returned to the deck and everything that gives any hint of winter has been stashed away for another season. We know there will still be some cool days and colder nights, but everything around us points to warmer, brighter, more promising days.

And so we, in our own individual ways, will start our own spring cleaning. Not with buckets and mops—we don't need to do that any more. But each of us has a need to breathe in that warmer, fresher air and let it fill us with a new spirit. We need to take a walk outside on the sidewalk instead of just in the halls, so that our lungs can expand along with our hearts. We need to shake off the dust of winter and let spring take over our faces as well as our lives.

That's what will keep us young.

APRIL 12

Last night was a sort of *déjà vu*—a flashback to earlier days when my husband and I were considerably younger and singing our hearts out with a talented and challenging vocal group. This time I was only listening, but mentally I was singing along with the chorus because Dean and I had sung this exciting work in concert 45 years earlier.

I was drinking in the music at the final concert of the Lima Symphony Orchestra season. The highlight of the evening was, for me, a presentation of Leonard Bernstein's *Chichester Psalms,* complete with full orchestra and a choir of about 75 voices. Although I did not have the score in front of me, nor did I remember the Hebrew words, the melodies were so familiar, so haunting, that I'm still humming them.

It's not an easy work to listen to, at least parts of it. But the erratic rhythms and jarring dissonances are countered with some beautifully-soaring melodies, plus the sweet and calming voice of a boy soprano singing the words of the 23rd Psalm. That's the melody that I keep humming today—"The Lord is my Shepherd" part—along with the ethereal ending of the piece.

Music has always been my heart's focus. To me it brings peace as well as excitement, calm as well as joy. What I heard last night will keep on resonating tomorrow and tomorrow.

APRIL 13

I have a fuzzy pink flamingo sitting at the edge of my bookcase, long legs dangling over the side. Or, I should say that the flamingo *was* sitting on the bookcase. It fell off yesterday evening, nearly into my lap. After my initial surprise, I got to laughing—and remembering.

Remember when plastic pink flamingoes first came on the scene? It must have been in the 70's when friends looked for a good excuse to place one, or several, in someone's front yard as a prank. Our good friends had done it to us (after we had played a rather unusual prank on them) and the battle of the pink flamingoes was on. Every so often the flamingoes would appear at one house or the other.

We finally outgrew such childish behavior (or so we thought) and put those plastic birds in storage. But at our 50th wedding anniversary open house, our friends appeared with a special gift—a warm and fuzzy "Precious Moments" pink flamingo. It has been perched at the edge of the bookcase ever since—a reminder of good friends and old times.

Now, as I write this, the flamingo is sitting on my computer desk watching me type out these words. I think I'll keep him here—for inspiration and to bring a smile once in a while. Maybe he was tired of being "put on the shelf" and fell down last night just to get my attention.

APRIL 14

This afternoon I pinch-hit for a friend. She was out of town and our retirement center's men's chorus needed a re-hearsal pianist, so I filled in. It's a small and rather new group, started less than a year ago, but the men love to sing and they practice faithfully. About once a month they sing for one or another of our gatherings here. It is always a treat to hear them sing.

Since we live in a retirement village, the age of these sing-ers is older than the usual men's choirs. One gentleman has long since celebrated his 95th birthday. One or two have not yet reached 80, and the rest are in their 80s. So this is not a young group, except young at heart, and every one of them is certainly in that category.

One of the younger members is the man who started it all. A relatively new resident who loves to sing, he saw the possi-bilities for finding some compatriots. Using his powers of per-suasion, he invited a few to get together. Most of the men had sung in choirs before, but most of them thought their singing days were over. Not so, as it turns out. They just needed an in-formal, non-threatening group to help let the music out that was just waiting for a chance to reappear. Now four-part har-mony fills the room with song.

It may not be the Mormon Tabernacle Choir, but it's close enough.

APRIL 15

Today was Memory Day in Ohio. Because of it I was in Columbus all day with about 350 others, meeting with our state legislators and advocating for caregivers and families touched by Alzheimer's disease. This is the fifth year I have attended and it won't be my last. It is a very special day with a group of very special people.

Fifteen years ago, when Ohio's first Memory Day was held, I paid no attention to that relatively new disease, Alzheimer's. Ten years ago my husband and I were busy living with the disease. Five years ago he died from the disease. Every year since, I have attended Memory Day to lend my support to all those who have the disease and for the people who care for them.

We really *do* get to speak with our legislators on Memory Day. After a luncheon where at least one of our legislators speaks, we are all assigned to small groups of from five to ten to meet in person with the senators and representatives, or one of their staff, from our voting areas. We sit around tables and tell our stories. And many of our legislators have their own stories to share about how Alzheimer's disease has affected their own families. They listen. We all learn.

We know there are many worthy causes, but for us who know Alzheimer's personally, Memory Day is very special. As long as I can still keep going, I'll keep going.

APRIL 16

Recently I was asked to be on a panel of three at a women's conference, our topic being "where do you find your inspiration?" This invitation has come at an opportune time in my life since I have been spending the past year discovering inspiration all around me, then writing my reflections about it. I am eager to share the excitement I feel when noticing all the little things that make a difference in my day.

I realize that I have plenty of time in my day to ponder and write. I don't have to go to a job, I don't have young children to care for. My daily schedule is not chock full of things to do and places to go. I can write without constant interruption.

But I have discovered that inspiration seldom comes when I'm just sitting around doing nothing. Special things happen at unanticipated moments. The only thing different for me now is that I can more easily recognize a special moment and to mentally take note of why it is special. There are times when I am able to sit right down and write about it, but oftentimes that special moment is stored away in memory where it simmers for a while before I put it all on paper.

Inspiration comes in its own time. When it comes, I must recognize it, drink it in and then find a way to express it in words. That all makes for a very good day.

APRIL 17

It's a picture-perfect spring morning. There are gentle ripples moving on the surface of the deep blue pond, forsythia bushes in their bright yellow dresses along the bank, trees in early spring bud, one starling with a beak full of grass heading for a nest-construction site, plus our female mallard patiently tending to her nest of eggs. All's well on this lovely morning.

My raised garden is beckoning. Last week I spotted too many sprouts of chives coming up in places where I don't want them. Some winter detritus needs to be cleaned up. There are probably some little grape hyacinths in bloom—I haven't checked for a few days. And soon the milkweed will start sprouting again. It's time to get out and dig in the dirt.

I am what we used to call a "gentleman farmer"—someone who dabbles in the dirt but doesn't have to make a living at it. When I was growing up, my mother's garden was more than a diversion. It was a necessity. Now I wax poetic about it but have never had to cope with the absolute necessity to feed my family from a garden. So my small garden is more of a pastime, plus a place to grow milkweed for our monarch butterflies.

Perhaps the monarchs are my "family" now. If so, my garden is a necessity—for them. They need what I provide. They are invited to the table. Let's hope they come.

APRIL 18

This was a day of celebration and renewal. Tomorrow will harbor remembrance of the past and contemplation of the future, but today was dedicated to smiles all around. This weekend is the time we celebrate the life of my brother while gathering to renew the relationships of those of his family left on this earth.

My brother Norm and I have always lived in the Midwest, but our families have scattered to the four winds. So today cousins flew "home" from California, Illinois, Maine, Manitoba, New Mexico, North Carolina, South Carolina, Washington and various parts of Ohio. We spent an afternoon and evening renewing acquaintances with relatives some of us had not seen since early childhood. Laughter, stories, smiles and hugs were the order of the day. Warm temperatures and sunshine added to everyone's spirits.

This same group of people will, no doubt, never all meet together again. But every person at that gathering today took home both physical and mental photographs of the day, plus renewed memories of both past and present. Parting company, we have good intentions of getting together again "soon," but that intention may not happen again until the next death in the family.

But even that is as it should be. Time goes on, life goes on, love and memory continue. We are part of each other no matter how far apart we live. We will remember, and be remembered.

APRIL 19

Today the life of my brother Norm was commemorated by the larger community. The church was filled with friends and family as we, through an outpouring of song and words, celebrated our common faith in God while remembering someone who had impacted our lives.

Since Norm loved music, classical in particular but most everything in general, there was plenty to appreciate. We were treated to good music, both instrumental and vocal, from Bach to "I'll Fly Away." The congregation sang hymns in beautiful four-part harmony. Norm would definitely have approved of it all.

And he would have laughed heartily at every story told at the reception after the service. Norm's quiet demeanor belied the jokester inside. He was able to laugh at himself as well as make others laugh at his occasional antics. So today his children and their cousins enjoyed sharing remembrances of growing up with such a man as their father and uncle.

It makes me wonder how I will be remembered. Will it be with laughter and song or in a more somber mode? I sincerely hope it will be the former. My brother and I were different in many ways but I think both of us lived our lives with smiles on our faces, songs on our lips and love in our hearts. That's a good way to live life, as well as a good way to end it. May it be so.

APRIL 20

Everything is quiet again, after a whirlwind weekend of family togetherness. I drank in every moment of celebration as I relished the hugs, the laughter and smiles as well as the solemn moments. And now, with my children back in their own homes again, I put my recollections on replay and live the weekend once more.

What would life be without memories? So much of what I'm thinking right now is an echo of the last three days. Those memories will keep me smiling for days and then gradually get stored back in the recesses of the mind to be brought out sometime later when someone says, "Remember when...?" And then these past days will be there again to elicit another smile.

Which brings me to the painful remembrance of what Alzheimer's disease did to my husband and, in effect, to our whole family. We all saw how, in slow stages, his memory slipped away. First, the ability to work with figures, to calculate, to make complex decisions. Then the ability to vocalize thoughts and ideas. Then the ability to recognize and respond. And finally the ability to move and breathe.

I hope and pray that I will be able next year, and the year after, and the years after that, to recall these past days and relish them once again. One death before death is more than enough.

APRIL 21

Our female mallard has been patiently sitting on her eggs for two weeks now—the halfway point in the incubation process. People walk by on the sidewalk—not often, but there is enough foot traffic to make me wonder if she will be frightened away. But she continues to sit there, perfectly still, until the intruder passes by. She still vacates the nest sometime in late afternoon, when I often see her with her mate. But he does not visit the nest.

The other evening there were several families enjoying the outdoors and I was happy to see that there was at least one adult watching the children. However, the following day I saw that there was an egg placed right in the middle of a large, flat stone about ten feet from the nest. An egg the color and size of a duck egg. Oh, no! Did the children find the nest when she was gone, then pick up that egg to show their parents? And then did they not know what to do with the egg, so just placed it on the rock? Questions—no answers.

Our mallard still sits on her nest. She has no way of telling me if she lost an egg and, even if she could, I wouldn't know what to do to help her. So I guess I'll just have to content myself with the knowledge that nature can, and will, take care of itself. With or without my meddling.

APRIL 22

Every person's schedule needs, at some point, a time to catch up. Today is one of those days for me. After a busy weekend, with thoughts only of the here and now and nothing of what happens tomorrow, I'm catching up with myself. Right now there are papers covering my table, two other files spread out on the bed. All part of an attempt to put order into files I need for a meeting tomorrow.

It's easy to stuff papers in a folder, set the folder aside for another day, then forget where you put it. That's what happened here. Some of the information I thought I had at my fingertips was, instead, in sundry other locations that needed searching through before all was found. Now, before putting everything back in some sort of order, I've decided to take a break and write this reflection—before I forget the feeling of frustration that comes with looking for something one needs but cannot find.

Perhaps you, reading this, are always organized and have never had that feeling. Or perhaps you are one who always has to search high and low and take it as an everyday occurrence. I am in the middle—usually quite organized and know where I can find things when I need them, but my blood pressure rises when something isn't where I think it should be.

Just sitting down and writing about this frustration has calmed me. Now I'm ready to tackle the clean-up process. Thanks for listening.

APRIL 23

Sometimes it takes the diminishing of one talent to allow another talent to shine. We have a resident here at Maple Crest, now in his mid-90s, who is sharing a once-unheralded talent. A retired professional musician, he is unable now to perform in concert as he once did. But he put on a program for us today that shows off another, still viable, talent. In fact, today's program was the third presentation he has given over the past year, and there are still more to come.

Photography was one of his hobbies, all the time he was traveling professionally as well as in retirement. So he has a mountain of color slides taken in the various countries around the world that he has visited. He periodically selects the "best of the best" and enthusiastically shares the beauty with his friends here.

Today we visited England, Scotland, Wales and Ireland. At other times we have traveled to the Far East, South America, Australia/New Zealand and the U.S. He selects all the slides, arranges them, writes the script to go with the photos, then runs the projector while someone with a stronger voice reads his narrative.

The younger crowd might think that a slide show of scenery is far too boring. They think they need blaring sound, flashing lights and hype. But all of us here are eager for our resident photographer to pull out another box of slides and advertise another program. We'll be there!

APRIL 24

Along with the tulips that are just now opening their bright petals to the sun, the scourge of lawn-lovers has arrived on the scene. Suddenly, yellow dandelions are popping their heads up along every roadside and un-sprayed plot of ground. A delight for young children but not so delightful to parents who love tidy lawns.

One of my childhood memories is of going out with my mother to the ditch between our house and the roadside. I carried the bucket, she carried the knife. Together we searched through the winter-limp leaves and grasses to unearth the biggest clumps of dandelion greens we could find. With her knife, she would dig down and pull out those clumps that had been bleaching among their cover of leaves—the most succulent of all the greens, turned pinkish-white and tender.

Back in the house, we cut away the less-tender top part, leaving only the bleached core. Then we washed and washed the dandelion greens to remove every speck of dirt and grass. Many cooks made a bacon dressing to put on the greens, but not at our house! My mother made a mashed potato/vinegar/cream dressing that made those dandelion greens the best dish one could ever imagine.

Herbicides have cleaned up most of our roadsides and any hardy dandelions are now off-limits for eating. But I can still remember the taste of dandelion greens at our table. How I wish I could duplicate it one more time!

APRIL 25

An unexpected visitor knocked on my door this morning and set my day a-glow. I had not seen her for a good many years and even our Christmas card exchanges had slowed. But, when I opened the door today, her smile was the same as forty years ago. I knew that the next hour would fly by.

That's how it is sometimes with old friends—the friends we were close to in an earlier stage of life, at a different location, among different circumstances. Through a series of moves and life changes for both or us, we had gradually drifted apart. And yet today it was as if those decades between were dissolved and here we were, chatting away as if our last conversation occurred just yesterday.

We probably won't see each other again, since she was just passing through Ohio on a trip with family. It was on a whim that they stopped after spotting the Bluffton water tower while passing by on the interstate. "Bluffton - that's where Joanne moved to," she told her daughter. "Do you think we could just pop in and see if she's home?"

I was. They came. We talked. And talked. An hour later, they left for the rest of their trip. My smile remains, along with all the new memories sprinkled in with the old. Enough to warm the rest of today and give my memory bank a few more images to store for tomorrow.

APRIL 26

Why am I smiling? After all, it's only 8:00a.m. and I'm not really a morning person. And yet, there's a smile on my face as well as in my heart.

It's the stillness of the pond outside my window that brings this warm feeling of contentment. After too many days and nights of wind and bluster, with the water constantly moving, moving, moving, the pond is calm this morning. Not a ripple.

Yes, I know that the water is really not completely still. Were I to venture out and sit along the bank, I would be able to distinguish movement. Not everything would be still above, on, or below the surface of the water. And if I really wanted to think even more profoundly about it, I would acknowledge that microscopic life—an underwater world of microscopic life—is constantly moving, moving, moving to keep this pond a place of beauty.

But now, this peaceful morning, is not the time to discuss scientific facts and to argue theories. Now is not the time to point out the physics of what makes the world go round. Right now is the time to smile, to savor, and then whisper a quiet "thank you, God" for a morning blessing.

The pond is at peace. I am at peace. That's enough for now.

APRIL 27

If you'll pardon me, I must again wax poetic over the glories of spring. This is my last chance now that I am nearing the end of my goal, my 365 days of reflections. Nearly a year ago I wrote the first of these daily ramblings. Tomorrow will be the last, the swan song. Or maybe a mallard song, since I have no swan but my duck is still sitting on her nest of eggs, awaiting her ducklings.

I just returned from a brisk walk—brisk because the air is chillier than I expected, the breeze is more than a light breeze, and I should have worn a heavier jacket. Nonetheless, the walk took me past a proliferation of new blossoms to add to the spring catalog. It also lifted my already-high spirits, so this day can be chalked up to be another Very Good Day.

Cherry blossoms are opening now, their pink shades blending with white flowering pears, bright yellow forsythia and a few magnolias that didn't get frosted a couple of nights ago. My raised garden contains a small ocean of tiny deep blue grape hyacinths, sprinkled with a few miniature yellow daffodils, all thanks to a small gift planter sent by my son Mark many Mother's Days ago.

If I had my choice of which season to keep forever, it would probably be spring. Definitely not winter, maybe not summer, possibly fall. But spring is here now and that's good enough for me.

APRIL 28

Here we are, at the end of the line. This last writing to complete my year-long goal of one reflection per day. What do I do now that my daily writings have come full circle? I look back to the beginning, last April 29, and I still resonate with the feelings I had then— my delight in spotting the belted kingfisher just outside my window, then letting my thoughts take wing in response.

But I also feel changed in ways I cannot fully explain. I have encountered more light throughout this journey than I ever thought possible. Light in the form of new insights and unexpected discoveries. Light in the form of little things that continue to make me smile. Flashes of remembrance at unexpected times. All of them keeping me young at heart.

So, my question returns. What next? I do expect to take a break and try to put away the feeling that I must write, write, write every day. Perhaps that will be harder than I think since I have trained my eye to look more closely, my heart to keep more attuned, my mind to put it all on paper. But it is time to step back.

It's spring, a time of renewal. A good time to end a project and then to get started on a new one. A good time to breathe in the freshness of a new idea, whatever that new idea may be. Who knows what will evolve in time? I look forward…

About the Author

Joanne Niswander began writing poetry in her teens, then abandoned it for music. A new awakening to prose came later in life, through her nature columns in the *East Lansing* (Michigan) *Towne Courier,* "A Lighter Shade of Gray" in *The East Toledo* (Ohio) *PrimeTime Press,* sixteen years of monthly columns in the *Bluffton* (Ohio) *News,* and occasional writings for the Bluffton Icon. She is the author of *An Alzheimer's Primer,* published in 2012.

She resides at Maple Crest, a retirement village in Bluffton, Ohio. If you wish to know more about her history, family, friends and idiosyncrasies, you will find nearly everything within the pages of this book.